BEYOND WHITE GUILT

BEYOND WHITE GUILT

THE REAL CHALLENGE FOR BLACK–WHITE RELATIONS IN AUSTRALIA

Sarah Maddison

First published in Australia in 2011

Allen & Unwin
Sydney, Melbourne, Auckland, London

83 Alexander Street
Crows Nest NSW 2065
Australia
Phone: (61 2) 8425 0100
Fax: (61 2) 9906 2218
Email: info@allenandunwin.com
Web: www.allenandunwin.com

Cataloguing-in-Publication details are available from the National Library of Australia
www.trove.nla.gov.au

978 1 74237 328 7

Typeset in 12.5/15 Centaur MT by Midland Typesetters, Australia
Printed and bound in Australia by McPherson's Printing Group

10 9 8 7 6 5 4 3 2 1

The paper in this book is FSC certified. FSC promotes environmentally responsible, socially beneficial and economically viable management of the world's forests.

Contents

Let no one say the past is dead.
The past is all about us and within.

From 'The Past', by Oodgeroo Noonuccal, 1970

Foreword

In 2010 I launched an exhibition at the Australian Museum in Sydney. It contained works by the noted Aboriginal artist, Gordon Syron. A few days earlier, I had been invited by Gordon to visit the Keeping Place, a large space near the Everleigh train sheds in which he and his wife maintained their unique collection of art by Aboriginal painters.

One painting in the collection caught my eye. It was part of a series that Gordon had produced, over the years, showing the fateful meeting between the ships of Governor Arthur Phillip's First Fleet, arriving off the heads of what is now Sydney Harbour, and a lone Aboriginal witness. He seems to stand defiantly on the water, confronting the ghostly vessels with their portents of change.

Executed in beautiful colours of dark blue and pale white, the painting was arresting both in its concept and its execution. Gordon Syron's most famous painting portrayed a courtroom in which all the actors (bewigged judge and barristers, the jury and attendants, clerks and members of the public) were black. Only the accused, sitting in the dock was white. It was a powerful allegory. And yet the sombre confrontation of vessels and witness on the January day in 1788 bore a more subtle message: What if?

What if the British officials had been more attentive to the demands of the American colonists? What if they had quickly given away their obduracy and agreed to accord to their American cousins rights equal to those enjoyed by Englishmen at home? What if the need to find an alternative dumping ground for the British convicts had evaporated, so that there was no requirement to send the prisoners to the far-off coast that James Cook and Joseph Banks had reported in 1771? What if Phillip and his captains had got lost on the long journey? What if they had succumbed, as so many Netherlands vessels did, to the dangers of the Roaring Forties or the perils of landfall in Australia? What if Phillip had not been such a skilled commander but had lost his human cargo to disease or mutiny? What if he had quickly suffered the failure in his large project in Sydney town? What if they had not explored Farm Cove and, in search of water, had pressed on to the New Zealand? What if, on arrival at Farm Cove, Phillip or his successors had negotiated a treaty with the original inhabitants, acknowledging and respecting their rights, treating them as the first peoples, as would later be done at Waitangi? What if the Aboriginals and other indigenes had been more numerous? More warlike? Less transfixed and overwhelmed by the astonishing vessels off the heads, with their pale human cargo and well-armed redcoats?

All of these questions are futile today because we know what happened. The First Fleet laid anchor in the pristine solitude of one of the largest and most beautiful spaces of water in the world. The home reports that followed made Australia a beckoning attraction to the waves of migration that have continued, right up to the present time. The droughts and flooding rains have hardly caused in a dent in the ongoing arrivals of humanity that pour into the Great South Land searching for adventures, opportunities and human happiness.

Of course, many of those who have arrived have suffered pain and disappointment. But the chief disruption, as events turned out, was for that first solitary Aboriginal witness and his descendants. This book lays out the way modern Australia can right the wrongs that have occurred in the intervening years, and decades, and centuries that have passed since that first dramatic encounter.

In the middle of this book, the author tells of an exchange she had with the great Australian philosopher, Peter Singer. She records, with candour, that at a conference he accused her of being inadequately concerned with the real-life challenges confronting Aboriginal women and children in the here and now. No doubt, there will be readers of this book who will likewise 'roll their eyes' at its title and put down its pages with distaste and exasperation. Rejecting the thought that they are racists. Embracing the idea that they live in a land of the 'fair go'. Clinging to the notion that it is completely unnecessary to re-live the moments when British power and Aboriginal presence confronted each other on the fateful shore of Sydney Harbour. As Sarah Maddison repeatedly explains, the Australian reaction to the indigenous people of the continent has been ambivalent from the first. Most of the newcomers hoped to find, in the image of the country they grew up in, or later adopted as their own, honourable stories of good deeds, generous acts and magnanimous engagement with others.

Whilst there had been such events in the evolution of Australian nationhood, a defect quickly arose in our relations with the first peoples. Many were killed for daring to protect their lands, possessions and families against the onrush of the explorers and settlers. Quite quickly, the legal system rejected their claims for acknowledgement of land rights. It denied respect for the culture and traditions of their Aboriginal forebears. They were not eliminated in the kind of genocidal extermination pursued by the Nazi rulers of Germany. But they were certainly denied true equality; many driven to the outskirts of townships; exposed to crippling diseases; introduced to the debilitations of alcohol; and effectively kept from the benefits of modern shelter, education and health care. Equal pay (or pay at all) was very slow in coming to them. Few indeed were admitted to universities, the professions, or leadership opportunities. The Constitution itself for a long time contained disparagements, notions of assimilation and elimination of cultural identity. For generations, these represented the accepted policy of successive Australian governments. In the long term, it was expected, the 'Aboriginal problem' would simply disappear because they would die out and be fully assimilated.

Although by the 1970s, this story of deprivation began to change, the author's thesis is that the change has been too slow. It has not been whole-hearted. It is deeply flawed by a stubborn refusal of white Australia to acknowledge the wrongs, so that we can all move beyond unarticulated feelings, collective guilt and discomfort into a true sense of solidarity and community with Aboriginal brothers and sisters. This will not happen, it is suggested, so long as Australians cling to the notion that everything has been fixed up. That the tide has turned. That reconciliation has been achieved. That a national apology has been given. And that enormous advances have been accomplished in land rights, shelter, education, health and opportunities.

The author acknowledges the power of the national apology delivered in the Australian Parliament by then Prime Minister Kevin Rudd, supported by Dr Brendan Nelson, John Howard's successor as the leader of the Coalition parties. The cadences of

Mr Rudd's speech, and its contents, made a large contribution to moving all Australians beyond the denial of inter-generational guilt, so long maintained. But land rights litigation remains slow, frustrating, expensive and often dispiriting. The achievements in housing, health and education continue to disappoint. The response to the stolen generation report has not yet provided tangible recompense for the families dislocated and the individuals deprived of the most basic of human rights. The Northern Territory Intervention continues its deeply wounding intrusion into the Aboriginal communities of that most significant part of Aboriginal Australia.

As it happens, the challenge to the constitutional validity of the Northern Territory Intervention was the very last judgment of mine, delivered during my tenure on the High Court of Australia. Eight weeks before the 2007 federal election, Mr Howard's government raced through the Australian Parliament a very large statute, ostensibly designed to respond to a report to the Northern Territory government *Ampe Akelyernemane Meke Mekarle or Little Children Are Sacred.*[1]

Purportedly, the purpose of the new law was to introduce strong measures aimed at stopping child abuse and protecting women and children. Those measures were supported, as the author points out, by the then Labor opposition in the Federal Parliament. The support has substantially been continued by the succeeding Labor governments.

The High Court of Australia rejected a challenge to the validity of the intervention law. A majority held, indeed, that the challenge was not even legally arguable. I disagreed, fundamentally because I read the Australian constitutional promise to provide 'just terms' for the acquisition of 'property' as including something more than monetary compensation. In my view, at least arguably, as advocated by the Aboriginal objectors, it extended to a requirement of proper consultation with the Aboriginal individuals and communities affected. All of which had been denied in the helter skelter rush to enact the legislation in time before the election. Some unkind observers suggested at the time that the law was rushed for electoral purposes, to 'wedge' the Opposition and to tap deep feelings in the electorate, adverse to Aboriginal Australians.

In my reasons, in the High Court, I remarked:

> If any other Australians, selected by reference to their race, suffered the imposition on their pre-existing property interests of non-consensual five-year statutory leases, designed to authorise intensive intrusions into their lives and legal interests, it is difficult to believe that a challenge to such a law would fail as legally unarguable on the ground that no 'property' has been 'acquired'. Or that 'just terms' had been afforded, although those affected were not consulted about the process and although rights cherished by them might be adversely affected. The Aboriginal parties are entitled to their trial and day in court. We should not slam the doors of the courts in their face. This is a case in which a transparent, public trial of the proceedings has its own justification.[2]

These words, and the outcome of the court case, were almost wholly ignored in Australia. For a long time, despite a change of government, the Racial Discrimination Act remained suspended in respect of all those affected by the Intervention. Signs outside Aboriginal townships referred to pornography, stigmatising entire communities. They remain firmly in place to this day. The bans and prohibitions of the earlier era of Protection Acts remained in force. Intrusions and affronts, as well as unequal treatment of citizens, continue to remain in place. A miserable number of houses have been built, as tokens of the 'achievement' of the major intrusions of federal police and defence personnel. The authors of the report on children, invoked to justify the Intervention, always insisted on the imperative need for prior consultation. I agree with those authors and with the then world President of Amnesty International, Irene Khan, that what happened was 'not merely disheartening; it was morally outrageous'.

Many who read this book will come away angry. A few because of the 'polemics' of the author. Others because of failings of others that she reveals. Maybe some, because of these words of mine. But anger and guilt are not, as such, the purpose of Professor Maddison's text. Repeatedly she insists that we can learn from other societies in whose name great wrongs have been done. However, the lesson of other instances is that resolution only really occurs where there is a national apology; but one that is conjoined with specific identification of what exactly occasions the apology. And appropriate recompense is needed beyond words which come cheap. Only words with action will create the means to establish a new and healthy relationship.

I have not agreed with everything I have read in this book. Few Australian readers will. But to find a path towards true reconciliation and justice remains a very important challenge for the as yet incomplete Australia project. For the time being, the image in Gordon Syron's painting should remain in our minds. The vessels, in full sail, portending the presence of great power. The Aboriginal observer, watching and waiting. Guilt and fear are not enough. This book challenges us to contemplate and embrace restorative justice. It should be possible for our continent of privilege to take up this challenge. But is there now the will to do so?

Michael Kirby
18 March 2011

Introduction: Australia's original sin

... we, too, peoples of Europe, we are being decolonized: meaning the colonist inside every one of us is surgically extracted in a bloody operation. Let's take a good look at ourselves, if we have the courage, and let's see what has become of us.

Jean-Paul Sartre, 1961

For over a decade I have had the good fortune to live in the inner west of Sydney, within walking distance of the Cooks River. Most weekends I take the opportunity to walk down to the river and either walk or run along the paths that follow the course of the waterway. The poor Cooks River has been brutalised since the arrival of the British in 1788, damaged by the agriculture and industry that grew on its shores, including market gardens, a sugar mill, tanneries and wool scours, which resulted in high levels of pollution and siltation. Today the river is known as one of the most polluted and most altered waterways in Australia.[1] While a friend of mine who grew up in the area can remember swimming there as a child, current pollution levels are such that only the hardiest of water birds dare enter. Regular warnings are issued against eating fish caught in the river, although every weekend there are a stalwart few who refuse to be dissuaded from casting a recreational line. Until recently, ugly and rusted steel piling covered over large sections of the river's bank, although work has now been undertaken to reconstruct a more 'natural' shoreline. Even with this improvement, however, there is little of the original river left to see. Bridges crisscross the water, on either side of which there are parks, sports ovals and a golf course that give way to houses backing directly onto the river paths. Some sections of the river are still lined by concrete walls. Walking by the river is very much a suburban experience.

Still, there is one spot along the river that reminds me that it was not always like this. At one point, when crossing a bridge back to my side of the river, I can see a rock ledge that juts out into the water. The ledge is overhung with mangroves, providing a perfect sheltered spot for fishing. Behind the ledge, and across the walking path, there is a deep rock overhang, creating a space underneath that would accommodate several people and give shelter even in bad weather. The ledge looks like it belongs to a different river altogether and is a startling contrast to the surrounding area. The first time I saw it—the first time I *really* saw it—I stopped in my tracks. What I saw that day was not just a pretty spot by the river. Instead I saw an ancient place that had survived dramatic change, a place that would have been well used by the original inhabitants of the area probably over thousands of years. In my mind's eye I could see a fire burning ready to cook the fish pulled from the river to feed a family who might later take shelter under the overhanging rock. I could see men, women and children gathering the clams and oysters that could once be found in the river. I could see a peaceful scene in which people content and at home in their environment enjoyed a relaxed afternoon by a pristine waterway that had fed them and their ancestors for generations.

What I could imagine that day was not just fantasy. It was from this area that the Bidjigal leader, Pemulwuy, led the local resistance against the British invasion. I also knew that around 1,500 Dharug people were thought to have lived along the

Cooks River for around 10,000 years until the British incursion in 1788. Evidence of their presence was recorded in other rock shelters, some still containing middens and rock art. What I could imagine that day was no doubt inaccurate, perhaps romanticised, but probably not very. What made me catch my breath, however, was not an imagined, long ago scene. For some years I had been researching Aboriginal politics and had travelled to many places in Australia to meet and interview Aboriginal leaders and activists. I had had the experience, in less suburban parts of Australia, to begin to appreciate the Indigenous connection to land and to understand—when I was in Arnhem Land, or Kakadu or the MacDonnell Ranges—that I was on Aboriginal land. What stopped me in my tracks that day by the Cooks River, however, was the reminder that even in my own suburb, amid the environmental change wrought by two centuries of European occupation, I was *still* on Aboriginal land. I caught my breath in guilt and shame, not because this was the first time I had reflected on that reality—it was not—but because I had allowed my consciousness of that reality to fade. As a white person I had that privilege. Unlike Aboriginal and Torres Strait Islander peoples, I could choose to 'forget' or to deny or repress the reality of my place here. But never for long. Periodically an experience like this would intrude upon my suburban existence and unsettle my sense of place. This is as it should be.

Acknowledging our guilt

White Australia was settled on a land that did not belong to us. Deep in our hearts every Australian knows this to be true. Australia was not conquered through war nor were treaties signed with the original inhabitants. Rather, the British who arrived in

1788 advanced a brutal program of violent dispossession that spread from Sydney Cove to all corners of the continent, eventually inflicting trauma upon every single Indigenous man, woman and child, with devastating effect. Academics Murray Goot and Tim Rowse have noted the evidence from public opinion polling which shows that 'most Australians' admit that it is accurate to observe that colonisation treated Aboriginal and Torres Strait Islander peoples very badly.[2] For many of us today this knowledge is a source of guilt. Some of us turn this guilt inwards, leaving us paralysed and helpless to address the contemporary manifestations of our history. Others turn this guilt outwards, expressing anger at this country's original inhabitants for their failure to grasp the opportunities that colonisation has brought. As a nation, however, we have failed to deal with the collective and intergenerational nature of our guilt. Since colonisation, the dominant response to the original inhabitants of this country has ranged from hostility to fear, and from curiosity to ambivalence, tempered at times by compassion, and eventually governed by frustration. Governments have reflected these changes in public sentiment through policy that has in turn mostly sought to obliterate or assimilate Australia's Indigenous peoples. Almost without exception, efforts to talk about the wrongs of our past and our guilt in the present have been characterised as not in the national interest.

Perhaps unsurprisingly, not one of the official responses to the complexities in the Indigenous–non-Indigenous relationship has been effective in bridging the gulf between those who were here first and those who have come later. Repeated failures of policy and of efforts towards reconciliation, accompanied by a pattern of heavy-handed interventions in Indigenous lives, demonstrate our fundamental failure to adapt. Our guilt prevents us from doing anything more than develop endless technical responses to the contemporary problems that our history has bequeathed us, leaving the relationship between non-Indigenous and Indigenous Australia profoundly 'stuck'. Resolving this tension remains a matter of pressing national significance, but to do so will necessitate a new way of thinking and talking about our past, and about how we might live together in the present and in the future.

Recent decades have seen a growing awareness of the fault-lines and conflict that characterise relationships between Indigenous and non-Indigenous Australians. Anthropologist Deborah Bird Rose suggests that there is an increased awareness of the 'ruptured alienation of settler societies', adding that the generations alive today may be the first to 'try to grasp the enormity of conquest, and to understand it as a continuous process', leaving us searching for ways in which 'we may inscribe back into the world a moral presence for ourselves'.[3] The Australian experience is part of an international trend to redress the past, which acknowledges that such a process is 'central to our moral self-understanding' as individuals, groups and nations.[4] Yet many in Australia still tend to avoid this work, often for complex social and psychological reasons, disavowing their responsibility and displacing it onto others; urban whites onto rural whites, rural whites onto Aboriginal people, governments and 'urban elites'.[5] Anxiety about these relationships in fact crosses boundaries of class and location, and cannot be ascribed to a neat ideological category. Rather, as a nation, we experience a widespread social conflict that is *about* Indigenous–non-Indigenous relationships rather than *between* particular racial groups.[6]

This book is intended primarily for those of us on one side of this relationship, although there is no widely used term for this group of people. The dominant or majority group in Australia may be referred to as white Australians, although there is some unease associated with this terminology due to an association with the White Australia policy with all its racist baggage.[7] Anthropologist Ghassan Hage still prefers to discuss 'White' Australians as he considers the term to be a 'dominant mode of self-perception' even if it is not consciously so.[8] Historian Henry Reynolds[9] refers to 'whitefellas' in deference to the common usage among Aboriginal people. The writer Donald Horne preferred 'ordinary Australians',[10] and 'mainstream Australians' is another term that has come into common political usage[11] although exactly who is and who is not 'mainstream' is never very clear. Anthropologist Peter Sutton[12] asks who might consider themselves 'vain enough' to calibrate the weights of different moral burdens that might accrue based on a cultural identity, asking whether recent immigrants are excused from a sense of responsibility about Indigenous dispossession or whether they 'acquire a guilty mantle as soon as they put a first step on Australian soil'. But historian Ann Curthoys counters such a question by pointing out that the 'continuing presence of colonialism has implications for all immigrants, whether first-generation or sixth'. Curthoys argues that all non-Indigenous people 'are beneficiaries of a colonial history. We share the situation of living on someone else's land.'[13] Or as critical race theorist Sara Ahmed puts it, 'non-white non-Indigenous Australians also walk on stolen ground'.[14] The extent to which different groups of non-Indigenous people in Australia are aware of our colonial history and the benefits that accrue to them will vary, and so to some extent it will be up to individual readers to determine whether this book is addressed to them. As I will discuss in Chapter I, however, it is not so much our past or the length of time we have spent in Australia that determines our collective guilt. Rather, our collective guilt is determined by what we do in the present.

In many ways I have written this book with my heart in my mouth. I understand, as anthropologist Gillian Cowlishaw has pointed out, that there is 'considerable room for bad faith' in what may be seen as an enthusiastic embrace of ideas of collective guilt and the need for restitution. Cowlishaw suggests that academic work in this area often displays a 'complacent superiority' through what may be seen as a 'self-assumed task of exposing the moral failing of our forebears'.[15] But this book—that stands on the shoulders of much work that has gone before to present only a broad analysis of history and policy—is less about our forebears than it is about those of us alive today. While the events of the past have shaped who we are in the present, I am less interested in our history than in what we do about that history today. In that sense this is a very personal book. I have grappled with these issues in my own life and am frustrated at the way our national struggles keep falling at the same hurdle. I have come to the view that it is our collective guilt that lies at the heart of our failure to truly engage with Aboriginal and Torres Strait Islander peoples on their own terms. Whether we internalise our guilt or deny it altogether, it is always with us. Our energies are too much directed at avoiding the discomfort that this guilt produces and not directed enough towards working through the guilt as a means of developing a revitalised view of our national self. Avoidance of this task—what I will talk about in this book as our adaptive challenge—will continue to present a profound obstacle to a more just Australia and a more confident Australian national identity. It is work that simply cannot be avoided.

Understanding our adaptive challenge

It is my hope that this book will do more than merely encourage readers to pick at the scabs of their own feelings of guilt. The chapters that follow explore some of the dimensions of our collective guilt and the ramifications of the continued denial of that guilt in the present. But this exploration of our collective guilt is, in part, an attempt to diagnose what US leadership expert Ronald Heifetz would call an 'adaptive challenge' and, having undertaken that diagnosis, this book proposes some of the adaptive work that we, as a nation, have to do.

Heifetz describes adaptive challenges as involving those problems 'for which there are no simple, painless solutions—problems that require us to learn new ways'. Problems, in other words, that require us to adapt, to develop our social and cultural capacity:

> Adaptive work consists of the learning required to address conflicts in the values people hold, or to diminish the gap between the values people stand for and the reality they face. Adaptive work requires a change in values, beliefs or behaviour. The exposure and orchestration of conflict—internal contradictions—within individuals and constituencies provide the leverage for mobilising people to learn new ways.[16]

What Heifetz is suggesting is that for progress to be made in complex situations, where many of the previous 'technical' solutions have persistently failed, change is required at a deeper level. In the Australian context I am suggesting that we are not talking about a change of policy or even a change of government. If we want to 'close the gap' between the values many of us profess to hold with regard to the status and life chances of Aboriginal and Torres Strait Islander peoples and the reality our nation faces, what needs to change is us. For the status of Indigenous peoples in Australia to change *we will all need to change.*

No matter how much effort we direct at the institutional political realm, a change of government or minister or policy will never be enough to address the challenge we face. Adaptive problems can create considerable social stress and a sense of urgency among some groups in society. Our first response in the face of such stress tends to be to look to authority and demand that 'they' make a difference. Heifetz describes this inclination as generating 'inappropriate dependencies'. Our dependency on authority to create change is inappropriate because time and again when the 'accepted dependencies' are applied to problems that cause persistent distress they reveal that they 'cannot do the job'. The response from authorities, such as governments, to this kind of pressure will often make the situation worse, or at least perpetuate the problem. Authorities are often under pressure to appear decisive, and as a result they are inclined to 'fake the remedy or take action that avoids the issue by skirting it'. Authorities are always more likely to deal with an adaptive challenge by diverting attention from the issue. By applying a technical solution rather than engaging in adaptive work the problem '*appears* to be taken care of'. The public response—our response—when authority fails or when the problem in fact worsens in response to the supposed 'solution' is to 'perpetuate the vicious cycle by looking *even more earnestly* to authority' for a new solution, often switching our support to someone new who promises new and better answers.[17]

Although Heifetz is writing generically of the challenges of adaptive leadership, the scenario he describes is an alarmingly accurate description of the cycle of Indigenous policy in Australia. In response to public distress about the so-called 'Aboriginal problem', over decades and decades governments have applied various 'fake remedies': protection, assimilation and, most recently, intervention—to name just a few. I have elsewhere argued that successive Australian governments have made bad Indigenous policy because they have failed to come to grips with the complexity of Aboriginal political culture.[18] This is certainly true, but it is only a partial diagnosis of our adaptive challenge. A deeper reason that governments continue to apply fake remedies in Indigenous affairs is that we let them. Our distress in the face of persistent Indigenous disadvantage, and our underlying collective guilt about its causes, lead us to engage in what Heifetz calls 'work avoidance'. It is easier for us to let authorities skirt the issue with fake remedies than it is for us to engage in our own adaptive work. This 'flight to authority' is dangerous not only because it occurs in response to such a complex and difficult challenge, but also because it immobilises some of our best personal and collective resources for doing the work that really needs to be done.[19]

Key to the problem of work avoidance is our avoidance of feelings of distress and discomfort—such as feelings of guilt. But in taking the first step in our adaptive challenge, that is, in beginning to diagnose what the problem really is, these unpleasant feelings can in fact form an important 'diagnostic principle'. Heifetz suggests that if social distress cannot be alleviated through the application of our technical know-how or our known policies and procedures, then the feelings themselves provide an important clue to what the adaptive challenge really is.[20] Avoiding our distress will lead us to make 'comforting misdiagnoses' of the problem, allowing certain groups—in this case, Indigenous people—to be scapegoated as being responsible for the problem.[21] What this response misses is that by making any one group in society responsible for a problem we neglect the fact that social problems actually involve the whole of society. I have no doubt that Aboriginal and Torres Strait Islander peoples have their own adaptive work to do and will face similar challenges with regard to work avoidance. But their adaptive challenges are not the subject of this book. Here I am focusing on the non-Indigenous adaptive challenge: how to acknowledge our collective guilt and where this acknowledgement might lead us.

Heifetz counsels that adaptive work often involves loss, and that often this loss is real and sustained. The adaptive challenge will not be the same for all groups within a society; there will be competing values at stake and different factions will each have their own experts. But to make progress in our adaptive work we will have to '*learn our way forward*', and often this will require that we make adjustments to our lives.[22] To learn our way forward we may need to rethink ourselves in some profound ways, questioning old beliefs, identities, values and our 'images of justice, community and responsibility'.[23] This is not easy work. It is painful and difficult. But if we do not do this, if we do not take up this adaptive challenge, we will continue to face obstacles. We are deluded if we think there will ever be a government that takes up this challenge without there first being a profound shift in our social values. Equally, we are deluded if we think that government or government policy is itself the problem. As Heifetz argues:

> The accumulation of evil never resides in one person at the top because no one gets to the top without representing the interests of the dominant factions in the system. The evil, if it is evil at all, lives in the routine ways in which people throughout the system collude in maintaining a dysfunctional status quo. Changing the status quo will always require more than simply changing the person of the authority figure. Adaptive work requires adjustments, learning, and compromise on the part of many among the dominant, complacent, and beleaguered.[24]

Why does guilt matter?

Guilt remains a profound and complex barrier to honest reflection and a national examination of the systemic racism that continues to marginalise Indigenous peoples in this country. But it also presents us with an opportunity. Anti-racism educator Frances Kendall sums up the challenge:

> By exploring the ways that we hold collective guilt and shame individually and in the national psyche, we are better equipped to look at the role that these feelings play in our refusal to address our history genuinely and to understand how personal and collective guilt blocks us from moving forward.[25]

Our sense of guilt about historical and contemporary injustice, whether we acknowledge this guilt or not, damages our ability to relate across cultures,[26] creating unbridgeable divides out of what should be unthreatening cultural differences. According to the contentious African American writer Shelby Steele, white guilt has created a 'moral vacuum' that comes from knowing that one's social group is or has been associated with racism, creating paralysis in the face of pressing social crises.[27]

But rather than being complacent about these challenges, or avoiding the discomfort that guilt produces, we can choose to act. We can make a commitment to exploring and understanding the dynamics of our collective guilt and we can use the insight that we gain in that process to develop less damaging, more engaged relationships with Aboriginal and Torres Strait Islander peoples in order that we might coexist more peacefully. In moving those relationships forward we will find new opportunities to rethink the institutional frameworks of this country, the place of Indigenous peoples in our national polity, the symbols with which we articulate our national identity, and the policies through which we intervene (or do not intervene) in Indigenous lives. These are enormous tasks, each one, and tasks that we cannot even begin as long as our collective guilt is in the way.

Guilt is a difficult concept to apply to the Australian context. I have no doubt that there will be some in the community who will simply roll their eyes at the title of this book, convinced that it either does not apply to them as individuals or that it should not be applied to Australia as a whole. While we may debate the extent of wrongdoing perpetuated against Aboriginal and Torres Strait Islander peoples in the invasion and conquest of this (their) territory, it is widely known and understood that their treatment at the hands of white settlers and colonial/governmental authorities was harsh, unjust and possibly genocidal.[28] Despite this reality, however, it is also true that confronting information about unjust or immoral acts committed by members of our own social group is highly unpleasant and poses a kind of threat to social and national identity.[29] Examining such information is all the more difficult for those we might call 'high identifiers': people who place a significant value on their group identity, who are strongly motivated to protect and enhance this identity even if it means denying the truth.[30] How the acknowledgement of past injustice translates into the contemporary experience of collective guilt is the subject of Chapter I.

But guilt also offers enormous potential as a driver of transformative change. Arguments for social change based in claims for justice are often simply not enough to motivate people to work to change a system or a society in which they continue to be privileged and to experience benefit.[31] Guilt is a more personal experience; it is a constant reminder that all is not right. Guilt signals that a relationship with an individual or group is damaged, and that action should be taken to repair that damage. It is often accompanied by a motivation to apologise for doing harm in order to repair the damaged relationship.[32] Guilt tells us that whatever we have done in the past is not enough, that there is more to be done to create a just and fair society.[33] Guilt brings with it a need for forgiveness and approbation, and can therefore help to move us from sentimentality to political action. Accepting collective guilt and using it to focus our attention on redress and restitution can be a powerful political tool.[34] In Australia, the experience of collective guilt has, for example, been shown to predict greater levels of support for reconciliation generally and for the apology to members of the Stolen Generations in particular.[35]

Some have argued, however, that because the experience of feeling guilty is unpleasant people will go to great lengths to avoid it, making it quite limited as a basis for collective action.[36] Experiencing collective guilt requires seeing oneself as belonging to a group that has acted immorally, suggesting that in some ways it may be an 'unlikely emotion to experience'.[37] But despite these psychological impediments, collective guilt *is* something that is widely experienced. Efforts to avoid or deny guilt do not erase its existence. *Denying* guilt is not the same as not experiencing guilt in the first place. It is a central concern of this book to argue that collective guilt is in fact a commonplace experience, and that our response to that guilt should be the subject of considerable attention. In the introduction to my book *Black Politics* I wrote of my own experience when first confronted with the reality of Australia's history. For me—and my experience is far from unique—the feelings of guilt I experienced were completely paralysing. It took some years for me to be able to work through the complexity of my own response and find a way to take action. And this is the key. While guilt may, for some people, not be a terribly useful emotion, if we are able to get past this response we may find that acknowledging our feelings of guilt can be the first step towards taking responsibility.[38]

The dynamics of collective guilt

In each of us there is a psychological need to feel good about ourselves, about 'who we are'. The extent to which our sense of who we are is bound to a social or national identity will determine the extent to which we experience collective guilt about the past. A desire to feel good about our group or our nation can lead us to develop explanations and justifications for immoral and unjust actions. For some people some of the time—and for some people all of the time—these justifications will hold and they will maintain a positive social or national identity. For many other people, however, those justifications will fail at some point. Confronted with historical fact or current-day inequality, many people will find themselves unable to sustain their justification for past actions by their group, especially where these actions violate present-day moral standards. The widespread experience of collective guilt is the result.[39] Our level of understanding of these emotional dynamics has been shown to be an important predictor for the actions that we take—or fail to take—in the face of knowledge about historical injustice.[40] But these dynamics are highly complex and multifaceted.[41] The ways in which we identify with our group—as white Australians, non-Indigenous Australians, or just as Australians—and what this identification means for our experience of collective guilt and our desire to act are difficult subjects that will be explored in the chapters to follow.

The challenges posed by our emotional responses to collective guilt are not just personal. Or perhaps it is more correct to suggest that our experience of collective guilt is another example of the personal being political. These experiences are not restricted to lay people. Politicians, judges, lawyers—all those with influence in the political realm—share the same psychological needs as the rest of us when it comes to addressing collective guilt.[42] Ministers for Indigenous Affairs past and present offer fascinating insight into the ways in which collective guilt informs policy, and in Chapter 3 I will explore the ways in which guilt continues to shape government policy. In much government policy we can see the tendency for guilt to motivate actions that alleviate one's own discomfort through interventions that may not address the root causes of present-day inequality and marginalisation.[43]

There is some debate over whether guilt or shame is the correct label for the discomfort that people feel when confronted with information about historical injustice. Both emotions are evident in the relationship between Indigenous and non-Indigenous Australians. Some suggest that feelings of guilt tend to accrue to the 'perpetrator' group in a society, who are more likely to feel collective guilt and moral responsibility for the harms their group has inflicted. In contrast, the 'victim' group in an historical relationship more often experiences feelings of shame, where they may feel that what has been done to them exposes them as weak or incompetent.[44] This is an interesting argument given the currency of the word 'shame' among many Aboriginal people in Australia, where people who are feeling embarrassed or humiliated *are* 'shame'.[45] Others make a distinction between guilt as the response associated with personal behaviour—what they should or should not have done in a given situation—and shame as the feeling that past wrongs in fact imply something deeper about who we are as a group. From this perspective it is thought that shame tends to produce a more passive response, a desire to hide or escape from the situation that creates this unpleasant feeling, rather than a more active drive to make reparations. The public humiliation associated with feelings of shame can also produce a 'corrosive anger' associated with denial of past events rather than a desire to face the past. Guilt is perceived as an emotional response more likely to motivate the acknowledgement of historical injustice and provoke action to repair the relationship.[46]

The response to feelings of collective guilt varies widely. Many people feel overwhelmed by information about what has been done historically 'in our names'. Moving from denial about the past to an acceptance of our collective guilt can leave us unsure of how to respond or take action.[47] However, US academic and scholar of whiteness Robert Jensen argues that these new feelings of guilt can become 'a way for white people to avoid taking action', because the paralysis that many people experience in the face of guilt makes it easy for them not to act. In some cases people make a display of their guilty paralysis, saying, 'Look how bad I feel—it immobilises me!', using their own 'psychological angst' as a means of escaping political responsibility.[48] Often the response involves adding to the burden of Aboriginal people, an experience I also wrote about in the introduction to *Black Politics*.[49] Responses such as these shape not only white action but also Aboriginal lives: as 'troubled whitefellas' listening 'tenderly in the wings for tales of black suffering' we do little more than contribute to a black 'victimology', reinforcing Aboriginal people's position as 'the nation's moral burden'.[50] None of these internalised responses to collective guilt are particularly useful, although I suspect many readers will recognise them in themselves.

Denial of guilt is another common response—perhaps the response most evident in public debate. Social psychologists attribute denial to an 'interpretative bias' that sees members of an 'ingroup' make negative attributions about the behaviour of an 'outgroup' and positive attributions for their own group's actions and outcomes. When there is a negative intergroup event, such as conflict between settlers and Indigenous people, the ingroup tends to blame external factors rather than accept that they played any causal role in the event.[51] Thus the problem is seen to lie not with the perpetrators of historical injustice but with the victims, and collective responsibility is denied. 'Exonerating cognitions' are formed that minimise the perception of harms done and instead blame the victims themselves for the harms they have incurred.[52] This form of denial is amplified in individualistic societies such as ours, such that even when harmful group actions are acknowledged as significant, responsibility is attributed only to individuals and collective guilt is minimised and downplayed. Denial is found to be strongest among those who belong to 'dominant' or higher status social groups, who are less likely to accept their collective guilt for racial injustice.[53] Refusing to see the social institutions—the patterns and structures beyond our personal experience—that made historical injustice possible and perpetuate that injustice in the present is one way of avoiding our collective responsibility to deal with our past and act in the present.[54] Those who deny collective guilt are more likely to endorse reparation strategies that aim to restore *psychological* equity—that is, action that can alleviate their own distress at present-day inequality—rather than *actual* equity in the relationship.[55] Choosing to restore actual equity may entail a far more fundamental reassessment of the origins and foundation of the relationship, which in the case of a settler colonial state such as Australia may be found to be immoral and unjust.

The public denial of our collective guilt was perhaps never clearer than when articulated by former Prime Minister John Howard at the 1997 Reconciliation Convention. In that infamous speech in which Howard thumped the lectern as the audience stood and turned their backs to him, Howard argued that reconciliation in Australia would not work 'if it is premised solely on a sense of national guilt and shame'. Howard insisted that it would be wrong to

> ... join those who would portray Australia's history since 1788 as little more than a disgraceful record of imperialism [...] such an approach will be repudiated by the overwhelming majority of Australians who are proud of what this country has achieved although inevitably acknowledging the blemishes in its past history.

It is not surprising that Howard is able to dismiss the atrocities of colonisation as 'blemishes'. As a member of Australia's most dominant ingroup, he is a high identifier with that group, and he is strongly individualistic in his world view. His psychological need to downplay Australia's collective guilt is high, and would no doubt have influenced his approach to reconciliation, to an apology to the Stolen Generations, and to Indigenous policy more generally.

But Howard's response is also premised on the view that experiencing guilt and shame is intrinsically negative and should be avoided. He also suggests that such emotions would be divisive and would detract from national unity. In contrast, social psychologists have suggested that these emotional experiences can be effective in 'facilitating positive outcomes in intergroup relations', stimulating efforts towards reparation and repair of the relationship.[56] In other words, acknowledging collective guilt is not just about feeling bad, but may actually present an opportunity for us to feel better. The Australian researcher of settler colonialism, Lorenzo Veracini,[57] reminds us that settler colonies like Australia are 'traumatised societies par excellence'. Contemporary international discourse on restitution for historical wrongdoing emphasises the important role of 'guilt, mourning and atonement in national revival and reconciliation', transforming 'a traumatic national experience into a constructive political situation'.[58] Collective guilt has a vital role to play in developing improved social conditions in the wake of a violent past.[59] Confronting the past and acknowledging our collective guilt may provide the impetus for constructing a revitalised national identity and associated social and political institutions. By taking account of past injustice in this work we may have the opportunity to experience ourselves as truly moral, rather than defensive and anxious about the past.[60]

Above all, we need to acknowledge that our collective guilt will not resolve itself. Irene Watson, a Tanganekald and Meintangk scholar, notes that Aboriginal people are 'observing much of the white Australian public expressing a fatigue of feeling guilt for an ever-present past'.[61] This insight must lead us to ask a compelling question: what are we to do about our guilt and our exhaustion in continuing to deny it? There is a cost to non-Indigenous as well as Indigenous people when the privileges of (white) society are based on lies about ourselves and our past. Not only is maintaining these lies exhausting, we will remain unable to 'lay claim to our full humanity until we find a way out of the web of denial'.[62] Letting go of the idea that we might ever achieve 'moral purity'—because history does not allow us this luxury—might be a useful starting point. Once we let go of purity, accept our 'moral stain' as US legal scholar David Williams describes it, then guilt may no longer be unbearable.[63] If we accept that we are guilty then we can ask the really difficult questions—about sovereignty, about national identity—without constantly having to defend our honour. Acknowledging our collective guilt can be a useful starting point for the hard work that is still to be done.

This book assumes at the outset that along with all we have to be proud of as a nation there is also much about which Australians should and do feel guilty. It does not attempt to explore whether or not this guilt is justified; rather, in Chapters 1and 2, it examines the nature and extent of this guilt, and the moral frameworks and historical narratives that have been developed in order to justify and minimise our guilt. Chapter 3 then explores the ways in which this historical denial and repression plays out in present-day policy. Chapter 4 begins to consider what non-Indigenous Australians might do in response to our collective guilt that could move us beyond our present moribund relationships. Chapter 5 examines the successes and failures of past efforts and Chapter 6 begins to map some strategies for the next phase of our engagement.

My aim in this book is not to generate feelings of shame. Shaming Australians from any walk of life is unlikely to contribute to our adaptive work. Shaming is more likely to promote 'anger, humiliation and denial' when what we are seeking is empathy and responsibility.[64] Shaming may, in fact, harden individuals in their positions of denial and promote greater efforts at work avoidance. What I most hope for is that Australia will soon commit to a renewed effort at finding its own mark on the spectrum of historical justice, 'between vengeance and forgiveness'.[65] Historical justice does not seek to punish the perpetrators of past crimes. Rather it seeks to repair the injustice done, to correct the record where necessary, and to advance changes in relationships and future behaviours.[66] We must do more than merely regret the past. Regret suggests merely that we wish certain events had not happened. A further step is required. In acknowledging and expressing our guilt we may be able to accept collective responsibility for historical injustice and begin to seriously develop a restorative, decolonising response that allows for the mutual recognition of sovereign peoples.[67]

Such a response is sorely needed in Australia. What I fear, however, is that until we engage in the adaptive work associated with our collective guilt about historical injustice in this country we will continue to stumble in this challenge; we will continue to turn to authority and avoid our own work because we want to avoid the distress and discomfort it brings. In doing this we will continue to hear our historical record defended and our guilt denied with the argument that a different approach would be divisive. But our collective guilt does not hold us together; it drives us apart. Our collective guilt perpetuates inequality, it feeds a defensive and often ugly nationalism, and it starves us of a moral presence in the world. Until we face up to our guilt we will never be the country we think we are.

Chapter 1

The long colonial shadow: Guilt, nationalism and the morality of genocide

A nation, like Australia, exists more in the hearts and minds of its citizens than it does in any constitution or parliament. As the renowned scholar of nationalism Benedict Anderson has suggested, nations are really 'imagined political communities'. Because most of us will never meet—or even hear or know of—the majority of our fellow Australians, we must imagine ourselves as sharing similar values and traits. What we imagine, regardless of any contradictory reality, is a community of equals, joined in shared struggle and blessed by equal opportunities.[1] We are challenged and disturbed by those who disrupt this imagined community and we strive through the telling of national stories to maintain an imagined unity and cohesion.

This imagined nation is in part constituted by the collective memories we share in public and in private.[2] The collective memories that constitute the imagined community of Australia include a history of colonialism; a history over which there has been much debate (as will be discussed in the next chapter).

Troubling aspects of this history have produced an insecure nationalism in Australia, the defence of which comprises one aspect of our adaptive challenge. David Williams describes the psychological threat that collective guilt poses to an insecure nationalism as being of 'nuclear proportions' as it indicates that a nation like Australia (or the United States, in the example of which Williams writes) is not only guilty of occasional wrong-doing, but is in fact 'rotten to the root': 'It was born in blood, and it feeds itself on land choked with the bodies of its victims.'[3] As the Australian anthropologist W.E.H. Stanner once pointed out, the tendency to excuse the destructive aspects of the development of European life on this territory now known as 'Australia' 'sticks out like a foot from a shallow grave'.[4] We are more comfortable when we do not confront the extent of our nation's guilt in causing harm in the imagining and creating of the Australian nation. We are more comfortable still when we can deny that current generations carry any trace of guilt for past acts. But despite this denial our experience of collective guilt persists. For reasons that this chapter will explore, our guilt not only persists in the present but is transmitted to each new generation, maintained by a form of defensive nationalism that will not allow an honest attempt to redress past wrongs.

Understanding collective guilt

The word 'guilt' can refer both to feelings of guilt and a determination of responsibility.[5] The dominant understanding of guilt is as an individual experience of (legal) liability, requiring some form of punishment that may lead to possible reform. This conception of guilt has a long history, with roots in Christian theology and Roman law and later consolidated in the individualism of the Enlightenment, which overrode any possibility of collective judgment. In this context, understandings of guilt in connection with 'collective responsibility, liability and atonement' tend only to be recognised by societies and by governments as 'an irrational conceptualisation of guilt', if indeed they are recognised at all.[6]

But collective guilt is a concept that transcends narrow legal individualism. While in the courtroom conceptions of blame may necessarily rest on individual wrongdoing, collective responsibility remains part of people's conception of morality and is therefore a feature of 'everyday justice'.[7] It is a psychological rather than a legal experience, in that it may not involve actually being guilty in any commonly understood sense of that term. Thus, although collective guilt is not the same thing as 'being guilty' in a legal sense, it is connected to feelings of a shared identity—the sort of shared identity that constitutes our imagined nation. Collective guilt, and indeed other shared emotions, is only possible as a social phenomenon—as 'guilt by association'—when people categorise themselves or others at a group level.[8]

But how is it that these feelings of guilt can be shared among a collective when the majority of individuals within that collective have not directly participated in the commission of any crime? German jurist and writer Bernhard Schlink suggests that, rather than collective guilt deriving from a sense of responsibility for someone else's crime, collective guilt arises from a feeling of 'responsibility for one's own solidarity with the criminal'. Schlink suggests that this conception of collective guilt casts a web that is 'high and wide', entangling every person who stands in solidarity with the perpetrators and who maintains solidarity with them after the fact. In the Australian sense it may be useful to think of national identification as a form of solidarity or what Schlink terms a 'community of responsibility'. Such a community is not something intangible or unintelligible, Schlink argues, but rather it is 'the tangible intertwining of relationships by real people as they communicate and interact'.[9] In this sense all of us who identify ourselves as members of the Australian nation may be caught in the web of collective guilt for the sins of our past and present by virtue of our social identification and interactions. The price of this solidarity or national identification is that, for as long as our community of responsibility maintains bonds of solidarity with the perpetrators of historical injustice, all the behaviour for which we might otherwise feel appropriate shame and disgust will also be credited to us. For as long as the options available for severing these bonds, such as restitution or reparations, have not been taken up, then the solidarity—the collective guilt—exists by default.[10]

Group, or national, identity is a crucial component in understandings of collective guilt. Our emotional responses to our national past, whether they be feelings of pride, guilt, or something else, do not stem from our personal participation in past events but rather from our shared membership in the category of offenders.[11] Despite the widely held view that guilty feelings should only be attached to those events for which we are personally responsible,[12] our Australian group or national identity is in fact central to our experience of collective guilt. Australians, and particularly white Australians, are part of the 'ingroup', the dominant social grouping in Australia most strongly associated with the colonisation of this land and the dispossession of Indigenous peoples. This identity is policed and reinforced through suggestions of what constitutes 'un-Australian' attitudes or behaviour. The reverse is also true. Collective pride in past events is often evoked as an important part of Australian national identity, whether or not we as individuals participated in these celebrated events. Very few Australians were actually at Gallipoli or on the Kokoda Track, and yet these events are commemorated as being about all of us, as moments in our history in which we all share, and which have passed on to future generations an important sense of who we are. Collective guilt operates in precisely the same way. When our sense of ourselves is connected to our forebears and ancestors, and where it is known that our forebears and ancestors committed harms and atrocities, it follows that collective guilt may be a salient component of our national identity.

Unlike pride, however, collective guilt produces feelings of distress rather than feelings of euphoria. Research on the phenomenon of collective guilt suggests that it is characterised by three interrelated properties: 'a focus of attention on the group self, a sense of group responsibility for an immoral act, and an extremely unpleasant feeling that people prefer to assuage through restitution or avoidance'.[13] It is this last that is of concern in this book, particularly with regard to the ways in which these unpleasant feelings get in the way of efforts to engage in adaptive work. There is a difference between *experiencing* collective guilt and *accepting* collective guilt. It is a salient aspect of Australian struggles in this domain that, despite a commonly *experienced* feeling of discomfort, we do much to avoid, deny and reject the notion that we are guilty of anything. Indeed some research has suggested that feelings of collective guilt can produce attitudes that are counterproductive to collective efforts to address the source of our guilt, such as the reconciliation process in Australia.[14] One common avoidance strategy is to insist that the crimes of Australia's history were long ago and that current generations have nothing to feel guilty about.

Guilt about the past

Bernhard Schlink suggests that guilt about the past not only infects the entire generation that lives through an era (in his case Nazi Germany), but also 'casts a long shadow over the present, infecting later generations with a sense of guilt, responsibility and self-questioning'.[15] Further, Schlink suggests that by not renouncing the actions of the original guilty parties 'a new sort of guilt is created'; new generations create their own guilt when, in the face of evidence or accusations concerning past atrocities, they maintain their solidarity bonds with the perpetrators.[16] If, as Schlink suggests, a nation of people constitute the sort of community of solidarity through which collective guilt is transmitted, then children and later generations become entwined and entrapped in 'the guilt of non-renunciation', which 'sits in wait for them until they become able to recognise the guilt of others, dissociate or not dissociate themselves from it, and therewith become capable of acquiring their own guilt'.[17]

In other words, the collective guilt of later generations is a distinctly different phenomenon to the guilt of the original perpetrators of an act. Intergenerational guilt involves our individual and collective choices about what we do *in response to* our knowledge of past atrocities, rather than our responsibility for the original acts. For as long as we choose an identity that is 'saturated by history'—as is very much the case in Australia—we continue to stand in solidarity with past generations and the crimes they have committed. The violence of our history generates a kind of 'psychic deformation' that is passed from generation to generation, able to 'hibernate in the unconscious, only to be transmitted to the next generation like an undetected disease'.[18] Schlink suggests that there is no external authority that can free subsequent generations of their share of the guilt bequeathed to them by their parents, arguing that 'over the generations, collectively experienced historical events become individual varied memories. The task of dissociation from specific historical guilt leads to the creation of one's own identity, an undertaking that every generation has to master.'[19] Collective guilt about historical acts is in fact a constituent part of our contemporary national identity.

In this sense the guilt of later generations is a political rather than a personal guilt. In as much as later generations continue to benefit from the resources and gains produced by historical injustices, and in as much as we choose to deny that the current circumstances experienced by Aboriginal and Torres Strait Islanders have causal links to these past injustices, then our response makes us guilty as a new collective, a new community of solidarity, not responsible for the original atrocities but guilty nonetheless.[20] Even if we recognise that we had no control over the original, blameworthy actions, we can perceive ourselves as responsible for the continuing negative repercussions from these historical events.[21] Our identity as contemporary Australians is not detachable from our history, for better or for worse, and there is a strong case to be made that current generations should still pay our nation's 'historical debts'.[22] As Gillian Cowlishaw has suggested, 'worry' about Aboriginal people and the injuries they have suffered in the past has become 'a distinctive element' of Australian national identity.[23]

These arguments about the transmission of guilt through the generations underscore the adaptive challenge facing Australians today. David Williams argues that the appropriate response to the recognition of our guilty inheritance is, indeed, guilt; 'not a soul-destroying, paralysing guilt, but a guilt born from a mature realisation that our past creates moral obligations that we won't ever escape'.[24] This mature realisation is not often in evidence. More common, in Australia and other societies experiencing collective guilt, are efforts by the dominant social group to reinforce their community of solidarity, to minimise past harms and current inequalities in ways that become part of mainstream culture and perpetuate the privilege and dominance of some groups over others.[25] In Australia, our ability to perpetuate this solidarity and deny our collective guilt is maintained through a vigorous form of nationalism that rejects both the sins of our past and our moral obligations in the present.

Guilt and nationalism

Clues about the extent of Australian feelings of collective guilt can be found in our somewhat defensive and often downright hostile expressions of nationalism. It is our collective guilt about Australia's past and present that prevents us from enjoying a more celebratory and generous nationalism. As each Australia Day rolls around there is a certain level of hysteria to the flag-waving insistence that we are a truly great country, the famous land of the 'fair go'. The fact that we choose to celebrate our national day on the anniversary of the European invasion of this country jars with our desire to erase that part of our history and celebrate only the nation-building aspects of it. Even our political leaders have experienced this incongruity. Historian Mark McKenna recalls Prime Minister Bob Hawke's discomfort at Australia's bicentennial 'celebrations'. In the wake of passionate

Aboriginal protests and the demands of the 'Treaty '88' campaign, Hawke, addressing a television audience of several million Australians, 'could not bring himself to mention the dispossession of Aboriginal Australians', speaking only of Australia as a successful nation of immigrants. The silences in the prime minister's speech underlined the dilemma of this intended day of celebration, namely that the historical injustices of our past continued to 'undercut any attempt to present Australia Day as the rallying point for national pride'.[26]

In and of itself, nationalism is not a 'moral mistake'. US sociologist Craig Calhoun suggests that we should approach an understanding of nationalism with 'critical attention to its limits, illusions, and potential for abuse' but we should not dismiss it completely.[27] Calhoun draws attention to what he describes as 'everyday nationalism', which 'organises people's sense of belonging in the world', and he rejects the idea that nations are 'mere figments of the imagination'.[28] The wider public likes nationalism, particularly for its role in asserting a positive national identity about which they can feel good. Nevertheless, an understanding of the potential benefits of nationalism in people's daily lives does not diminish the pitfalls of what Benedict Anderson terms 'official nationalism', which he describes as 'a self-protective policy, intimately linked to the preservation of imperial-dynastic interests'. Such policy, he suggests, is designed first and foremost to serve the interests of the state.[29] And while the wider Australian public may dislike the racist and sometimes ugly manifestations of 'official' nationalism, such as were evident at the Cronulla riots in 2005, the separation of these positive and negative aspects is not always possible.[30]

The defensiveness produced by Australia's fragile nationalism leaves us poorly equipped to engage in adaptive work. It is the very form of our nationalism—a settler nationalism—that means our past, present and future are 'intrinsically bound up with the relationship between settlers and Aborigines' making the legitimacy of the nation's connections with the territory on which it was formed our 'most vulnerable point'.[31] The Indian political psychologist Ashis Nandy has suggested that Australia's tendency to see itself as a colonial power, when in actual fact it is a colonised society, means that there has been an ongoing struggle for our supposedly rightful status as 'a European colonial power with a civilising mission'. This struggle has fostered a fear that 'even faint streaks of yellow, black, or brown detract from Australia's nationhood', which in turn has promoted the active denial of cultural space to others. This anxiety is now a feature of Australian political culture, playing out in electoral battles and other ideological contests concerning, for example, our acceptance or rejection of asylum seekers.[32] As will be discussed further in Chapter 3, this anxiety around nationalism in settler colonial states such as Australia and the United States is based in 'a sovereign's dread of a rival sovereign's claims'.[33] Such fear, and the insistence on a uniformity among members of a nation, is outdated and, according to Canadian political philosopher James Tully, 'has no place in the world of today'.[34]

The extent to which individuals in a collective are motivated by fear to protect their social or national identity depends in part on the degree of importance or value that they invest in this identity. This is what is known in social psychological terms as group identification, and it follows that those who are highly identified with a group, particularly a dominant group or 'ingroup' within a nation, are more likely to ignore or downplay the negative actions of their ingroup.[35] High identifiers—people who invest a high degree of value in a social identity such as 'Australian'—are far more likely to defend a nationalist sentiment, including through the denial of past atrocities and current injustices. People may feel an attachment to their national group that allows them to experience feelings of guilt and moral responsibility or, in the case of high identifiers, they may have a psychological need to glorify their national group that presents a serious obstacle to accepting negative information about their group or national history.[36] High identification gets in the way of people's ability to accept negative information about their group or nation's past, and makes them less likely to confront the sins of the past, make amends, and incorporate these negative aspects of history into a healthier, more authentic and more robust national identity.[37]

The rejection of intergenerational responsibility is one part of the defensive nationalism that is constructed in an effort to ward off acknowledgement of our collective, historical guilt. Former Prime Minister John Howard's efforts to argue against intergenerational responsibility, for example claiming in his speech to the 1997 Reconciliation Convention that 'Australians of this generation should not be required to accept guilt and blame for past actions and policies over which they had no control',[38] are just one example of a leader attempting to defend our national vulnerability. This is an example of the way in which high national identification can become a way of avoiding the work that needs to be done. Indeed, the negative national response to former Prime Minister Paul Keating's leadership in acknowledging past wrongs done to Aboriginal people in the name of Australian nationalism can be characterised as a reaction to his 'politics of guilt', understood by many to be divisive and threatening to Australian nationalism. Howard, himself a very high identifier and therefore already inclined to downplay the wrongs of Australia's past, offered some relief to those made uneasy by Keating's naming of Australian guilt, instead advocating a reassuring version of Australian history that promoted pride in what he argued is an honourable history.[39]

This aspect of Australian nationalism is a significant cause of the impasse experienced by non-Indigenous Australians in their relationships with Indigenous Australians. The myths that are built into our national identity—myths about the frontier as 'a site for the making of the nation',[40] about explorers and settlers, about the 'outback', about Anzac, and about a fair go—are difficult to question without being accused of being 'un-Australian' by trying to undermine our sense of national pride.[41] It is confusing to be told that our feelings of guilt are not just baseless and incorrect but somehow also a form of treason. Such pronouncements present a substantial barrier to the adaptive work there is to be done.

There have, of course, been moments in our nation's history that presented opportunities to rewrite Australian nationalism. Elizabeth Povinelli suggests that the Mabo and Wik judgments provided one such moment, when, in the years following:

> ... Australian subjects sent themselves a national postcard addressed to the general question of historical accountability: How should Australian nation-building be remembered and from whose perspective? What would this nation-building look like from the perspective of Aboriginal history? Would it seem like a bloody, illegitimate ordeal, a rotten deal forged on the back of blind prejudice and material greed? Indeed, should the eventfulness of colonialism be figured in the past tense? Did colonialism happen or was it happening? In the present, could the nation—or each and every person within that nation—be responsible for events of the past? And could responsibility be decided decisively in the manner of a court case? Could copping the sins of the past liberate the present from that evil, or would it create new problems—opening, for instance, the state's coffers for reparation claims? On radio and tele-

> vision, in beer and parliament halls, in newspaper columns and amid columns of cheering and jeering demonstrators . . . public pundits, parliamentarians, and other citizens debated a new counterintuitive model of national cohesion registered in these two High Court cases. They argued about whether a patriotic nationalism could arise from the sackcloth and ashes of public accounting of a nation's shame . . . .[42]

Povinelli suggests that 'finding' native title in the wake of Australia's colonial history was a decision with far more than legal implications. Rather, the Mabo and Wik decisions provided a 'litmus test' concerning Australia's preparedness to take responsibility for the suffering experienced by Aboriginal and Torres Strait Islander peoples because of our 'national dream'.[43]

In retrospect it is manifestly evident that Australia failed this test. In response to a moment in which it was possible to choose a different path—to break our bonds of solidarity with the perpetrators of past acts including Indigenous dispossession, and to renounce the violence of colonisation—Australia chose instead to reaffirm these bonds. The nation was won over by a leader promising that we could be 'relaxed and comfortable', that any suggestion of past or present guilt was unjust, that we should instead rejoice in a proud history, and that any notion of collective guilt was in fact 'offensive to the greater story of Australia's success as a nation'.[44] Perversely, however, in making the choice to opt out of a meaningful form of reconciliation, the nation chose guilt. A new generation became identified with a nation that had not reconciled its historical injustices, leaving the adaptive challenge unaddressed. In the process our collective guilt became highly politicised and contested,[45] opening new divides in our national identity rather than unifying the nation, as those who downplayed our guilty past had promised. The apparent success of Howard's strategy of avoiding the real work of the reconciliation process rested on his ability to maintain a public morality that could justify our colonial history.

Australia's genocidal morality

A history of harm being perpetrated by one group against another is not unique to Australia. History is made up of such conflict and brutality, and almost without exception group members tend to perceive their own group's damaging actions as morally justifiable. Legitimising historical injustice in this way has the effect of protecting group members from the guilt that they might otherwise experience when confronted with the harm they have done. Indeed, it is probable to expect that people will be 'strongly inclined' to protect their social or national identity by developing an understanding of their group's actions 'from the vantage point of the "moral high ground" '.[46]

The 'civilising mission' that accompanied colonialism, advanced by both colonial governments and the missionary regimes that were hot on their heels, is one example of this pattern of behaviour.[47] Today, however, the mission of 'civilising' Aboriginal and Torres Strait Islander peoples through dispossession, containment, servitude and the banning of Indigenous languages and cultural practices—not discounting the violence and abuse that were often used to police these regimes—can be argued to be genocidal. The taking of Aboriginal children from their families has also been described as genocidal, although for some this terminology seems inflammatory in the Australian context: genocide brings to mind Hitler and the Jews, not Australia and the Aborigines.[48] But the concept of genocide, defined by the legal scholar Raphael Lemkin as 'the destruction of a nation or of an ethnic group',[49] is much wider than the popular understanding of the practice as one of mass extermination. The United Nations has developed Lemkin's original conception of the term to encompass 'any of the following acts committed with intent to destroy, in whole or in part, a national, ethnical, racial or religious group, as such:

(a) Killing members of the group;
(b) Causing serious bodily or mental harm to members of the group;
(c) Deliberately inflicting on the group conditions of life calculated to bring about its physical destruction in whole or in part;
(d) Imposing measures intended to prevent births within the group;
(e) Forcibly transferring children of the group to another group.'[50]

As Canadian sociologist Christopher Powell has argued, the concept of genocide extends to the destruction of the foundations of life of the national group, including the destruction of language, culture, religion and social institutions, with the intended aim of annihilating the group. And by annihilation we may not necessarily be referring to extermination. Rather, we may think of practices intended to absorb or assimilate a minority group into a dominant group as being genocidal in intent, what Powell refers to as 'slow genocide'.[51]

Given both the breadth and the specificity of the internationally accepted definition it is, as Ann Curthoys has suggested, 'a little curious' to find that in Australia today, where colonisation produced population losses on an extraordinary scale, there remains such a strong reaction to the suggestion that genocide is a concept that might explain our past.[52] Neverthless, the high identifiers appointed to defend our national honour continue to furiously reject any assertion of genocide in Australia. Keith Windschuttle, for example, argues that 'There were no gas chambers in Australia or anything remotely equivalent. The colonial authorities wanted to civilise and modernise the Aborigines, not exterminate them.'[53] But an absence of gas chambers is hardly the point. Windschuttle's assertion of what he sees as a benign effort to supplant Indigenous culture with the more civilised and modern values and behaviours of the settlers in fact fits the definition of genocide outlined above. And as the Australian writer Carmel Bird has argued, 'a state cannot excuse itself by claiming that the practice of genocide was previously lawful under its own laws or that its people did not (or do not) share the outrage of the international community'.[54]

Nevertheless, the historical injustices that are an unavoidable fact of Australian settler colonialism are often justified as being in accord with the morals of the time and therefore understandable, or at least excusable. The public morality that permitted these historical injustices—injustices that include regimes of dispossession and forced migration, the chilling acceptance that Aboriginal people were a dying race, and the callousness of policies of child removal—is what Christopher Powell describes as a 'genocidal morality'. Powell argues that a genocidal morality can share many features of 'more pedestrian moralities', including that an action may be framed as a duty or obligation pursued for its own sake; that it can be justified via claims that it is being undertaken for the greater good and the promotion of social solidarity; and that it can integrate the individuals into a group or national whole through their knowledge of the moral framework and their relation to it. Powell understands morality as 'a particular kind of social institution', with different norms and dynamics depending on the social location. Contrary to everyday understandings of what is 'moral'—understandings that often equate morality with goodness—Powell suggests that morality can take many forms, in some instances opposing genocidal acts, and in others facilitating or justifying these same events. As a consequence, there have been eras and events during which genocide has been framed as a moral obligation or duty to something (a regime, a nation) beyond any individual element of hatred or greed.[55]

The moralising framework of settler states was used to justify atrocities committed against Indigenous peoples as a civilising project in which violence could be excused by the 'great weight of moral necessity' of the colonial project as a whole. The genocidal morality in settler colonies including Australia, Canada and the United States witnessed the approval of genocidal acts in the name of nation-building and in light of the presumed superiority of Western civilisation.[56] This does not excuse the perpetrators of genocidal acts, but it does move away from an essentialist position that suggests that those involved in the commission of genocide are themselves either good or evil. It points to the power of public morality to influence the views of citizens, who may be drawn into the commission of genocide through their belief that such acts will serve the greater good. This argument in fact grants greater agency both to those involved in the original genocidal acts and to the generations that follow, each of whom, one would hope, is in possession of the critical thinking abilities that might allow them to question the morality that justifies immoral acts. Although, as Powell suggests, morality cannot always protect us from being perpetrators of genocide, a critical awareness of morality as a social structure rather than some intrinsic or extrinsic essence may open up a new space for adaptive work.

Today, our collective failure to substantively break with this morality suggests a further dimension to our adaptive challenge. What are the implications in the present for continuing to align ourselves with—and defend—a genocidal morality? As the art historian and critic Bernard Smith suggested in his Boyer Lectures in 1980, a new awareness of 'what actually occurred' has created a significant problem for 'the integrity and authenticity of Australian culture today'. Smith asks how we can 'redeem' our culture from 'the guilty awareness that these acts of genocide and attempted genocide were being enacted most vigorously at that very time when our own white Australian culture was being conceived and born, and that its very growth presupposed the termination of a black culture . . . '.[57] In other words, Smith was asking how we might break the bonds of solidarity with the perpetrators of historical injustice on this territory.

The assertion of Indigenous rights claims, and the guilt and discomfort expressed by many non-Indigenous Australians in response to these claims, has the potential to challenge the genocidal morality that has characterised Australia since invasion. This potential, according to Gillian Cowlishaw,[58] goes some way to explaining the 'tenacity and fervor' of those high identifiers who continue to deny Australia's adaptive challenge through the downplaying of both the most heinous aspects of our past and the extent of Indigenous suffering today. Their refusal to acknowledge the 'entrenched inhumanity' that has been exhibited to Aboriginal and Torres Strait Islanders since the European invasion of this territory is an attempt to maintain the moral framework that has justified the many expressions of this inhumanity. But as historian Raymond Evans has argued, although 'patterns of denial run like coarse threads through the unfolding drama of Australian land-taking', over time coming to 'predominate in the Australian psyche', the success of this denial could only ever be 'shifting, tenuous and never total':

> For there are, contemporaneously, so many sources that break that silence in order to thwart its intended conspiracy—the words of individual whistle-blowers, both named and anonymous, who need to enter their protests, sometimes stridently, sometimes cautiously; sometimes in small tangential voices, sometimes in persistent and unrelenting ones—against what was regarded in their time as well as our own as being both questionable and unjust: the uncompensated seizure of another's territory, the theft of children, the rape and sexual enslavement of women, the imposition of terror and the manifold, cursory killings of the original inhabitants. These are the kind of historical messengers that today's media love to shoot down.[59]

Despite ongoing efforts at denial it is evident that Australia was 'caught out . . . red-handed playing the genocide game . . . using our own version of history and our own versions of the law to legitimate our questionable actions'.[60]

The moralising framework that underpins and perpetuates such efforts at denial continues to call into question the 'moral legitimacy' of settler colonial states. International relations theorist Paul Keal defines a morally illegitimate state as one that:

> . . . either had its origins in the dispossession of Indigenous peoples whose descendants continue to be dispossessed in important ways, and have unresolved claims against the settler state, or one in which there continue to be practices that discriminate against and threaten the survival of Indigenous peoples within its borders. It is, in short, one that has harmed or continues to harm particular peoples and has yet to negotiate a mutually agreed reconciliation.[61]

Keal contrasts this form of moral illegitimacy with what he terms 'political legitimacy', arguing that a country like Australia might never see its political legitimacy at issue, maintaining functioning governments and good international standing.[62] Or as Canadian political philosopher James Tully suggests, legitimacy and justice are not necessarily equivalent; a legitimate state is not just if those members suffering an injustice cannot seek to have the injustice rectified.[63] Political legitimacy cannot override the persistence of moral illegitimacy, which can only be overcome by states that direct considerable effort towards securing the rights of Indigenous peoples and seeking reconciliation with them.

Here there are two different, but complementary, views of the way in which moral frameworks can inform our conceptions of collective guilt, national identity and the dimensions of Australia's adaptive challenge. On the one hand, an understanding of 'genocidal morality' helps to explain how Australia's historical injustices took place and why later generations have been unable to break the bonds of solidarity with the perpetrators of genocidal acts, thus ensuring that our guilt about the past is perpetuated in the present and future. On the other hand, we can see Australia as morally illegitimate when measured against international human rights standards, which demand of us our most sincere effort to address past and present injustices involving Indigenous peoples. Settler states like Australia have, for the most part, not really begun to face up to the significance of our public justification for genocidal acts—a failure that suggests some deep connections between a genocidal morality and our broader social and political culture.[64] Examining these connections is a part of our adaptive challenge, and it will be a process that raises some difficult questions about how we feel about the nation that we live in and—for the most part—love.

Loving this country

Nations everywhere need a story that is 'vibrant and relevant', and that will give 'direction, meaning, and purpose to the national life'. National stories promote national cohesion and, in some important ways, they make sure that 'a nation's spirit is alive and well'.[65] Seen in this light it is perhaps understandable that the Australian national story would chime so strongly with our official nationalism. Indeed, the telling of heroic and celebratory tales of Australia's colonial and military past is often held up as a unifying practice, and critics of these narratives are tagged with that ugly label 'un-Australian'. Political leaders and other high identifiers who become our central story tellers may not recognise the ways in which they are meeting their own psychological needs, but they would almost certainly argue that a positive and celebratory national story is good for the country, or at least that segment of the country with which they identify. That there is a 'vacuum' at the heart of our national story, a vacuum created at least in part by Indigenous challenges to Australia's legitimacy, goes some way to explaining the promotion of the Anzac myth as intrinsic to our story of national pride and heroism, as other days of national 'celebration' have proved more problematic[66]—an issue to which I will return in Chapter 6.

Australian political theorist Tim Soutphommasane has described patriotism as a 'Janus-faced phenomenon' that includes both 'a dubious national loyalty' and the motivation for citizens to 'make sacrifices for the improvement of their country'. While he advocates a form of patriotism that is both progressive and inclusive, Soutphommasane acknowledges that contemporary Australian patriotism is 'confused', sustaining a 'cultural aggression' rather than citizenship such that it has, at times, been 'indistinguishable from racial chauvinism', fostering anxiety, fear and hate, sentiments which 'have been given succour by a renewed sense of loving our country'.[67] This two-faced patriotism is both the greatest asset and the greatest barrier to our adaptive challenge. We will only engage in adaptive work when we value what is at stake. But the desire to make our country a better, more just and morally legitimate place will founder on the need to first admit that it is not already just and moral. Nevertheless, Soutphommasane argues, it is possible to acknowledge the wrongs of the past, and to accept collective guilt in the present, while still loving our country.[68]

I really love this country, but my love for Australia is a complicated love. Most of what I write and speak about publicly is highly critical of government and often expresses shame or disappointment in the direction a policy has taken or what I see as injustice or inequity. During the years of the Howard governments I would have been labelled a 'Howard hater', but my criticism of Australian politics and political culture pre- and post-date John Howard. For a long time I would have been uncomfortable expressing my love of country, thinking that it would somehow align me with the sort of aggressive and official nationalism that, as this chapter has outlined, is highly problematic. Now I am more comfortable expressing what I hope is always an engaged and thoughtful love, rather than a blind and obedient love. This love of country can energise and motivate us, help us renew our belief that this place can be just and fair, and provide us with emotional strength and resilience in order that we may persist when the work is difficult.

The adaptive social change practitioner Adam Kahane has developed this way of thinking over the decades of his own work in complex and 'stuck' situations. Kahane draws on Martin

Luther King's argument that while 'Power without love is reckless and abusive', so too 'love without power is sentimental and anemic'.[69] Kahane suggests that if we 'recognize our interdependence and act to unify with others'—that is, if we are motivated by love—but we do so in such a way that we 'hobble our own or others' growth', the outcome will 'at best be intellectual and at worst, deceitfully reinforcing of the status quo'. In contrast, if those of us concerned with social change and adaptive work do not understand the ways in which we are interdependent with others—that is, if we are concerned solely with power—the outcome will 'at best be insensitive and at worst, oppressive or even genocidal'. Kahane argues that power without love produces scorched-earth war that destroys everything we hold dear. Love without power produces lifeless peace that leaves us stuck in place.[70] So while our love of country can be a powerful force for change, we must combine this love of country with the power of critical analysis and a preparedness to confront the reality of our collective guilt.

The risk, if we do not do this, is that our love of country will blind us to the true complexity of the challenges we face. Patriotism can be seductive, drawing us towards a premature conclusion in our adaptive work rather than holding us in the spaces and relationships that are most stuck, difficult and uncomfortable. We may be seduced into believing that our love of country and our superficial efforts are worthy enough, helping us to avoid having our good intentions criticised or finding that historical injustices present a greater barrier to reconciliation than we were prepared to admit.[71] Reverting to a blind nationalism may also help shield us from the fact that our good intentions are not yet universally shared, that those of us in cities may be more 'eager to plead guilt to past injustices' while many of our fellow Australians in rural and regional areas are 'less sympathetic and sorrowful'.[72] Reverting to this form of nationalism may be comforting: 'We tried', we can all say, as we have said so many times in the past. But such a reversion is merely work avoidance. The adaptive challenge will still be waiting for us, and in avoiding it once again we will merely reinforce our bonds of solidarity with the perpetrators of historical injustices, leaving in place our genocidal morality, confirming our collective guilt in the present, and creating new layers of intergenerational guilt. All of which is to suggest that our good intentions are simply not good enough.

Chapter 2

History and identity: What we lose by denying our past

In his 1968 Boyer lectures, the anthropologist W.E.H. Stanner spoke of the 'great Australian silence' about the atrocities and injustices perpetrated against Indigenous people. Stanner argued that the level of inattention to the place of Aboriginal and Torres Strait Islander peoples in Australian history books could not be explained by mere 'absent-mindedness'. Rather, Stanner suggested that this neglect had been structured into the Australian identity, creating 'a view from a window which has been carefully placed to exclude a whole quadrant of the landscape'.[1] Historian Tom Griffiths suggests that Stanner was not just urging the nation to face up to suppressed facts about our colonial history, but also that we break this silence as part of 'an essential exploration of the white Australian psyche'. As Griffiths goes on to argue, we need to pay as much attention to our national silences as we do to the 'white noise' that tends to drown them out.[2] While rhetoric that suggests we can simply draw a line under the past and create a more positive future is appealing, it is also simplistic. History matters: both recent history and long-ago history. If we cannot face some of the uncomfortable truths about the past—if we cannot break our national silences—we will remain unable to engage in adaptive work in the present and future.

There was once a time when history was believed to be an objective recording of 'facts' open to only one interpretation. It was also in the past, so there was really no point dwelling on it as nothing could be done to change past events. Recorded history tended to be a 'winner's history', told from the perspective of the victors and ignoring or minimising the experiences of the vanquished. Over time, however, the 'elasticity' of history began to be recognised, and it became increasingly important to our identity and daily life. Recognised as socially constructed and therefore open to interpretation, history also became subject to increasing debate, a 'crucial field of political struggle'.[3] Histories of material exclusion accompanied by symbolic and cultural stigmatisation have, perhaps inevitably, become highly politicised.[4] The sorts of high identifiers discussed in the previous chapter tend to feel an imperative to 'prop up' the historical narratives that show us in the most positive light, reinforcing our sense of ourselves as noble and good and fostering an identity that can be celebrated. Those who would advance a more critical view are often derided for undermining our national identity.[5]

It we are to move beyond our collective guilt and make some real, adaptive changes in Australia we must begin with an honest stocktake of the harms we have done. As the Christian ethicist Donald Shriver argues, 'justice to the past is a form of justice in the present and for the future'. While we must find a balance between 'burying the gruesome past' and burying ourselves in the memory of it, we must also find a way of doing justice to the past that will 'drain the memory of its power to continue to poison the present and future'.[6] It would be a mistake to assume that there is wide agreement about harm, racism or injustice in Australia's history and it would be a crucial error to suggest that these concerns are somehow less relevant today.[7] Dealing with the past can be a strand of the 'official nationalism' discussed in the previous chapter or it can be part of a project of healing and reconciliation. We cannot make the past 'unhappen' no matter how distressing it may be. We can, however, focus on restoring the condition of the persons, or peoples, who have been harmed.[8] The issue really should not be whether we recognise the injustices committed in Australia's past but *how* we might do this, acknowledging that the way in which public memory is constructed is never neutral.[9]

The brutality of colonialism

A good place to start might be an honest conversation about what the colonisation of this territory has meant—and continues to mean—for Aboriginal and Torres Strait Islander peoples. I say continues to mean because recognising that colonisation is not an historical event but an ongoing process is crucial to our adaptive challenge. One of the most frequently deployed strategies designed to minimise or avoid our collective guilt is the rationalisation that colonisation happened 'a long time ago'. It is true that the bonds of solidarity that perpetuate our collective guilt in the present were in fact forged in a settler solidarity that once seemed crucial for survival. As Henry Reynolds has argued, 'The shared guilt of the punitive expedition, the complicity in killing, bound participants together in close confederation'.[10] But recognising the myriad ways in which colonialism persists in the present—through the failure to properly recognise Indigenous prior ownership and sovereignty and through all other measures that maintain an overt or covert assimilationist agenda—is an important first step in defining the scope of our adaptive challenge.

The historian of anthropology Patrick Wolfe suggests that colonialism occurs in three phases: confrontation, what he calls carceration, and assimilation.[11] Contrary to the commonly held view, the use of the phrase *terra nullius,* or land belonging to no one, to describe the Australian continent was not initiated at the time of invasion.* The doctrine of *terra nullius* was not a motive for invasion, but over time became a rationalisation for the greed for land that spawned a brutal 'zero-sum conflict' which in turn established a pattern of violence that was 'systemic to settler-colonisation'.[12] Indeed, the nature of the settler colonial project requires the active and forceful domination of an invaded territory's original inhabitants through the repression of their culture, identity and history, the persistence of which challenges the legitimacy of the colonial mission.[13] Indeed, it is evident that settler colonies were and are premised on the elimination of Indigenous societies.[14] There is, as W.E.H. Stanner[15] has pointed out, more than an accidental correspondence between the destruction of Indigenous life and the construction of European life on this territory. Rather there is a 'functional concomitance' to these dynamics. Although profoundly disturbing—and therefore often denied or avoided—the knowledge that invasion and colonisation *require* death and dispossession is, as Deborah Bird Rose argues, 'unavoidable'. Rose suggests that while we are experts in building 'hegemonic silences' to contain the facts of our past that are 'too demanding or too demeaning' to deal with,

---

**Terra nullius* did not in fact become a doctrine of Australian law until the *Mabo* judgment of 1992 when the High Court attributed it as legal doctrine (evidenced by Crown actions of the past) in order to refute it.

we nevertheless continue to 'fetishise the violence' of the past through the reification of frontier excitement and glamour.[16] As a nation we like to recall the thrill and the danger of being strangers in a strange land, while cordoning off our memory and discussion of the brutality and degradation experienced by those who were already here.

The brutal patterns of colonisation are not unique to Australia. Colonial genocide and oppression have been repeated around the world, in almost all cases reducing the Indigenous peoples of new colonial territory to a very small minority, often on the verge of extinction.[17] Settler societies are in fact premised on the violent and traumatic displacement or destruction of the original Indigenous inhabitants of a territory.[18] The supposedly scientific but in fact always political category of 'race' — measured by blood quantum and shades of skin colour—has been used to ensure that the population of 'full blood' or 'authentic' Indigenous peoples was always on the decline, reinforcing the idea of white settler superiority and the apparent dying out of a genetically inferior race.[19] Settlers engaged in a dual war 'against Nature' and 'against the natives' clearing the land in order to establish what they thought to be 'civilisation'.[20] That in the process the settlers engaged in acts that were profoundly un-civil by any standard one might wish to apply is an unremarked irony.

As the settler state embedded itself in the soil of *terra Australis* the violent conflict of the confrontation phase eventually gave way to (in)carceration and assimilation. By the time Australia federated as a nation in 1901 the official policy had become what was benignly referred to as 'protection'. The protection era saw the creation of reserves and missions on which Aboriginal people were contained, often removed considerable distances from their traditional lands, with different clans and families thrown together in sometimes conflictual situations. The carceration period was no dirty little secret: between 1901 and 1946 all Australian States passed legislation that would control Aboriginal people's independence of movement, marriage, employment and association and that authorised the removal of Aboriginal children from their families. Protection policies assumed that Aboriginal people were merely an ancient remnant who would inevitably die out. During this period Aboriginal people were further 'protected' in poorly paid or unpaid domestic and agricultural labour, unable to leave without permission from the 'boss' or the official government protector, and often never even seeing the meagre wages they earned[21]—a scenario not dissimilar to the slavery endured by other dark-skinned people in other parts of the world.

The missionary regimes that took up much of the settler state's labour regarding the 'civilisation' of the natives overlaid the 'protection' of Indigenous peoples with a proselytising Christianity that denigrated Indigenous culture and spirituality. Writer and activist Lorna Lippmann has argued that the early government settlements and church missions onto which Aboriginal people were herded were 'the antithesis of traditional living'. Aboriginal people were often cajoled and at times brutally relocated to these areas, where several large, frequently unrelated groups lived under the 'petty autocracy' of white staff in substandard conditions not dissimilar to refugee camps.[22] Yorta Yorta leader Paul Briggs has discussed the 'despair' that many Aboriginal individuals and families experienced due to the 'dismantling' of their culture through their containment on missions and as fringe dwellers in town camps near rural townships, saying:

> You've come out of country, you've come onto mission stations, you've come to live on the edge of town on the river banks and the tip sites, you've come into public housing, and it's slowly just pulling families and identity and culture apart because of the pressure to conform and live white, act white, think white, so that you can get on and get access to services.[23]

On many missions Aboriginal people were prevented from expressing any form of their traditional language or culture. Ceremony was forbidden and even names were replaced with Christian names. The intent of these practices of control and containment may not have been aimed at physical extermination as in the past, but they were genocidal nonetheless.

Over time national policy changed again and by 1951 Australian settler colonialism had moved into its third phase with the formal adoption of a policy of 'assimilation'.* The underlying assumption of assimilation was that, rather than dying out, Aboriginal people would be absorbed into the white population to live like other Australian citizens. Ostensibly, assimilation was a commitment by the state to the 'advancement' of Aboriginal people, rather than a view of their inevitable demise.[24] Many non-Indigenous people at the time believed that assimilation equated to advancement, and that full engagement and participation in white society would offer Aboriginal and Torres Strait Islander peoples the best way out of poverty and social marginalisation. It was soon clear, however, that 'advancement' was really code for 'more white, less black'. Assimilation policy was also riven by internally conflicting ideas exacerbated by a hangover from the protection era. As Aboriginal

---

*Many States had adopted assimilation policy earlier than this.

historian Frances Peters-Little has noted, Aboriginal people were often expected to assimilate into white society while still subjected to segregation laws that restricted them to reserves and missions.[25]

This brief recounting of certain aspects of Australian colonialist policy from the past inevitably also documents the historical and human injustice that is a part of the colonial project. Despite the fact that the protection and assimiliation phases of colonialism were considered to be beneficial for Aboriginal and Torres Strait Islander peoples at the time, it is evident that such an interpretation cannot be sustained today. Legal scholar Roy Brooks provides a lengthy definition of human injustice that draws on international human rights measures and is worthy of consideration in the Australian context. Brooks defines human injustice as:

> ... the violation or suppression of human rights or fundamental freedoms recognized by international law, including but not limited to genocide; slavery; extrajudicial killings; torture and other cruel or degrading treatment; arbitrary detention; rape; the denial of due process of law; forced refugee movements; the deprivation of a means of subsistence; the denial of universal suffrage; and discrimination, distinction, exclusion, or preference based on race, sex, descent, religion, or other identifying factor with the purpose or effect of impairing the recognition, enjoyment, or exercise, on an equal footing, of human rights and fundamental freedoms in the political, social, economic, cultural, or any other field of public life.[26]

If we accept a definition such as this there can be no doubt that the Australian settler state is guilty of human injustices both in the past and in the present. The colonisation of this territory involved all of these elements in the past, and continues to involve in the present (at a minimum) the denial of due process of law (in too many instances to list here, but notably in the suspension of the *Racial Discrimination Act* between 2001 and 2010 for those Aboriginal people affected by the Northern Territory 'Intervention'—discussed in the next chapter); and many forms of discrimination and exclusion based on Indigeneity that effectively impair the recognition and enjoyment of Indigenous people's human rights.

Yet the feeling of moral disgust at the recognition of ourselves as perpetrators of human injustices jars with our national identity and the official nationalism that is propped up by a more celebratory telling of our national story. This ongoing need for denial sits at the crossroads of the hope that animated many of our ancestors in their quest for a better way of life, and the 'hope-destroying' reality of the colonial destruction of Indigenous people and culture.[27] While this story of colonial brutality is not unique to Australia, it seems we have been particularly successful in developing what Stanner described as a 'blazing and odious rationalisation' for the 'ugly deeds' of our history.[28] Continuing to justify or minimise past brutality is a part of the genocidal morality discussed in the previous chapter, which continues to pervade Australian society and politics. Claiming that historical policies and practices were benevolent rather than violent—claiming that they were for the 'good' of Aboriginal and Torres Strait Islander peoples whether they realised it or not—is another strategy that maintains our bonds of solidarity with past perpetrators of these acts and thus reinscribes our collective guilt in the present. One recent example of these strategies at work was during the so-called 'history wars'.

The history wars

Heated debate about the interpretation of national history is not unique to Australia. Countries as diverse as Japan, France, Germany and the United States have all debated aspects of their own histories, particularly the legacies left by colonisation and war. In each case the battle seems to be waged between nationalists who would prefer a celebratory telling of the national story and those who take a more critical view, who are often accused of undermining national identity and unity. Allegedly at stake in these debates is a sense of national pride; a fear that shame will 'overpower the national conscience' and that the unpleasant, embarrassing and often downright disgusting aspects of a nation's past will make any form of pride in the present an impossibility.[29]

In the Australian context, the so-called 'history wars' became a battleground in the larger 'culture wars' waged over the content of our national identity during the period of the Howard governments from 1996 to 2007.[30] 'Race' has been the 'big battleground' of these culture wars.[31] The battleground was set by the assertion of a new historical narrative concerning the origins of the Australian nation. During the last 30 or so years of the twentieth century Aboriginal people increasingly demanded that history also be told from their perspectives. Public reports such as the Royal Commission into Aboriginal Deaths in Custody,* *Bringing them Home*** and other efforts to

*The Royal Commission into Aboriginal Deaths in Custody (RCIADIC) was established in 1989 in response to public concern over the deaths in police custody and prisons of 99 Aboriginal people between January 1980 and May 1989.

** This inquiry produced the seminal report, Human Rights and Equal Opportunities Commission, *Bringing them Home: Report of the national inquiry into the separation of Aboriginal and Torres Strait Islander children from their families*, Sydney, 1997. The inquiry had been instigated by the Keating Government in 1995 in response to Indigenous demands for greater recognition of the impact of child removal policies.

foreground Aboriginal and Torres Strait Islander experiences contributed to a new and contested account of the extent of historical injustice. Indigenous people expressed this counter history through oral testimony and written life stories, which had a considerable impact on the law and public life.[32] Some non-Indigenous historians also took up this challenge, writing with a belief that Australia was capable of better and in the hope that a well-expressed argument might persuade large numbers of Australians to redirect their sympathies and reshape their social and political institutions.[33] This new, more critical history of colonisation and its impacts brought into question both the founding stories about how this nation came to be, and the assertion that this 'new' nation was a place of justice and egalitarian opportunity.[34]

This trend towards a more critical historiography was reflected in the legal decisions and political currents of the early 1990s. In the 1992 *Mabo* decision the High Court determined that although the communal ownership of land by Aboriginal people could not be recognised as a proprietary interest in common law, it did constitute a unique form of title to land that had existed prior to colonisation. This decision was later codified (in a very limited form) in the *Native Title Act (1993)*. The prime minister of the day, Paul Keating, seemed determined to address the genocidal aspects of Australia's history, including Indigenous dispossession and child removal. Keating's 1992 Redfern Park speech went further than any previous political statement had done to acknowledge the wrongs of Australia's treatment of Aboriginal and Torres Strait Islander peoples. By the mid 1990s public discussion was dominated by debate about the vices and virtues of Australian history in ways that made many non-Indigenous Australians deeply uncomfortable.[35] In the face of a more critical assessment of our past there was a renewed assertion of the 'rightfulness' of colonisation, the challenges of 'pioneering' and settlement, and the modern day economic, social and political benefits accruing from the struggles of the past.[36]

Feeding the flames of this backlash was an essay by the historian Geoffrey Blainey, who argued that critical historians took what he termed a 'black armband view of history'.[37] Blainey contended that the 'balance sheet of Australian history' in fact suggested that there was more to be celebrated than regretted. In 1996, just a few months after his election as prime minister, John Howard advanced this point of view in a public lecture, claiming that 'the "black armband" view of our history reflects a belief that most Australian history since 1788 has been little more than a disgraceful story of imperialism, exploitation, racism, sexism and other forms of discrimination'. In contrast, Howard claimed that 'the balance sheet of our history is one of heroic achievement' and that 'we have achieved much more as a nation of which we can be proud than of which we should be ashamed'.[38] The balance sheet analysis seems particularly crude, as though an accounting of triumphs in one column can overcome an accounting of human costs in another, requiring us all to carry a 'moral abacus' in order to evaluate our history in mathematical terms.[39] I have always wondered what such an exercise would look like as something other than a tidy metaphor. Just how many deaths can be considered collateral damage for the founding of a colony? How many dispossessed and distraught people are balanced by the expansion of agriculture? How many children is it acceptable to remove from their families in order to entrench a settler state in someone else's country?

In the years that followed, historians on both sides of the 'war' debated whether there had ever been a deliberate policy to exterminate or eradicate Indigenous populations in the colony; where and whether massacres had taken place; the number of deaths that had resulted; whether or not smallpox had been introduced to Australia by the British and if so whether this had been deliberate; and the number of Aboriginal children removed from their families by missionaries and government agencies and the circumstances of their removal.[40] Raymond Evans notes the 'delicious irony' of describing what were essentially analytical differences as 'wars' while 'simultaneously denying that repetitive physical conflicts embedded in our history, in which many thousands of people died, can ever be typified by such an excessive term'.[41] But in denying the warlike nature of our national origins, the Aboriginal deaths that were seen as a necessary part of building the Australian nation continued to be dishonoured 'through chilling debates about how much blood has been shed and whose bloodshed counts'.[42] Those taking offence at a more critical view of Australia's colonial past seemed determined to 'smudge history into the sand' through a series of denials that, paradoxically, have also continued to feed the 'fundamental guilt that lies like a shadow over the European psyche', a guilt that 'will not be shifted until the colonial project is completed or abandoned'.[43]

Associated with the history wars, the question of historical responsibility became overtly political in debates around whether or not Australia as a nation should apologise to the Stolen Generations. The question of an apology was raised following the release of the *Bringing them Home* report from the National Inquiry into the Separation of Aboriginal and Torres Strait Islander Children from Their Families. The report, tabled in

Federal Parliament on 26 May 1997, concluded that, 'between one in three and one in ten Indigenous children were forcibly removed from their families and communities in the period from approximately 1910 until 1970'.[44] The report recommended that all Australian governments should officially and publicly apologise to the 'stolen generations'[45] for the harms done by past policies. The Howard Government both disagreed with the figures in the report and rejected the idea of a government apology, responding with a 'defensive, mean-spirited suspicion'.[46] Howard also 'recoiled' from a negative depiction of Australia's British heritage, consistently refusing to give an official apology on behalf of the Australian parliament to those of the Stolen Generations.[47] It seemed the prime minister feared that a national apology would be an acknowledgement of collective guilt, perhaps leading to the rewriting of his preferred, more celebratory version of our history. Howard's leadership on this issue fostered wider defensive sentiments and a widespread rejection of collective guilt.[48]

The vitriol and 'plain nastiness' in these debates about Australian history was extraordinary and served to yet again reveal the depth of feeling invested in the 'moral calculus of settler colonialism' and in preserving a sanitised version of our history.[49] The focus of critics on contesting the numbers of Aboriginal people killed in massacres or the numbers of children taken became a useful obfuscation for the deeper, unavoidable question of guilt. This continued obfuscation has meant that as a nation we have as yet barely entered 'the labyrinthine pathways of denial and disclosure'.[50] The 'wars' were always more concerned with the moral and political implications of our history than the realities of colonial conquest.[51] As Tim Soutphommasane observes, the celebratory, patriotic narrative in

Australia does better without recalling the treatment of Indigenous peoples at the hands of the original colonisers or their successor society.[52] Through the sorts of 'legitimatory narratives' that characterise the views of those who reject a 'black armband' view of history, official nationalism in Australia has attempted to proclaim its own 'virgin birth'.[53] The assimilationist logic of this view attempted to (re)construct a history in which the prior occupation of the land by Aboriginal people was effectively erased, and in which any such suffering as might be conceded was effectively minimised. Deborah Bird Rose describes this form of ideologically driven, monological telling of history as 'violent', not just for the ways in which it ignores the victims in the narrative, but also in the way that it attacks our own 'moral presence in the world'.[54]

Why we prefer not to remember, and why we cannot forget

What the exponents of the history wars neglected was the fact that societies cannot free themselves of guilt about the past simply by repressing or attempting to forget historical injustices.[55] The 'amnesias' about our past,[56] and the narratives that spring from this type of wilful forgetting, can only ever be fragile and temporary. The very presence of Aboriginal people in our communities makes it impossible to forget. Add to this the efforts by Aboriginal people, from at least the 1980s until the present, to challenge the official version of our history by insisting on acknowledgement of their prior occupation, their direct familial experiences of invasion, dispossession and racism, and their ongoing struggles for recognition, reparation and survival.[57] Non-Indigenous Australians have struggled in response to these challenges. Some form of 'moral engagement' between our present and our history is an essential part of our adaptive challenge and this engagement must both acknowledge past violence and the 'moral burden' that such acknowledgement entails. Frustratingly, for those who would rather we could simply put the past behind us and move forward with a confident stride, a moral engagement with our past also 'resists closure'.[58] Our adaptive work will be an ongoing proposition rather than something that can be finalised and filed away.

Many have suggested that what lies beneath the angry rejection of the 'black armband' view of history and any suggestion that genocide has been practised on this soil is a deep fear. Those who would tell a celebratory story of our history fear 'being cast out', both through the direct loss of land and through the loss of legitimacy of the non-Indigenous sense of home in what is still somebody else's country.[59] There is a fear that what we have done to others may one day be done to us.[60] There is a need to cover up the nature of our arrival and conquest in this territory, in order to feel a sense of belonging to this land.[61] And there is anxiety about the implications of admitting that Aboriginal people are contenders for 'the more powerful anchor' of Australian national identity, displacing the comforting imagery of the white man and his dependants.[62] Acknowledging the shameful aspects of our past is threatening to aspects of our national identity and our sense of ourselves as a just and egalitarian nation. We fear losing the 'familiar and comforting map of the past',[63] to be replaced with a pirate's map of buried bones and stolen treasure.

One crucial legacy of the history wars is a divisive politicisation of our national history along ideological or partisan lines. People who hold a more conservative world view are more likely to be high identifiers, with a clear preference for avoiding anything that might disrupt the status quo, violate norms or cause social unrest. Their high identification with the ingroup makes it more likely that they will ignore information that comes from 'outgroup' sources and does not comply with what they perceive to be the interests of their group. They are more likely to minimise their group's responsibility for past harms. In contrast, those with a more progressive world view are more likely to be open to change and are more likely to pay attention to information that may be unfavourable to the ingroup.[64] Certainly it has been the case that conservative politicians have been more likely to align themselves with efforts to promote a celebratory telling of our national story, whereas those on the other side of the chamber have, on occasion, expressed some greater willingness to take responsibility for historical injustices. As Ann Curthoys points out, however, a rejection of a more critical version of Australian history is not confined to conservative historians and politicians. Many other non-Indigenous Australians have also rejected the idea that they are 'invaders' or beneficiaries of violent or genocidal practices. Their preference has also been to reassert an historical narrative of which they can feel proud.[65]

Understanding our colonial history is important for a number of reasons. First, it matters greatly to many Indigenous people that we do. In conversation with Indigenous people all over Australia I have heard them speak of their frustration with the way history is taught in this country, and the great silences that are often maintained over local and national histories that continue to have impact for many Indigenous individuals, families and communities. Acknowledging historical injustice is also a first step towards addressing that injustice. Admitting that past policies were damaging is also to admit that the individuals harmed by these policies deserved better. Aboriginal and Torres

Strait Islander peoples should not have been treated as they were. Understanding and acknowledging this fact, acknowledging our collective guilt in the wrongdoing of the past, also implies that we acknowledge the dignity and rights of Indigenous people in the present and future.[66]

But just having knowledge of past events is not enough. If non-Indigenous people want to understand the experiences of Indigenous people today we need to understand the ways in which trauma from past policies and historical acts continues to affect them. The late Wiradjuri and Kamilaroi writer and poet Kevin Gilbert once observed that it is not possible to 'look down on black people while you understand the historical reasons that have reduced them to what they are'.[67] Aboriginal trauma expert Judy Atkinson has argued that policies of child removal, for example, have produced 'profoundly hurt people living with multiple layers of traumatic distress'. Atkinson suggests that alcohol and other drugs are often a self-medicating choice, and in many cases no other treatment is available.[68]

In recognising this it seems entirely appropriate that our response to knowledge of human injustice should be one of guilt, shame and discomfort. There are many responses we might have to a recognition of this guilt. We may try to ignore it, we may turn away in bewilderment, or we may experience feelings of 'moral disgust'. Alan Atkinson suggests that only the last of these possible responses is likely to be productive because disgust at least proves that 'we are human and we can think'.[69] While the history warriors, the high identifiers, and the conservative politicians might ask us to turn away from that guilt, they do us a disservice. Rejecting our historical guilt is the coward's way out and ultimately it does nothing to help us move forward, nothing to help us face our adaptive challenge. Recognising historical injustice may be distressing and uncomfortable but it is the only way in which we can come to know and understand 'the incubus which burdens us all'.[70] Rather than turning away, I would suggest that we need to sit with our guilt for a while, read some more, really understand our historical legacy. We need to experience our discomfort in a deep rather than a superficial way and allow ourselves to be affected by the human dimensions of our historical legacy evident among many still-traumatised Aboriginal people today. But as Ronald Heifetz cautions, distress can also produce unexpected responses. In their desire for order and a return to emotional equilibrium, people may become cruel, they may sacrifice their empathy, compassion and mental flexibility.[71] We need to be alert to the ways in which our guilt and discomfort affect us.

But this is not an invitation to wallow or become bogged down in our guilt about the past. We need also to be alert to the ways in which acknowledging collective guilt for historical injustice, and the distress that this may cause, can cause us to become ineffectual. Nor do I suggest that non-Indigenous people take their burden of guilt to Indigenous people and ask them to absolve us, as I once so naively did.[72] Our guilt is our responsibility. Once we have acknowledged our collective guilt and have had some time to experience it and understand what it means for us, there are choices to be made. It is right to feel guilty but it is not enough. Our individual experiences contribute to a collective response, our private feelings become public. There is more work to be done.

Our history in the present and future

The way we deal with the past is not confined to the history books. Our national identity in the present and our visions for a shared future are also rooted in our history. The question then becomes not whether we should acknowledge the past, but how. History books will be one part of the answer, but so are questions of public commemorations, museum exhibitions and, more substantially, constitutional or other legal reform that address the question of prior ownership of the land. We have choices about the way in which we engage in 'memory politics'[73] and the way in which we choose to recognise past injury will inevitably rewrite aspects of our history and reshape some of the ground on which we stand.[74] Although our individual memories are not something we can necessarily command, as a collective we can choose what we publicly remember and what we attempt to forget.[75] John Howard's famous dream of an Australia in which everyone could be 'relaxed and comfortable' suggested that we should put a shroud of amnesia around that which makes us uncomfortable or distressed.[76] This approach merely avoids the reality that doing adaptive work will often involve discomfort. In the past, our inability to persist through feelings of unease, in order to really understand the genocidal aspects of our history and their implications in the present, has meant that this work has remained constantly on hold.

Acknowledging the past, however we choose to do that, will not magically transform us into a nation of reconciled citizens, and nor will it mean a rapid transformation in the quality of life experienced by many Aboriginal and Torres Strait Islander peoples. This has not been the case in other countries that have attempted to reconcile a tragic past, such as South Africa, but nor has it been the case that such countries have been plunged into turmoil by choosing to make a painful and honest examination of their history.[77] Indeed, in the Australian situation, the long-awaited apology from former Prime Minister Kevin Rudd did not unleash a storm of litigation as the critics had suggested. What it did do was give a small group of Indigenous Australians and their families the comfort of some long overdue recognition and respect. But at the same time, however, we must remain alert to our tendency to limit our recognition of past injustices to a 'sanitised, romanticised, or victimised Aboriginality'. Our collective guilt is about real people; our guilt and shame must go beyond the impersonal and the voyeuristic in order to be understood in more deeply human terms than have characterised past expressions of public goodwill towards Aboriginal and Torres Strait Islander peoples.[78]

Examples such as the national apology underscore the fact that efforts to acknowledge historical injustice, however uncomfortable they must be, should not just be focused on our own feelings about the past. Efforts to amend past injustices can focus on building interpretations of the past that both parties to a conflict can share, and in which there is space to negotiate identities and mediate national histories. This is work that must be undertaken in dialogue with Aboriginal and Torres Strait Islander peoples, as we determine what versions of our contested historical narratives can be legitimated with limited space and resources.[79] Such dialogue will take us beyond the ideas of democratic 'inclusion'. Indeed, inclusion is barely conceivable for many Aboriginal and Torres Strait Islander peoples for as long as historical injustices have not been addressed. Historical violence, marginalisation and oppression have shaped identities in terms of opposition and conflict.[80] We cannot pretend that this is not the case. We cannot just 'include'. We need to find ways of engaging in the underlying adaptive challenge that makes these relationships so complex.

There are risks to how we approach this task. In the German context Bernhard Schlink has observed that the legacy of debates about a contested history can lead to a kind of 'banality' on the topic for the next generation. In Germany, as in Australia, breaking down the resistance of those who would prefer to continue repressing knowledge of historical injustice meant that the topic had to be raised again and again. Over time, when in Schlink's view there remained no one who needed convincing that the past could not in fact be repressed his generation continued to congratulate themselves on their 'moral fortitude' as if continuing to discuss the past 'still demanded courage, still justified pride, still could not happen often enough'. The 'ennui' in the next generation that resulted, their 'careless and cynical tone' when speaking about the past, can be politically dangerous in the present.[81]

In Australia we seem caught between two dynamics. On the one hand there are still those who seek to repress the past and who prefer tales of historical heroics over an acknowledgement of past wrongdoing. On the other hand, we have a generation of young people who have grown up during the history wars and who may well feel that Australia's contested history has been discussed all too frequently. It will be a challenge to engage this generation in the adaptive work required of them if they are to be part of a future informed by dynamics other than collective guilt. If this generation is not a part of this work they will in effect be reinforcing the bonds of solidarity with the perpetrators of historical injustices in this country, thereby ensuring that our collective guilt is perpetuated into the future.

In dealing with the past we need also be aware of the way we are imagining this work as a contribution to the present and the future. Imagining a different future for Australia is clearly an aspiration for many of us concerned to achieve greater justice and equity. But we must be wary of a future orientation that allows us to claim the moral high ground without dealing with our past, deflecting us from our moral responsibility in the present. Building a future 'in a society built on destruction' can allow past 'regimes of violence' to continue. Focusing solely on future achievement, on the idea that there might be a future in which we will have left behind the conflicts, contradictions and suffering of the present, allows us to 'turn our backs on current social facts of pain, damage, destruction and despair', which we will now only acknowledge as belonging to the past.[82] Acknowledging historical injustice, allowing ourselves to feel guilt and disgust about the genocide practised in the past, is an essential component of our adaptive challenge. But our adaptive work cannot be solely directed towards an imagined future. We must also understand what this history means in our present.

If what we are imagining is a more unified nation in which Aboriginal and Torres Strait Islander peoples feel more included then we may be thinking more about our own desires than theirs. While modern democracies tend to aspire to the hallmarks of 'nationhood', with a shared national identity, language and public culture 'reinforced by a steady diet of nation-building policies', this risks repeating the assimilationist drive that has been the cause of so much harm in the past. One lesson we must take from our contested past is that Indigenous cultural differences have been excluded from 'the national imaginary'.[83] These exclusions have contributed to the view that Indigenous cultures were inferior to British culture, that Indigenous peoples were less civilised, and that 'for their own good' Aboriginal and Torres Strait Islander peoples should be encouraged or coerced to live more Westernised lives. The next chapter will examine the ways in which this view of Indigenous culture has informed policy and practice in the past and in the present

Chapter 3

Intervention and redemption: Conquering the rights agenda

Many of the worst historical injustices perpetrated on Indigenous peoples, including policies of assimilation and child removal, have been justified as being 'for their own good'. The federal government 'intervention' into Northern Territory Indigenous communities continues this mode of interaction with Indigenous people in Australia. The intervention has been the most controversial approach to Indigenous affairs in recent decades, requiring the suspension of the *Racial Discrimination Act (1975)* for several years due to the explicit targeting of Aboriginal people in select communities in the Northern Territory under the new regime. The justification for this approach has been that Aboriginal people must be coerced into better behaviour—they must be saved from themselves—for their own good. This chapter argues that 'saving' Aboriginal people keeps both Indigenous and non-Indigenous Australia locked in a contest over Indigenous autonomy, and looks at the adaptation that will be necessary in attributing a new value to Indigenous cultures and ways of life.

In recent years much policy debate in Indigenous affairs has focused on Noel Pearson's articulation of the 'rights' versus the 'responsibility' agenda among Aboriginal leaders. Those articulating the rights agenda, with all of its inherent challenges to Australian sovereignty, have been subjected to often-vitriolic public attacks. In contrast, those advocating Indigenous responsibility have been embraced, as their argument does little to unsettle the settler state. This chapter considers what Australia might have to give up in engaging in adaptive work that recognises Indigenous rights and moves towards the legal recognition of Australia's First Nations peoples.* It argues that legal recognition of Indigenous peoples is a core component of our adaptive challenge.

Good intentions are not enough

The previous chapter sketched the evolution of Australian policy towards Aboriginal and Torres Strait Islander peoples through the eras of confrontation, (in)carceration and assimilation.[1] In the latter of these two periods, attitudes and practices towards Indigenous people were justified as being 'for their own good'. For much of Australia's post-invasion history, the subliminal theme in our white noise has been concerned with our 'civilising' mission, our goals of dragging a so-called 'primitive race' into the project of modernity with nary a thought for the damage we might do along the way. Our mission was not just moral, it was

*The term First Nations refers to the Indigenous peoples of Canada who are neither Inuit or Métis and has been adopted by many in preference to the terms 'Indian' (which still has legal status) or Aboriginal. A similar term has recently been formally adopted in Australia through the creation of the national representative body, the National Congress of Australia's First Peoples.

essential. Maintaining these narratives has been comforting and reassuring, but it is also work avoidance.

The development of Australian settler colonial society is most often presented as an inevitability. The work of 'discovering', 'exploring' and 'settling' this land—carving out swathes of bush for agriculture, digging deep into the soil, first for gold and later for other minerals—is valorised by extolling the courage and endurance displayed by those involved in these 'nation-building' endeavours. As the previous chapter discussed, much effort has been made to repress the parallel narrative of the costs incurred by Aboriginal and Torres Strait Islander peoples while their land was being invaded and colonised. But as W.E.H. Stanner once pointed out, however, the particular course of colonial expansion in Australia need not necessarily have followed the path it did. Stanner argues that:

> The disposal of land, the development of law and order, the distribution of political power, the recognition of human rights, and the administration of justice must all have taken a different course, had it not been for the suffocation of conscience.[2]

Stanner goes on to suggest that if a different path had in fact been followed, one that was informed by conscience and a sense of justice for Australia's original inhabitants, then 'a number of chickens would not now be coming home to roost'.[3]

Indeed, many of these 'chickens' seemed to be coming home to roost quite early in Australia's history. The devastating effects of uninterrupted policies of assimilation and cultural destruction have been obvious, if overlooked, in settler colonial societies including Australia for many, many decades.[4] At no point, however, has the settler state been made accountable for this destruction. Rather, and somewhat perversely, even the most damaging of Australia's policies towards Indigenous people have been excused as failed attempts at improving their quality of life. But as anthropologist Elizabeth Povinelli asks, 'if courts and publics do not blame shameful events on bad people but on the good intentions of good people, how are the good intentions of present people protected?'[5] In other words, as long as we maintain the 'good intentions' justification—as long as we avoid the work of actually scrutinising the role of past policies in the colonisation of this country and the many ways in which non-Indigenous people continue to benefit from these processes—then those of us who today might want to engage more productively have nowhere to go.

Political theorist Michael Freeman suggests that failure to properly take account of past wrongs acts like 'the imperialist ghost in the liberal-democratic machine'.[6] No matter how passionate our quest for justice in the future may be, our inability to recognise the harms done by past policy leaves us destined to repeat our mistakes. This can reduce the role of the well-intentioned individual to one who merely bleats about our 'national shame'. Indeed, speaking of national shame can be offered as evidence that we do truly 'mean well'. By calling attention to the past failings of 'the nation' we avoid our own guilt.[7] It is another strategy of work avoidance and, worse, its effect may be to make us as individuals feel better, while in this 'conversion' of bad feeling into good feeling we do little more than repeat the same forms of structural violence we were seeking to address.[8] This complicated interaction between individual feeling and the contemporary political response is evident in some recent debate on the current and future direction of Indigenous policy.

The sense that Australian governments should do 'something' that improves the lives of Indigenous people is still strong, but guilt about past injustices and ongoing policy failure pervade contemporary decision-making. Since 2004, however, when the former prime minister John Howard advanced the view that that 'experiment' in self-determination in the form of the Aboriginal and Torres Strait Islander Commission (ATSIC) had 'failed',[9] there has been an increasingly dominant view that pursuing any policy directed towards genuine Indigenous self-government must be the wrong approach. As anthropologist Melinda Hinkson points out, the underlying logic argues that if self-determination is seen unambiguously as an approach that has failed 'then Aboriginal people are to blame for their own demise'.[10] Intervention is therefore justified. Arguments suggesting that *meaningful* self-determination has never been tried in Australia, and which point to the weak and compromised philosophical underpinnings of the Australian version of this policy, are ignored.[11] Australia's tentative steps towards a limited form of Indigenous autonomy have been backtracked at breathtaking speed and government has instead set off down the seemingly new path of 'intervention', signposted in the language of responsibility over rights. Many have pointed out that this 'new' path looks very much like the earlier path of assimilation policy, which most would agree was a dead end. The response, however, is the old refrain that the 'new' paternalism of government policy is again 'for their own good'.

Intervening in Indigenous lives . . . again

In 1972 when the Whitlam Government introduced the formal policy of self-determination, Aboriginal and Torres Strait Islander peoples hoped they had seen the end of assimilationist policy in Australia and the start of a new era of autonomy and developing self-government. Nearly 40 years later, however, it appears that these hopes had been very much misplaced. Following the abolition of ATSIC in 2005 the Howard Government introduced a set of 'new arrangements' in Indigenous affairs involving the 'mainstreaming' of ATSIC's 21 programs between six existing federal agencies and the introduction of the new policy of Shared Responsibility Agreements, another part of what the government dubbed a 'quiet revolution' in Indigenous policy.[12] Shared Responsibility Agreements (SRAs) entailed a community making certain commitments towards achieving their nominated goal and the government, in turn, making commitments of their own—usually the provision of services or funding. The rhetoric of shared responsibility sounded good to many non-Indigenous people troubled by guilty feelings about continuing poverty and disadvantage in many Aboriginal communities. Rather than engaging in a more unsettling examination of the historical and structural underpinnings of these contemporary circumstances, policies such as shared responsibility meant that Aboriginal people were required to take at least some of the blame, while the Australian Government could be cast in the role of 'a benevolent patriarch engaged in community-based behaviour modification'.[13]

Howard's view of the Australian state as a paternal figure required to 'care' for Aboriginal people had long been evident. As noted in the previous chapter, for example, in 1997 he rejected the findings of the *Bringing them Home* report from the National Inquiry into the Separation of Aboriginal and Torres Strait Islander Children from Their Families, which had concluded that 'between one in three and one in ten Indigenous children were forcibly removed from their families and communities in the period from approximately 1910 until 1970'.[14] Howard contradicted these findings and instead argued that many

Indigenous children 'were taken in circumstances where under today's laws they would be regarded as being properly and lawfully taken from their families in the interests of their own protection'.[15] Indeed, there is a history of the image of vulnerable Aboriginal children being used to displace white guilt and justify continuing human injustice through Indigenous policy. As Melinda Hinkson has noted, the image of the vulnerable and suffering Aboriginal child has 'an unparalleled potency', allowing urgent action to be demanded and justified by the 'essential moral righteousness' of the spectre of child abuse and neglect.[16]

Nowhere is this more evident that in the most recent Australian approach to Indigenous policy: the Northern Territory Emergency Response, more commonly referred to as 'the Intervention'. The Intervention was announced by John Howard and his Indigenous Affairs Minister Mal Brough on 21 June 2007 as a response to the *Ampe Akelyernemane Meke Mekarle 'Little Children are Sacred'* report released six weeks earlier by the Northern Territory Board of Inquiry into the Protection of Aboriginal Children from Sexual Abuse.[17] The new policy contained governmental interventions unmatched by anything introduced in the past 40 years.[18] Allegedly to tackle the issue of child sexual abuse, the Howard Government undertook to apply a range of 'emergency' measures to all people resident in remote Aboriginal communities in the Northern Territory. Specifically it would:

- introduce widespread alcohol restrictions on Northern Territory Aboriginal land;
- introduce welfare reforms to stem the flow of cash going towards substance abuse and to ensure funds for child welfare are used for that purpose;

- enforce school attendance by linking income support and family assistance payments to school attendance for all people living on Aboriginal land and providing meals for children at parents' cost;
- introduce compulsory health checks for all Aboriginal children to identify and treat health problems and any effects of abuse;
- acquire townships prescribed by the Commonwealth Government through five-year leases including payment of 'just terms' compensation;
- increase policing levels in prescribed communities, including through secondments from State and Territory jurisdictions;
- scrap the permit system for common areas, road corridors and airstrips for prescribed communities;
- marshal local workforces through Work for the Dole to undertake ground cleanup and repair of communities;
- improve housing and reform community living arrangements, including the introduction of market-based rents and normal tenancy arrangements;
- ban the possession of X-rated pornography and introduce audits of all publicly funded computers to identify illegal material; and
- appoint managers of all government business in prescribed communities.[19]

The rapid passage of the 500 pages of legislation that would bring in the intervention measures required the suspension of the *Racial Discrimination Act (1975)* (RDA) by prescribing the intervention as falling under the 'special measures' provision of the Act. The legislation was fully supported by the then Labor Opposition.

The measures in the Intervention, and most particularly the quarantining of welfare payments, constitute paternalism *in extremis*. Aboriginal people had been judged incapable of managing their own lives and government had declared itself forced to intervene for their own good, and particularly for the good of the children. Indeed there could be no stronger demonstration of state paternalism than in the delivery of some of the early measures in the intervention by uniformed members of the Australian army, terrifying some women in remote communities enough to flee into the sandhills in fear that their children were to be taken away. There is a continuity here between earlier policy eras in which the 'captured' Indigenous population was subjected to paternalistic institutions of 'care' designed to 'civilise, modernise and assimilate' them and today's return to these outmoded forms of race-based paternalistic discipline still justified as necessary forms of 'practical care in exceptional circumstances'.[20]

The Intervention legislation passed in August 2007 and in November that year Australia saw a change of government. The incoming Labor government had supported the introduction of the intervention measures while in opposition and later decided to continue and expand aspects of the policy. Indigenous Affairs Minister Jenny Macklin chose to ignore the findings of the independent review she had ordered of the Intervention program, despite the review team's finding that the policy had 'diminished its own effectiveness through its failure to engage constructively with the Aboriginal people it was intended to help'.[21] Nevertheless, Macklin did undertake to reinstate the RDA by the end of 2009. In the meantime the policy came under considerable international scrutiny and condemnation, with United Nations Special Rapporteur on the situation of human rights and fundamental freedoms of Indigenous people, James Anaya, declaring that measures in the Intervention 'overtly discriminate against aboriginal peoples, infringe their right of self-determination and stigmatize already stigmatized communities'.[22] Irene Khan, the Secretary General of Amnesty International, found the fact that Indigenous people in Australia were experiencing human rights violations 'on a continent of such privilege' to be 'not merely disheartening, it is morally outrageous'.[23]

Ultimately Minister Macklin found it impossible to meet her own deadline for the reinstatement of the RDA, instead announcing in November 2009 that the government would 'strengthen the Northern Territory Emergency Response (NTER) to provide the foundations for real and lasting change in Indigenous communities'.[24] In this instance, 'strengthening' included a commitment to 're-design' income management as a non-discriminatory measure essentially by widening its application beyond the prescribed communities initially targeted by the policy. The wider application of income quarantining was to commence in all areas of the Northern Territory in July 2010, to be completed by 31 December 2010. This would be the 'first step in a national roll out of income management in disadvantaged regions', with the minister retaining the power to proclaim any area in Australia a 'declared income management area'. These measures, contained in the *Social Security and Other Legislation Amendment (Welfare Reform and Reinstatement of Racial Discrimination Act) Bill 2009*, were passed in May 2010. For some analysts, the expansion of the welfare quarantining measure amounted to little more than a cynical attempt to 'normalise' the policy by potentially applying it to disadvantaged sections of the non-Indigenous community.[25] Other Intervention measures that continued in the prescribed communities alone included restrictions on alcohol and pornography, the retention of government business management powers, and the five-year leases over townships as a 'special measure' under the RDA. The RDA itself became a more restricted piece of legislation with the passage of the May 2010 amendments as, without the inclusion of a 'notwithstanding clause' in the new legislation, any provisions in the amended legislation that are inconsistent with the RDA will continue to override the RDA.[26] This situation has led analysts such as the retired jurist Alastair Nicholson to claim that the new legislation merely perpetuated the 'paternalism and racial discrimination inherent in the NTER'.[27]

Policies such as the Northern Territory Intervention are deeply comforting for those discomforted by the idea that the struggles experienced by Aboriginal people today may still be linked to our colonial past. Writers such as Peter Sutton suggest that contemporary problems of so-called 'community dysfunction' are the result of pre-colonial cultural norms and individual relationships between people damaged by alcohol and violence.[28] Indeed, as Hinkson has pointed out, Indigenous policy is 'increasingly being framed by suggestions that Aboriginal people need to undergo forms of cultural redevelopment'.[29] These suggestions are not new, having long been championed by conservative commentators such as Ron Brunton and Gary Johns and others associated with organisations such as the Institute of Public Affairs and the Bennelong Society.[30] Ignoring the fact that the same patterns of postcolonial Indigenous struggle and disadvantage are evident the world over, in widely diverse Indigenous cultures, the collectively guilty conscience is easily persuaded by the suggestion that the fault is not really ours but theirs. This is a triumph of colonial liberalism. Where anti-colonial movements had created a crisis of legitimacy for settler colonial orders through their refiguring of paternalistic policies of care as acts of continued domination, settler states like Australia have contained the crisis by allowing limited notions of 'culture' to become incorporated into the liberal order without rupturing the state framework. In this way the 'locale of the crisis' is shifted and the concept of culture itself becomes problematised, particularly where it proves itself resistant to change or 'modernisation'.[31]

This defensive shift in the orientation of Indigenous policy perpetuates the earlier colonial order in the present. The paternalism evident in policies such as welfare quarantining has even been described as 'a return to the ration days'.[32] Through reinscribing these colonial attitudes in the present, our bonds of solidarity with perpetrators of historical injustice are reaffirmed. Our collective guilt gets in the way of our ability to listen to what Aboriginal people are saying about what is hurting them and instead we propagate their trauma in the present day. Frustratingly for governments hoping that making Indigenous policy 'for their own good' will displace white guilt about the past, an Aboriginal or Torres Strait Islander point of view will often suggest something very different. Despite over two centuries of brutality, oppression, dispossession and marginalisation, Indigenous people keep talking about their rights, their sovereignty, their prior occupation of this territory and their continuing connection to and responsibility for the land. And every time they do so, we are reminded of our illegitimacy.

Rights or responsibility? Creating the cultural deficit

Key to the level of public backing, or at least complacency, about the Intervention has been the vocal advocacy for paternalistic interventions by the influential director of the Cape York Institute for Policy and Leadership, Noel Pearson. While Pearson did express some concern about aspects of the Intervention, he concluded that, 'Whatever one thinks of Howard and Brough, their strategy is justified on the basis of the fate of the children.'[33] Indeed, recent years have seen much debate over the current direction of Indigenous policy framed around Pearson's views on the tension between Indigenous rights and Indigenous responsibility. Pearson has talked about the 'institutionalised dependency' that he believes has been created by regimes of 'passive welfare' in Indigenous communities. He argues that the collapse of social norms in Indigenous communities is a recent rather than historical phenomenon, dated to the rise of what he terms 'victim politics' in which the 'increased recognition of black rights' was accompanied by 'a calamitous erosion of black responsibility'.[34] Pearson and his colleagues at the Cape York Institute suggest that 'the current problems of Indigenous people are very much the result of passivity problems created by *earlier interventions*'.[35] Perhaps surprisingly, however—given his recognition that earlier interventions in Aboriginal lives have been so problematic—Pearson's proposed solution envisages the creation of greater community responsibility through further intervention and individual coercion. Such proposals are at best speculative, although currently under investigation through a multi-million dollar trial of Pearson's proposed Family Responsibilities Commission in four Cape York communities. Such a trial is not without risks. As Judy Atkinson has noted, there is a long history of 'multiple, protracted and many-layered' interventions by governments and others into Aboriginal lives. These interventions have, at many levels, 'acted as traumatising agents, compounding the agony of already traumatised individuals and groups' and have 'increased the dependent conditions of the oppressed'.[36]

The tension between the concepts of rights and responsibilities that Pearson articulates, with his emphasis on the primary importance of responsibility, has found fertile ground with government and others. Pearson has expressed the view that some explanations for continuing Indigenous disadvantage such as 'structural violence in history', although not necessarily incorrect, are 'beyond contemporary policy reach'. Pearson advocates a form of pragmatism that is very reassuring for the settler state, arguing that 'we have to deal with what we face now'.[37] His core proposal—that problems in Indigenous communities can be resolved through the exercise of greater Aboriginal responsibility within the current political and institutional context—is comforting. Changing our national self-understanding and our political institutions to allow for the full recognition of Indigenous rights and the exercise of Indigenous self-government is put in the too-hard basket. Non-Indigenous Australians can comfort themselves that the problem is 'them' and not 'us'. 'They' need to change, not 'us'. Maybe we don't need to feel guilty after all if the problem is either *their* culture or *their* failure to maintain social norms since the arrival of the Europeans.

Anthropologist Peter Sutton has put it slightly differently, suggesting that there has been too much emphasis on 'considerations of strict justice' at the expense of 'considerations of care'. According to Sutton, what he calls 'do-goodism' may indeed take the form of 'saccharine sympathy' but may also be enacted through 'self-redemptive legal and political crusading on behalf of marginal citizens that proceeds on the assumption that emotional wounds will be healed by laws and documents and covenants signed in Geneva'. Sutton suggests that what he terms the 'unscientific mumbo jumbo' involved in talking about Indigenous rights 'beggars belief', relying on 'a kind of magical cause-and-effect relationship, as if a treaty between "races" will keep children safe in their beds at night'.[38] Sutton, like many others in the field, is concerned with high levels of violence among Aboriginal people, particularly where such violence involves women and children. He rejects, however, what he describes as a 'myth' that the recognition of Indigenous rights will in any way be able to 'put food in the bellies of toddlers in the bush, or prevent local acts of violence or abuse'.[39] This is strong and emotive stuff, reassuring white Australia—intentionally or otherwise—that our interventions in Indigenous lives are indeed 'for their own good'. What Sutton neglects in his analysis, however, is that the 'colonial rage' expressed by Aboriginal people, often evident in their violence towards one another, has its roots in the historical injustice of our past.[40] Further, as fellow anthropologist Jon Altman has noted, where Pearson has identified both the decline in Indigenous social norms and out of place and ineffective government intervention as problematic, Sutton is 'more limited in his understanding of the state apparatus'. The result, according to Altman, is worrying. Sutton's 'treatise against Indigenous culture' comes at a time when such an argument is likely to win many supporters who are 'all too willing' to use such an analysis as justification for the continuation of 'monolithic assimilationist solutions'. As if, Altman notes, 'such approaches have not been tried, and failed, before'.[41]

But this dichotomy between care and justice is entirely manufactured. What could be more caring than delivering justice and acknowledging rights? Sutton's argument neglects the growing body of international evidence suggesting a very strong link indeed between the recognition of Indigenous rights and an improvement in Indigenous life circumstances, for example in the extensive data collected by the Harvard Project on American Indian Economic Development.[42] Not that there is anything 'magical' about any such cause and effect as Sutton seems to think. Recognising Indigenous rights may go some way towards alleviating the painful disconnect between the way in which Aboriginal and Torres Strait Islander peoples experience themselves as sovereign beings and their daily confrontation with the reality of the settler colonial order. More tangibly, however, recognising Indigenous sovereignty, whether it be by treaty or through constitutional reform, creates a starting point for the conditions in which Aboriginal and Torres Strait Islander peoples can do the hard work *they* need to do to rebuild their nations and communities and turn their lives around. It is one of the great conceits of the colonial order to believe that we might hold better solutions to these challenges than do Indigenous peoples themselves.

The barrier to the recognition of Indigenous rights is our collective guilt. We cannot acknowledge Indigenous sovereignty as long as maintaining the fiction of our legitimacy and the narrative of our heroic nationalism remains so important to us. So instead we persist with our interventions in Indigenous lives, evoking the figure of the vulnerable child as justification that our actions are for their own good. What are we so afraid of?

Indigenous sovereignty and the colonial project

Talk of Indigenous sovereignty is an implicit and explicit challenge to the legitimacy of the settler state. According to the political mainstream the fact of this sovereignty is 'an impossibility', it is a threat that might 'fracture the state's very foundation'.[43] We can imagine ourselves as a democratic polity only by 'the complete disavowal' of Indigenous sovereignty, through a persistent narrative the currency of which 'should not be underestimated'.[44] At the same time, our continued denial of the continent's prior occupation by Indigenous people perpetuates our moral illegitimacy.[45] The continued assertion of 'prior, ancient, autochthonous [indigenous] belonging' makes a mockery of the white claim to 'ownership, superiority, and hegemony' and, according to Gillian Cowlishaw, is 'one source of white hysteria, fear, and racial hatred'.[46] Claims of Indigenous sovereignty expose our collective guilt.

The question of Aboriginal and Torres Strait Islander sovereignty is more than just an intellectual debate or an ideological contest. Indigenous people raise the question of sovereignty as part of what political philosopher James Tully describes as a 'struggle for recognition'. Struggles for recognition take place whenever and wherever one group of people subjected to a dominant set of norms concerning recognition experience the prevailing circumstances as 'unbearable'. The struggle is over 'the relationships of communication and power through which we are governed', going to the heart of the experience of being an Indigenous person in a notionally postcolonial state.[47] The intensity of such struggles derives from the fact that the settler's legitimacy continues to rest on the denial of colonial history. What worries white Australia is that in the struggle for recognition Indigenous people will drag our denied historical narrative into the glare of the national spotlight. The continued and contested place of our past in the present poses an 'existential threat' to our sense of moral legitimacy as a nation.[48] Our response to this threat has been to cast the source of the threat as an aggressor. We behave, as Deborah Bird Rose[49] has argued, 'as if Aboriginal people sought explicitly to destroy white Australians' comfortable attitude towards history'. We prefer to interpret their evident psychic and physical wounds as evidence of an imagined cultural deficit that they need our help to overcome, rather than as injuries sustained in the war for their country. Our continued rejection of their claims and our denial of historical injustice 'reinflicts past harm and sustains present injuries'.[50] But our collective guilt traps us in our limited response. As we continue to deny Indigenous sovereignty, we also sustain efforts to 'graft' Aboriginal and Torres Strait Islander peoples onto a new national history. These efforts have included policy interventions such as the removal of Aboriginal children and advancing other assimiliationist endeavours in an attempt to do away with the threat altogether.[51] In this context it is not surprising that a government made up of conservative high identifiers would introduce a policy framework that revives the assimiliationist agenda.

For Aboriginal and Torres Strait Islander peoples, however, the fact of Indigenous sovereignty does not need to be argued or proved, it just *is*. It is a constant, unavoidable and undeniable reality even while the struggle to have this reality recognised continues. For as long as sovereignty is denied, non-Indigenous Australians continue to do damage to Aboriginal and Torres Strait Islander peoples. Further, we continue to reinscribe our own collective guilt through our refusal to break the bonds of solidarity with the original perpetrators of the colonial injustice that denied Indigenous sovereignty in the first instance. The ongoing denial of Indigenous sovereignty not only results in 'the continued decline and genocide of Aboriginal lives', it also represents a 'missed opportunity to engage with thinking beyond the possible'.[52] For as long as we remain caught in our need to deny historical injustice we render ourselves incapable of imagining a fundamentally different relationship between Indigenous and non-Indigenous people in Australian territory. Thinking beyond the possible is perhaps another way of describing adaptive work. Rather than reverting to the 'technical solutions' that have so often tried and failed, we could instead begin to think together of new possibilities, a new sense of ourselves that recognises the injuries of our history. How else will it ever be possible for us to make progress as a morally legitimate nation? As Irene Watson asks, 'how does a thief recognise the victim of the theft if not to give back what they have stolen and to no longer hold claim over the object of the theft?'.[53]

The problem in settler societies like Australia is that the colonial project is not over. As Patrick Wolfe has argued, 'invasion is a structure not an event'.[54] The invasion of this territory did not end with the arrival of the boats and colonisation did not end at Federation. If we accept Wolfe's argument, discussed in the previous chapter, that settler colonies are premised on the elimination of Indigenous societies, then the continued assertion of Aboriginal and Torres Strait Islander sovereignty makes it clear to the settler colonial order that their work is not done. In other words, Australia is now engaged in a process of 'internal colonisation', which James Tully defines as 'the vast array of more mobile and changeable techniques of government by which Indigenous peoples and their territories are governed'. These techniques are implicitly designed for 'guiding the conduct of Indigenous people, directly and indirectly, and responding to their resistance'.[55] Indigenous policy such as the Intervention is one clear example of internal colonial strategy, but much past policy has also contributed to the construction of Australia's structures of invasion, to our techniques of internal colonial governance. As a nation we persist with such an approach because of the 'unresolved contradiction and constant provocation' at the foundation of our ongoing colonial project; that is, that we continue to exercise jurisdiction over territory that Indigenous people 'refuse to surrender'.[56]

Why policy will never succeed

A fundamental principle of Heifetz's framework of adaptive change is that adaptive challenges cannot be resolved through technical means. Heifetz argues that:

> When people are challenged, the first line of defense is to apply the responses already in their repertoire. Given the high number of major problems people have sorted out through history, applying solutions from the repertoire makes obvious sense. The solution for new problems, however, may lie outside the repertoire, which is exactly when adaptive work is needed.[57]

We can see that the repertoire has failed when a problem does not resolve, or even worsens, over time, and when we find ourselves endlessly recycling past technical solutions rather than diagnosing and tackling the underlying adaptive challenge. When this happens it is evident that the technical solutions are 'fake remedies', diverting attention from the real and more difficult work to be done. This is both work avoidance and a part of the bureaucracy's 'self-replication process'. As anthropologist Tess Lea notes, ideas about success and failure are 'measured against a yardstick of under-conceptualised and idealised western cultural abstractions'. Our settler colonial imagination is limited in its capacity to imagine 'what a good life is and what it takes for an Aboriginal person to have one'.[58] We struggle to think beyond the possible.

Focusing our attention at the level of state political institutions is crucial to understanding why policy fails. The analysis in this book is focused at the level of collective, rather than individual, guilt. It is in the way we function at the national, collective level that our guilt gets in the way of making the required social and political changes that will enable Aboriginal and Torres Strait Islander peoples to take control of their lives. Our adaptive challenge is also a political challenge. What Elizabeth Povinelli describes as 'late liberalism' can be understood as 'a set of techniques' that have transformed an extensive critique of the colonial governance of difference into a 'crisis of culture'. Once we understand this 'we can begin to understand whether we are in the midst of a political event, what kind of political event it is, and thus what it might be to engage politically in Aboriginal Australia'.[59] But this understanding continues to be inhibited by the contemporary implications of white Australians' imagined self-image as victims of the colonial project and our constructed history of the nation as 'won through suffering'.[60] We make policy in a framework dominated by strategies of internal colonisation. While some of the strategies for addressing our guilt at the collective level must start with individual change, these strategies are still aimed at generating bigger, broader, deeper, national change. Suffice to say that, as James Tully has argued, any resolution to these struggles in

Australia (as in other postcolonial orders) must be worked through 'by means of dialogue among those in the field who are subject to the contested norm of mutual recognition'.[61]

At the individual level, many of the 'bureaucrats and bleeding hearts' that Tess Lea describes go into the field of Indigenous policy and service provision not because they are tyrannical, mindless or openly racist individuals who see working for the state as a useful method of continuing to constrain or manage Aboriginal aspirations towards sovereignty and autonomy. Rather the opposite. Lea argues that the majority of the professionals in the field are motivated by a desire to 'make a difference', to 'turn things around'. Their jobs are difficult and under-resourced, leaving many to 'lapse into despair that there are no defensible grounds for further intrusion into Aboriginal lives and that anyway, community dysfunction is too complex and deeply embedded to overturn without an impossible return to pre-invasion circumstances'.[62] They are, in many cases inarguably, well-intentioned. But as the discussion in this chapter has made clear, good intentions while necessary for opening up new dialogue can never be enough and on their own can in fact result in further damage. In the current policy moment, in which Indigenous culture has been recast as the source of social ills and interventionist policies have been constructed that aim to 'change the everyday practices, internal social organisation and structural position of a whole people', as Gillian Cowlishaw suggests, the bureaucrats engaged in implementing such policy 'cannot know what they do'.[63] That such an approach must inevitably inflict damage is justified in Lea's acknowledgement that 'the idea that Aboriginal people *need our help*' is 'a foundational assumption' for the majority of 'helping whites' and indeed for the bureaucracy itself.[64] This belief in the indispensible nature of their work, with all its undertones of the guilty collective conscience, is based in a belief that the settler colonial Australian state has the answers. It robs all who hold this view of the ability to think beyond what is possible in administering their care and good intentions.

None of this is to suggest that policy-making and program delivery should stop. The immediate needs on the ground remain great and in the short term it remains an imperative of both care and justice that every effort be made to meet these needs. But this work must be undertaken in recognition of the fact that until the national container into which we pour our good intentions changes shape, the impact of any policy or program will be severely proscribed. The recent example of the Intervention is a case in point. The apparent aim of this 'new' policy has ostensibly been to produce greater 'responsibility' among Aboriginal individuals and communities. The effect, some would say unsurprisingly, has in fact been to reinforce 'an old and familiar sense of being governed by external and somewhat alien powers', thereby reinscribing a relationship with the state that 'cannot increase a sense of responsibility or social health among adult men and women'.[65] Despite the fact that 'the promise of one day getting things right' continues to underwrite what Lea calls 'tropes of interventionary necessity',[66] the current political and institutional context in fact means we are absolutely and completely unable to get anything 'right' at the level of policy. If history has taught us nothing else it ought to have taught us this. But collective guilt has proven a profound learning disability and we are obtuse in our denial of the ongoing colonial project. Yet the message is really very simple. If we persist with a process of internal colonisation Aboriginal and Torres Strait Islander peoples will continue to pay the price. Better surely to break the bonds of solidarity with our colonial forebears and shape a new national container.

I do not disagree with Pearson's argument that Indigenous people have the right to take responsibility for their own lives. Where I disagree with him is that I do not believe it is possible for Indigenous people to take the kind of responsibility he imagines within a national political context in which their wider rights are constantly under threat. I do not contend that changing the Constitution will instantly change Indigenous lives—that would be a ridiculous proposition. But I do believe that until the Constitution changes—until Aboriginal and Torres Strait Islander peoples have been recognised as First Nations with an inherent right to govern themselves—nothing else will change. As Pearson himself notes, 'Aboriginal people are lepers in the Australian democratic process'.[67] For as long as they are compelled to go cap in hand to the settler to argue their cause and plead for their autonomy they will remain subjects rather than sovereigns.

Anthropologist Emma Kowal distinguishes between two paradigms in Indigenous governance that sit in tension with one another. 'Remedialism' rests on the view that Indigenous lives 'can be improved through reasoned intervention' and at a basic level seeks to 'change' Indigenous people in order to reduce inequality. The logic of remedialism underpins initiatives including strategies to 'close the gap' in statistical inequality and the Intervention in the Northern Territory. In contrast, 'orientalism' foregrounds Indigenous particularity and cultural difference, emphasising the primacy of culture in any program designed to assist Indigenous people. According to Kowal, the self-determination era was largely informed by an orientalist discourse. Today, these two paradigms create a 'hybrid discourse'

Kowal describes as 'postcolonial logic'. The tension within this logic, which Kowal describes as 'a permanent undercurrent of the Australian postcolony', is confusing for well-intentioned non-Indigenous people who must now worry both about avoiding assimilationist policy while simultaneously advancing Indigenous development across measurable indicators. This is indeed a 'complex moral landscape', and one that often leads well-intentioned non-Indigenous people to seek and grasp simplistic solutions that appear to bridge the epistemological divide between the two ideas.[68]

Indigenous policy in Australia is made in the context of a 'hyper-mediated public sphere' in which it is becoming increasingly common for public and political focus on the challenges facing Aboriginal and Torres Strait Islander peoples to take the form of 'moral panics'.[69] In the face of these panics, and in the context of heated, emotional and often polarised debates about what direction Indigenous policy should take, too many Australians find themselves bamboozled, bewildered and paralysed. Unsure of what is 'right' and terrified of being wrong, they say and do nothing. Individuals who in other spheres possess effective skills in critical thinking prefer to be told what they should think. When a clear answer is not forthcoming they prefer not to think about it at all. Again, guilt gets in the way of an effective engagement with the place of the past in the present and the adaptive work that needs to be undertaken if we are ever to be able to think what has so far been impossible.

The next chapter considers what non-Indigenous Australians actually bring to these debates, and the responsibilities they avoid by acting as 'empty vessels' on these issues. As Tully has argued, however, the first step in transforming the way we think and act in response to ongoing struggles for recognition must be to reject the idea that there can be any monological answer, any one solution handed down from on high.[70] Time and again, our technical repertoire has proven itself unequal to the challenge we face. Policy will never be the answer. We must do the thinking and the work ourselves.

Chapter 4

Not just empty vessels: Moving beyond moral ambivalence

In 2009 I was lucky enough to be invited to the Byron Bay Writers' Festival where, among other panels, I shared the stage with the ethicist Peter Singer along with writer Irfan Yusuf and the performance artists Wire MC and Choo Choo. Our topic, perhaps ironically in retrospect, was 'Not in my backyard: community politics and social consciences'. As a part of our discussion the topic of the Northern Territory Intervention was raised, and I took the opportunity to ask the audience about their views on human rights. The audience was vigorous in their agreement that human rights were an ideal to be supported. Why, then, I asked them, had there been such overwhelming complacency about the fact that one group in our population had had their rights 'suspended' in order to deliver a race-based policy? Here Peter Singer intervened to suggest that my response was 'polemic'. After all, he argued, didn't women and children in Aboriginal communities deserve to have their rights protected too?

I was shocked at Singer's response, and disappointed that someone I regard as a serious and important thinker appeared to have been captured by the discourse of moral panic swirling around the Intervention policy. The idea that human rights can be assembled in some sort of hierarchy in which women's and children's rights trump Indigenous rights or the right to be protected from racial discrimination seems nonsensical to me—quite aside from the lack of any credible evidence to support the view that the measures in the Intervention were then or are now protecting women and children from anything. At the same time, however, I recognised Singer's response all too well. While he was quite emphatic in his views, I know many other Australians who have found this suggested trade-off between categories of rights quite confusing. Maybe it is okay to suspend certain Indigenous rights protection mechanisms in some circumstances? If the end result is an improvement in physical and material circumstances then perhaps the idea of rights doesn't actually matter as much as we thought? But really, most people seem to think, we're not quite sure, so we won't say anything at all.

Questions and confusions such as these have produced a strange silence among many otherwise thoughtful and politically engaged people. Noel Pearson, although generally a supporter of the Intervention framework, has observed this phenomenon more broadly. In relation to the legacies of Indigenous economic exclusion Pearson notes that those he calls 'progressive people' have 'virtually stood mute'. While he concedes there have been 'some exceptions' he suggests they have been few. For the most part, Pearson argues, 'the progressives have stood silent', preferring 'to talk about something else other than what we need to do about those children'.[1] Over the years I have also had many conversations with students and others wanting to understand more in order to feel able to take action in an area where they recognise injustice. Why, I have asked them, do they feel they need special guidance in this area? Do they feel similarly paralysed when they see injustice in another field? What happens to their critical thinking skills when confronted with the present-day repercussions of our colonial past?

Of course my own journey was not dissimilar to the one such students are beginning. In the introduction to *Black Politics* I wrote of my own experience after a 'typical white Australian upbringing':

> I lived in a white middle-class suburb and had white middle-class friends. Although there may well have been some Aboriginal children in my primary school I do not recall them. I remember the grainy black and white films of semi-naked Aboriginal people hunting and gathering in the desert as the entirety of my education about the way that Aboriginal people lived before Captain Cook 'discovered' Australia. I am sure many white readers will recall childhoods similar to this ...
>
> It was not until my first job in the welfare sector, as a youth worker in the inner-Sydney suburb of Waterloo, that I really began to come to grips with what it meant to be Aboriginal in contemporary Australia ... It seems shocking to write this now, but at the time I had just not ever really contemplated the impact of our colonial history on the people most affected. As a 20 year old, the 200 years since European arrival seemed like ancient history. But I can vividly remember the conversation where all that changed: I was talking to a young person about their family and they mentioned that both of their parents had been brought up in an institution. I had a sudden—if belated—realisation that I was only one generation away from the time when Aboriginal children were removed from their families. I realised I knew almost nothing about this history and started to read everything I could get my hands on. But like many white 'do-gooders' before me, my response to this growing awareness was a paralysing guilt. The more I learned about Australia's colonial history the worse I felt. In desperation I went to speak to an older woman I knew and poured out my guilt to her. (I cringe at this memory now as I think of the burden of guilt that white people are forever taking to

> Aboriginal people. What are we looking for? Absolution?). To this woman's absolute credit she did not send me away to get over myself. She quietly put her arm around me and said, 'Don't be guilty daught, just be really, really angry.'[2]

My experiences are far from unique, although I recognise my good fortune in receiving the advice that I did. Being alert to the pitfalls of guilt so early on gave me an opportunity to approach my learning in a different way. I certainly had a lot of learning to do, but as the beneficiary of a university education I also had some skills that allowed me to read, research and think critically about Australia's history and contemporary reality.

A great many other Australians also have these skills, and many would like to know and understand more in order to do their bit in improving Indigenous–non-Indigenous relations. Too often, however, their sense of guilt is so paralysing that they feel unable to initiate change, leaving them confused by different points of view. This paralysis is compounded by the inevitable racism that they have internalised—as we all have—growing up in a racist society. This chapter argues that non-Indigenous people do not come to these relationships as empty vessels, and nor do they need to drain the energy of Indigenous people figuring out 'what they should do'. Rather, the chapter suggests that core values concerning human rights, dignity and autonomy, combined with skills in critical thinking and a willingness to engage with complex ideas, are an adequate basis from which to begin some adaptive work.

Why the confusion?

In their study of opinion polling and other studies assessing public opinion in Indigenous affairs Murray Goot and Tim

Rowse challenge the idea that Australia is a nation divided about Indigenous issues. There are certainly divisions and certain topics in particular that exacerbate these divides, but Goot and Rowse suggest that in fact Australians are divided '*within themselves*'. Time and again, opinion polls have shown Australians to have a 'collective philosophical ambivalence' about the direction of policy or wider reform in Indigenous affairs. Even in the leadup to the 1967 referendum—an event widely considered to represent a high water mark in the public expression of support for Indigenous equality—Goot and Rowse detect two distinct strands of thinking. On the one hand, a large group of Australians were focused on what Aboriginal people were thought to have in common with non-Indigenous Australians, leading to support for ideas of equality of entitlements among all Australians. On the other hand there was a group more concerned to emphasise the differences between Indigenous and other Australians. The interplay between these two discourses was 'made complex by the ways in which both styles of thinking remained relevant to Australians concerned with the issues raised by assimilation'.[3]

As the discussion in the previous chapter suggests, Indigenous policy in Australia remains an area of heated debate. Emma Kowal describes the current environment as one of 'paradigm shift' in which 'the boundaries between help and hindrance, racism and anti-racism, are shifting and unstable'. For 'progressive Whites' this ongoing crisis about culture is also an 'identity crisis' and Kowal suggests that this inner turmoil is one reason that those concerned to make a difference in Indigenous affairs will tend to grasp at 'any formulation that offers a resolution, however provisional or fragile'.[4] Even the 'experts' can find themselves bewildered and silenced by feelings of guilt—and the attendant sense of confusion and complicity—in the face of complex debate, such as in the case of the 'eerie silence' among Australian anthropologists following the 2007 announcement of the Intervention in the Northern Territory.[5] This silence prompted heated and angry exchanges on the Australian Anthropological Society email list, which were further inflamed by the publication of Peter Sutton's *The Politics of Suffering*, also discussed in the previous chapter. Sutton's own interpretation of this phenomenon is slightly different,[6] arguing that those concerned with justice rather than care allow their 'political feelings and political values' to dominate their 'emotional feelings and moral values'—as though the former were not driven by the latter. Whatever the interpretation, it seems that both experts and everyday Australians frequently find themselves paralysed in their interpretation of Indigenous status and circumstances and in their views on the ever-changing policy response.

But regardless of an individual's political, moral or emotional beacons in this confusing landscape, it is virtually impossible for any Australian to today claim that they do not know of our contested history and the questions it raises in the present. Over the last 60 years in particular, Australians have become increasingly aware of what Bernard Smith once described as 'the locked cupboard of our history'.[7] In relation to policies of child removal for example, cultural studies theorist Meaghan Morris argues that Australians 'cannot not know' that such policies were applied to Aboriginal people for 'a systematically racist, deliberately ethnocidal purpose' on a 'horrifically large scale'. Morris concedes, however, that 'only now' is the extent of the scale of the trauma and disruption that child removal created beginning to 'filter through' to 'the *white* Australians in whose idealised name it was practised'. According to Morris this belated recognition means that Australians have only recently 'begun to develop a collective capacity to comprehend, to empathise, to imagine that trauma and disruption'. Morris also describes this somewhat belated understanding as part of a 'politics of remembering', suggesting that many, if not most, white Australians were unaware of child removal policies

> ... *not* because we did not *know* it was happening (we did) but because we were unable or did not care to *understand* what we knew; we could not imagine how Aboriginal people felt. So we whites have not 'just found out' about the lost children; rather, we are beginning to *remember* it differently, to understand and care about what we knew.[8]

This different form of 'remembering', however, itself proves problematic. A deeper, more empathic awareness of our history places us all in 'an increasingly embarrassing position',[9] which in turn seems to heighten a sense of confusion and uncertainty. This moral ambivalence about historical injustice is one of the enabling features of internal colonisation in the present. While we maintain our bonds of solidarity with past perpetrators, as 'carriers of internal colonisation' we also develop the 'habit' of perpetuating silences about suffering and resistance whenever they rub up against the 'official mythologies' that normalise contemporary circumstances. In this way, as psychologists Helene Lorenz and Mary Watkins suggest,[10] 'Many of us have learned all too well what not to say and when not to speak.'

The depth of the Australian silence

In revealing the 'great Australian silence', discussed in Chapter 2, W.E.H. Stanner relied on a survey of books examining Australian history and politics, 'the sort of books that probably expressed well enough, and may even have helped to form, the outlook of socially conscious people between say, 1939 and 1955'. What Stanner found in the almost complete absence of Indigenous people—let alone Indigenous perspectives—in these texts was a 'cult of forgetfulness practised on a national scale'. He observed that having been able to 'disremember' Aboriginal people for so long, Australians were 'now hard pressed to keep them in mind even when we most want to do so'. In reviewing this situation in the late 1960s, however, Stanner expressed confidence and optimism that the silence he had revealed would not be able to be maintained in the face of the research under way at that time.[11]

Over four decades later it seems that Stanner's optimism was only partially justified. In a similar, more recent review of political studies in Australia, Tim Rowse noted an almost identical absence of Indigenous people and perspectives at least until the early to mid 1980s. Rowse suggests that the 'slow dawning' of attention by political scientists cannot be explained by arguments that Indigenous people were too marginal to Australian politics to warrant this scholarly attention. Clearly this was not the case, and the success of the 1967 referendum would be just one example to support this claim. Rather, Rowse contends that Australian political scientists were 'slow to pluralise "culture" ' with regard to democratic governance, leaving the study of all things Indigenous to the field of anthropology.[12] Further, it would seem that when the national silence observed by Stanner was finally broken it was only to see it replaced with the 'white noise' of the 'history wars', which primarily served to further confuse rather than to educate the wider Australian population.

Anthropology, as the discipline by definition devoted to the study of human society and culture, was never silent in the way that historians and political scientists were. However, anthropology has also occupied a difficult place in the settler colonial intellectual order. The early anthropology as practised in Australia was interested in Indigenous peoples as 'primitive', often meaning that those who had been subject to the earliest onslaught of colonialism through an intense occupation of their land fell outside the interests of the discipline. This in turn created a 'strange dissonance' in which anthropologists did not recognise dispossessed Aboriginal people who had been relocated to reserves, although the state administration did, subsequently making policy in the absence of any anthropologically informed debate.[13] Further, early Australian anthropologists tended to speak *for* Aboriginal people rather than enabling Aboriginal people to speak for themselves.[14] The focus on a certain experience of Indigeneity reinforced views that it was Aboriginal people themselves who would need to change and to modernise, rendering anthropology and its practitioners as a kind of 'sympathetic collaborator' in the colonial project.[15] Like many other academic disciplines, by the 1960s and 1970s anthropology was to engage in a project of auto-critique, questioning the extent of its complicity in colonial practices and contemporary race relations, and the discipline as a whole has certainly benefited from this reflection. But this critique can perhaps only ever be partial. For example, Indigenous scholars such as Aileen Moreton-Robinson draw attention to the ways in which the work of white feminist anthropologists remains bounded by non-Indigenous epistemological assumptions and white Australian culture, meaning that they can only ever offer 'partial truths' about Indigenous women's lives.[16]

The inadequacy of the academic analysis of Indigenous affairs for much of the twentieth century goes some way to explaining the frustration many Australians have experienced when they finally grasp the depth of their ignorance in this area. Henry Reynolds has written specifically on that question in his book *Why Weren't We Told?*, in which he attempts to respond to this precise question, asked of him innumerable times by people who have listened to him speak. Reynolds detected in his interrogators a sense that what he had to say had been 'personally significant' to them. He also heard from them a sense of frustration:

> ... they felt that they should have known these things themselves, and didn't. They wished they had known them before. They believed their education should have provided the knowledge, the information, and hadn't done so. They felt let down, cheated, sold short.[17]

Many, like me, probably also felt guilty.

It might be hoped that the mainstream media would provide a lens through which those Australians who are aware of their ignorance may gain insight about Aboriginal and Torres Strait Islander cultures and aspirations. The 2008 Reconciliation Barometer produced by Reconciliation Australia indicated that while 49 per cent of respondents drew on their own personal experiences with Aboriginal and Torres Strait Islander peoples for their knowledge about Indigenous people and cultures, another 29 per cent nominated the media as their main source of information.[18] Sadly, however, the media does not always provide a fair or balanced view of Indigenous lives, often reporting in an uncritical manner on government policy or replicating the racist views sometimes evident in the wider community. Australian media history in this regard is telling, with the long running (now defunct) magazine *The Bulletin* maintaining the slogan 'Australia for the White Man' on its cover until Donald Horne became its editor in the 1960s. Today *The Australian* newspaper is thought to carry the flag of a defensive nationalism that often excludes Indigenous perspectives, and the mainstream media more broadly still tends to ignore good news stories in favour of what Mick Dodson has described as a story of 'failure, despair, violence and abuse'.[19] Such a skewed perspective, combined with the minimal reporting offered to critics of current government policy and the inadequacy of Australian curricula, contribute to a poorly informed population.

Today many non-Indigenous Australians seem to feel silenced by their lack of knowledge about Aboriginal and Torres Strait Islander cultures. They feel that they can only have an opinion when they have learnt—even passively 'been taught'—more about Indigenous lives than however much or little knowledge they presently hold. Henry Reynolds recalls that his own education did not properly prepare him to 'be an adequate citizen, a well-informed voter and a participant in public life'.[20] Some decades after Reynolds was at school I have seen first hand—both as a parent of teenagers and as a lecturer in Australian politics—that our high school curriculum still does not adequately prepare students for a serious engagement with Indigenous issues. It remains to be seen whether the new and highly contentious national history curriculum will do a better job. But the absence of a solid school-based education in this field should not stand in the way of further learning and reflection for anyone who is interested. Reynolds has noted that there is now a vast quantity of 'books, articles, films, novels, songs and paintings' that have 'filled out the space once claimed by Stanner's Great Australian Silence'.[21] With so much to read, watch and listen to that every one of us can access through a trip to the local library, why do so many still seem to feel unable to think critically and independently when discomforted or confused by debates about Indigenous issues? Perhaps, as Gillian Cowlishaw suggests, what is needed far more urgently than a new history curriculum is 'a mirror to examine ourselves and *our* society' rather than new tools or tropes for 'explaining *their* cultural difference'.[22]

Why can't we talk about racism?

Problematic race relations have divided the Australian settler state since its inception. Race-based tension and conflict has always been a feature of Australian society, with hostility from white Australians directed not only towards Aboriginal and Torres Strait Islander peoples but also successive waves of immigrants and refugees right up to the present time. The writer Albert Memmi has argued that colonial racism rests on three ideological components still in evidence today: first, the gulf between the cultures of the coloniser and the colonised; second, the exploitation of these cultural differences for the benefit of the colonialist; and, third, the use of these supposed differences as standards of irrefutable fact.[23] In this context it is odd that we find it so difficult to talk about racism. Given that the objects of racism understand racist sentiments so intimately, who is it that we are so determined to hide them from?[24]

Educator Shelly Tochluk suggests that for 'most whites' being labelled racist 'will spark a more defensive reaction than almost any other slight'. Our defensiveness gets in the way of the kinds of conversations we most need to be having, the kinds of conversations that 'ask us to consider ourselves related to that term'.[25] Despite this desire to avoid talk of racism, however, racism is something that each of us carries to a greater or lesser degree, 'in our minds and hearts and bodies'. Even when we pretend we have eliminated it, most of us know that we still carry it. And because those of us who want to support struggles for Indigenous justice also know that we are supposed to be 'appropriately antiracist', we also carry a fear that Indigenous people will 'see through us'. As Robert Jensen suggests, this fear sparks a set of paralysing questions:

> What if they [non-white people] can look past our antiracist vocabulary and sense that we still don't know how to treat them as equals? What if they know about us what we don't dare know about ourselves? What if they can see what we can't even voice?[26]

Our defensiveness on the issue of racism has led to any discussion of the term being 'carefully suppressed', particularly among educated city-dwellers. But underneath this suppression, it remains the case that 'racism and bigotry are things we all know about'.[27]

Our anxieties underscore the fact that our discussion of racism in Australia has become overly simplistic. Noel Pearson has pointed out an unhelpful dichotomy in public discussion of racism where it is assumed that there are only two possible sides: 'those who are racists and those who are not, those who are subject to racism and those who are racists, those who believe that racism is a major social ill and those who do not, and so on'. For Pearson, the divide seems to come down to an unsophisticated delineation between 'those who believe Australia has a problem with racism, and those who believe that Australia is not a racist country'.[28] In contrast, Pearson identifies six positions taken by Indigenous and non-Indigenous people in Australia with regard to 'race and history concerning the country's original peoples'.[29] Of relevance here is the position he describes as *denial,* in which a large constituency of non-Indigenous Australians continue to deny that racism in Australia against Indigenous people is a problem because the members of this constituency are 'defensive about their own identity and heritage'. Also relevant here is the group Pearson describes as being *morally vain* about race and history in Australia, a group he suggests 'largely come from the liberal left and are morally certain about right and wrong and ready to ascribe blame'. While Pearson does concede that moral vanity is perhaps an 'unfair characterisation', he nevertheless accuses this group of using issues of race and history 'as a means of getting the upper hand over their political and cultural opponents', having as their primary concern 'not the plight or needs of those who suffer racism and oppression, but rather their view of themselves'. In contrast to these two positions Pearson proposes *acknowledgement* 'of the past and its legacy in the present' as 'the optimum position for non-Indigenous people to take' with respect to race and history, and further suggests that non-Indigenous people take *responsibility* 'for the fact of racism, and work to answer and counter it.'[30]

The challenge in the argument for non-Indigenous acknowledgement and responsibility, however, lies precisely in the debates between those who would deny the racism entrenched in Australia's history and those who Pearson describes as morally vain. I would suggest that both groups are, to some extent, captured by the dynamics of our collective guilt. The discomfort this guilt produces leads some to respond with an angry rejection, while others cope by blaming Indigenous people rather than acknowledging their own complicity and internalised racism. Neither response is particularly helpful in addressing the wider adaptive challenge that we face.

To this view Ghassan Hage adds the suggestion that the tendency to think about racism only as a 'mental phenomenon' leads us to neglect the actual practices that are supported and enabled by racist ideas. In other words, Hage is pointing to the connections between 'what racists are thinking and what they are doing'.[31] Racist ideas have certainly informed much of the human injustice perpetrated in Australia. Social Darwinism, for example, was used to justify a view of Indigenous people as inferior to white people. Notions of social evolution were 'eagerly embraced on the frontier', providing both 'intellectual explanation and moral justification' for 'the brutal work of pioneering'.[32] Racist ideas were an essential foundation to the entire colonial project. For Hage the crucial link between racist ideas and racist practices, both now and in the past, has been the idea of territory. In the past these concerns may have been centred on establishing the colonial presence in Indigenous territory. Today such worries are more mundane, focused instead, for example, on perceptions of neighbourhood safety. Racist ideas tend only to inform racist practices when they are accompanied by a belief that we have a privileged relationship to a territory (or a neighbourhood), and this relationship is perceived to be under threat. For this reason Hage suggests it may be more useful to reconceive of 'racist' practices as 'nationalist' practices, even if it is racist ideas that inform them.[33]

Whiteness and anti-racism

Recent years have seen a rapidly developing field of scholarship dubbed 'critical whiteness studies'. Whiteness is described by Ghassan Hage as being 'an everchanging, composite, cultural construct' with its roots in European colonisation through which white identity has been universalised as a social position of cultural power, set in opposition to the racialised black and brown identities of the colonised.[34] Writers in the field argue that whiteness—as opposed to other markers of ethnicity—and associated white privilege, tend to be normalised and invisible. Effort is made to draw attention to the fact that 'white skin is privileged by institutions and practices and provides material and psychological entitlements to white people'.[35] Examples of these privileges and entitlements may be as seemingly trivial as 'being able to swear or wear second hand clothes without it being blamed on the bad morals or poverty of one's race' through to more profound benefits, such as 'not having to educate one's children about racism to protect them'. In a deeply racialised world these structural and cultural privileges are most often considered to be natural and therefore unproblematic, while other markers of non-white ethnicity are distinguished by their difference to the white norm. The invisibility of whiteness tends to mean that the unfair privileges and dominance enjoyed by people with white skin are generally not even considered as an explanation for race-based inequities.[36]

Drawing attention to whiteness in this way has been an important and challenging insight. There are questions, however, about what people with white skin should do with the discomfort produced by this new awareness. Robert Jensen suggests that rather than loving our whiteness we should first learn to hate it. Jensen clarifies what he means:

> I don't mean white people should hate themselves for having pale skin, for something we were born with. I think we white people should sometimes hate ourselves for what we do, or don't do, in the world, for the choices we make about our white skin ... We live in a white supremacist

> society and benefit from white privilege. We should hate that fact, and if we haven't done enough to change that world, well . . .

And there, says Jensen, is the rub. The fact that whiteness still allows and even normalises the domination of some groups over others 'should cause us discomfort, everyday'.[37] Ideally, this discomfort will at the very least prompt those of us who are white to undertake sustained self-examination that will deepen our understanding of the ways in which race and white privilege continue to affect our lives and our individual and collective relationships with Indigenous people.[38] The point is not for non-Indigenous Australians to feel bad about themselves. Rather, as a means of dealing with feelings of guilt, it is possible for non-Indigenous Australians to simultaneously maintain a positive view of their group while also interrogating their whiteness and acknowledging the need to address past injustice in order to enable adaptive change. These two positions are not incompatible.[39]

Even for white people themselves, Australian whiteness is not without its problems. These problems are tied to the question of moral legitimacy that in turn stems from our colonial past. What has often been termed the 'cultural cringe' in Australia is an expression of the cultural connections to Britain that many non-Indigenous Australians retain. This type of 'yearning for identity' is common in settler colonial states, where emulating European cultural practices enables the denial of much that has taken place in the colonised society. Privileging particular expressions and symbols of whiteness in this way offers the coloniser 'a sense of certainty and stability', and supports the reclamation of power from those who have been dispossessed.[40] But maintaining a sense of Britishness in Australia also produces a certain incoherence in the settler self, an incoherence that proves problematic for the imagining of a unitary nation. For the imagined Australian nation to make sense, it must continue to rely on 'a racialised social formation predicated on whiteness'.[41] Australian white identity is based on control of the land, of cultural expression and of language, necessitating the public performance of 'authority, respectability, and ownership'.[42]

Developing a deeper understanding of the myriad ways in which whiteness and white privilege continue to shape our national identity, and therefore how this identity continues to exclude Aboriginal and Torres Strait Islander peoples, should enable us to perhaps use our privilege to make personal, community and systemic change.[43] But translating a new-found understanding about ourselves into effective action is not without potential pitfalls. Even white anti-racists are 'shaped by settler-colonial histories and contemporary political discourse'.[44] Simply attempting to address inequity through anti-racism can lead to a focus on the subject of racism (Indigenous people), which still allows white 'complicity in the dynamics of racism' to remain unexamined.[45] Making a choice to become involved in anti-racist work does not allow 'good whites' off the hook, and the good intentions underlying such a choice should not—as the previous chapter made clear—be considered adequate as an objective guide for good behaviour or good policy.[46] Even—or perhaps especially—in anti-racist work good intentions are not enough. We need to draw on something more.

Values to guide understanding and action

One of the sustaining myths about Australia concerns our purported egalitarianism: we are, in theory at least, the land of the 'fair go'. The persistence of this myth underscores both the 'power of comforting deceits' and the continued marginalisation of Aboriginal and Torres Strait Islander peoples from Australia's traditions and opportunities.[47] Since the arrival of the British and the onslaught of settler colonialism Australia has provided Indigenous people with anything but a fair go.

It is possible, however, that a more critical stance on Australian values about egalitarianism could also prove to be a resource in our adaptive work. Heifetz has suggested that values, which are shaped by 'rubbing against real problems', are an important aspect of adaptive work. Understanding different values enables us to understand different dimensions of a problem, and to see different opportunities that may not be obvious if we only consider one perspective. For these reasons it is important to include not just different but *competing* value perspectives if we are serious about making adaptive change.[48] Heifetz points out that social systems tend to honour a certain mix of values. Within this mix there is always competition, which goes some way to explaining why adaptive work tends to involve conflict. Confronting a shared situation with competing value perspectives is challenging and difficult, and in extreme cases the conflict can become violent with tragic consequences.[49] But this is the work that needs to be done in postcolonial Australia.

Understanding Indigenous perspectives on ideas of Australian egalitarianism may open up different understandings of a cherished Australian value. It is possible, for example, that the myth of Australian egalitarianism could be built upon in order to generate wider understanding about Indigenous poverty and marginalisation. Inequality between Indigenous and non-Indigenous Australians violates idealised norms of egalitarianism. When this inequality is understood as part of an intergroup relationship, embedded in our history and maintained through white privilege, and where it is understood that non-Indigenous group identity is inextricably linked to Indigenous experience, then the more likely it is that this inequality will be seen as illegitimate, providing impetus for social change. It is discomforting to understand that one's group identity is dependent on another's exploitation, and the more this situation is perceived to be at odds with Australian values the more likely it is that people in the advantaged group will be supportive of change.[50]

James Tully also suggests that both Indigenous and non-Indigenous people share a basic value regarding the right of peoples to govern themselves in ways that conform with their own laws and ways, that are also able to coexist with the laws and cultural ways of others.[51] Again Indigenous and non-Indigenous perspectives on these values will be different, and most likely competing. It achieves nothing, however, to simply normalise the white value perspective and thus suppress or marginalise the Indigenous point of view. Both are features of the contemporary Australian political landscape and allowing one perspective to be suppressed is just more work avoidance. Heifetz suggests a series of questions to be asked when analysing a community's response to a difficult reality:

> Are its members testing their views of the problem against competing views within the community or are they defensively sticking to a particular perspective and suppressing others? Are people testing seriously the relationship between means and ends? Are conflicts over values and the morality of various means open to examination? Are policies analysed and evaluated to distinguish fact from fiction?[52]

The capacity to recognise shared but competing values and to use them as the basis for engaging in adaptive work is greatly complicated by the construction of Aboriginal and Torres Strait Islander peoples as 'others', who are somehow unknowable. In many ways this construction of 'others' seems inescapable, but it can be ameliorated by efforts to know and understand each other as well as possible.[53] By keeping a distance—that is, by remaining ignorant of Indigenous lives—non-Indigenous people are able to ignore the hardship that many Indigenous people face. In ignoring this suffering non-Indigenous people are also able to deny their obligations to people damaged by colonisation:

> It allows us to hold back from asking whether we share responsibility for the acts and policies that caused this harm and suffering. It enables us to avoid asking whether we should take on some responsibility for responding to the damage that has been done . . . Our resulting insensitivity and lack of awareness undermine the possibility of constructing better relationships in the aftermath of wrongdoing.[54]

Australia's history is all too full of examples of non-Indigenous people causing harm by acting in ignorance. The officials who carried out policies of child removal, for example, driving away cars 'full of terrified "mixed-race" children' certainly did so with 'a post-World War Two awareness of the implications of racial hygiene'.[55] And yet their construction of Aboriginal people as 'others', with a somehow lesser relationship with their children than the white officials had with their own, allowed them to cause harm and suffering while distancing themselves from the responsibility for this damage. More recently, too, we see examples of Aboriginal people being treated as so 'other' that non-Indigenous people feel able to neglect a basic level of care. As recently as 2006 there were distressing news reports of an incident in Brisbane involving an 'Elder in residence' at Griffith University who was ignored for five hours after collapsing at a bus stop. This well-dressed, elderly woman, who had never drunk alcohol in her life, was left lying in a pool of vomit for five and a half hours because passers-by assumed that—as an Aboriginal person—she must be drunk or drug affected. Eventually it was two Japanese students who stopped to investigate her wellbeing and call an ambulance.[56]

Again, however, those interested in engaging in adaptive work should consider how they go about gaining knowledge of Indigenous lives. Indigenous knowledge is certainly a crucial aspect of any critique of whiteness and white privilege,[57] and there is much to be learned from Aboriginal and Torres Strait Islander peoples about their experiences of colonialism, racism and poverty and about their aspirations for their futures. As Deborah Bird Rose notes, Indigenous people 'at the margins of the nation' are able to 'speak from perspectives that are almost invisible from the centre'. Unfortunately, however, there are also too many examples of non-Indigenous people attempting to 'find their own redemption' through their consumption of Indigenous culture and teaching 'as if those we had conquered should now save us'.[58] Many Indigenous people have made the point that they are tired of being asked to educate white people about what it means to be Aboriginal or Torres Strait Islander. Murri historian Jackie Huggins, for example, has pointed to the 'constant demands placed on Aboriginal people to be educators' and argued that 'It is too much to be expecting Aboriginal women to be continually explaining their oppression—as if somehow it is their fault and they have to talk and write their way out of it'. Huggins suggests that 'it is time for non-Aboriginal people to begin their journey of discovery by themselves'.[59] Frustratingly, the paralysis caused by white collective guilt often seems to render 'well-intentioned' non-Indigenous people 'unable to read and think for themselves, a feeling that can seemingly only be alleviated through asking Aboriginal people, "What can I do? How can I help?" '[60]

Beginning a process of learning and engaging is something for which we can each take responsibility. There is a vast and rich field of writing by Indigenous and non-Indigenous writers about Aboriginal and Torres Strait Islander history, politics and culture to which non-Indigenous people are certainly capable of helping ourselves. Our individual adaptive work begins there, and with the internal debates that engaging with new perspectives will provoke. These internal debates allow us to evaluate a range of different perspectives, weigh up different options, and test competing points of view. These debates are 'both a burden and a blessing'.[61] Fundamentally, however, they are a first step in learning to think critically and *for ourselves* about issues in Indigenous affairs.

Initiating this internal process, however, is necessary but it is not enough. This process must be more than personal development: reflection must lead to action. Even if the majority of white Australians made considerable progress towards eliminating every trace of racism within their own minds and bodies it would not necessarily have any tangible effect on the system and institutions through which the white privilege of settler colonialism operates.[62] The theory has certainly been that race relations are as much a feature of attitudes and behaviour as they are of public policy,[63] and in a democracy one would indeed hope that public policy reflects some measure of public belief. But personal development cannot take the place of political engagement.[64] As the previous chapters have made clear, there is much at stake for the settler colonial order in Australia in maintaining the status quo. Knowing and understanding more—learning to think more critically—is an important step. But as Henry Reynolds has argued, 'knowing brings burdens which can be shirked by those living in ignorance. With knowledge the question is no longer what we know but what we are now to do, and that is a much harder matter to deal with.'[63] The next chapter considers past efforts at taking action, seeking to understand where they have succeeded and why they have ultimately failed.

Chapter 5

Referendum, reconciliation and apology

Australian history is replete with attempts to acknowledge past wrongs and efforts to make things right. This history has not been without its moments of success. Some of the most transformative moments have come about when Indigenous and non-Indigenous people have worked together on adaptive challenges. From the 'dancing with strangers'—the curious social interactions between Gadigal and European—in the early days of the colony that historian Inga Clendinnen[1] documents to the shared efforts to expose racism evident on the 'Freedom Ride' bus tour through western New South Wales[2] organised by black and white university students, there have been intercultural connections between Indigenous and non-Indigenous Australians since the beginning of colonisation. While many of these connections have been violent and exploitative others have been adaptive, whether intentionally or otherwise. The work of the Federal Council for the Advancement of Aborigines and Torres Strait Islanders (FCAATSI) in generating support for the 1967 referendum was one such adaptive moment, as was the grassroots reconciliation movement that culminated in the mass bridge walks for Corroboree 2000 and, most recently, the 2008 apology to the Stolen Generations. Each of these was a moment when change seemed possible, when—all too briefly—there was a sense of hope and excitement that Australia might rethink itself as a more just nation in the future through a full acknowledgement of all that has been wrong in our past.

And yet in each case this hope ultimately came to nothing. Faced with the challenge of acknowledging our collective guilt, political will failed. There was bitterness and backlash from high identifiers determined to defend the historical legacy, and political cowardice from leaders who promised much but ultimately delivered very little. In the case of the derailing of the reconciliation process it can even be argued that as a nation we made a substantial retreat from the momentum for change that was evident in the early 1990s. This chapter considers some of the moments at which transformational change has seemed possible and explores the factors that have limited this potential. It also considers how we might build on the strengths in relationships that these moments have created in order to make more substantial progress on our adaptive challenge in the future.

We have not been blind

As the earliest and most brutal periods of the colonisation of this territory gave way to a sustained encroachment across the land there was some change in attitude towards the original inhabitants. While racism and contempt continued in quite overt fashion, underlying these attitudes there was often to be found a parallel 'awareness of indebtedness' to Aboriginal people.[3] Historians in the nineteenth century, while often 'crudely racist' in their views of Aboriginal people, also worried over the 'moral implications' of frontier conflict, as Ann Curthoys has suggested:

> Nineteenth-century observers were generally aware of the rapid population decline among indigenous people that seemed to follow Europeans everywhere, and spent their time not denying its existence but rather trying to work out why it happened and how it might accord with God's will.[4]

Henry Reynolds has also pointed to the long history of 'unease' about the morality of the colonial project, and suggests that each generation has seen a number of people prepared to speak up about their concerns, often at great personal cost. Reynolds argues:

> Some were so troubled by what they saw around them that they devoted themselves to the amelioration of Aboriginal suffering or to the denunciation of violence and brutality. In doing so they courted the anger, hostility and even the hatred of their contemporaries. They voiced the unspeakable, exposed carefully cloaked self-deception, dragged out hidden hypocrisies. For their pains they were seen as self-righteous, disturbing, dangerous, obsessive or mad.[5]

This same pattern of denunciating the past and highlighting the work to be done in the present is evident in more recent generations as well. Clyde Holding, the Minister for Aboriginal Affairs in the Hawke Government of the 1980s, spoke of needing to 'bring Australia to terms with itself', acknowledging that the 'genocide that took place upon our Aboriginal citizens' had 'scarred the Australian community'. Holding also contended that the 'perception of Aboriginal people as being something less than human' had been necessary to the colonial project, and meant that in the present day many people found it 'easier to maintain that perception' such that these racist views had become 'almost built into us in some ways'.[6]

Still more recently, professor of law and former Australian of the year Mick Dodson has described events including Paul Keating's Redfern Park speech, the Sea of Hands* and the bridge walks in 2000 as each being 'a marker and a catalyst of a new relationship founded on equality and respect'.[7]

What we can see in this pattern of intercultural engagement and the ongoing struggle to recognise the wrongs of our past is the complexity of what lies between Indigenous and non-Indigenous Australians. On the one hand we have the horrors of our history: a history of invasion, violence, domination, dispossession, death and exclusion, covered over with denial and silence, all of which continues to lie between us. On the other hand it is evident that there have always been powerful connections between Indigenous and non-Indigenous Australians, connections that rest on love, respect, solidarity, sympathy, support and a desire to work together to make progress in the present and the future. Deborah Bird Rose suggests that the complexity of what lies between us, a complexity that is 'neither wholly violent nor wholly non-violent', is what also creates the possibility of dialogue. Rose argues that it is our 'entanglements' that 'give us grounds for action'.[8] James Tully makes a similar point, arguing that Indigenous and non-Indigenous people have walked a

---

*The Sea of Hands was created in 1997 as a physical representation of the Citizens' Statement on Native Title, a petition circulated by the organisation Australians for Native Title and Reconciliation (ANTaR) to mobilise non-Indigenous support for these issues. Today, over 300,000 Australians have signed their names on one of 120,000 plastic hands that make up the Sea of Hands, which is Australia's largest public art installation. The Sea of Hands has been installed in every major city and many regional locations throughout Australia, and continues to gather signatures everywhere it appears.

'multiplicity of paths' together, producing intercultural institutions and relationships that 'provide the starting ground for a new dialogue of equality'.[9] This chapter considers some of the paths that have been walked in Australia.

The limits of 'yes': The 1967 referendum

It took ten years of activism by both black and white Australians to see the 1967 referendum pass successfully. The final campaign, organised and led by the Federal Council for the Advancement of Aborigines and Torres Strait Islanders (FCAATSI), asked the Australian public to simply 'Vote yes for Aborigines'.[10] They responded with the highest majority ever: 90.77 per cent of Australian voters did indeed vote 'yes', although questions remain about what it was they believed they were saying yes to. Many Australians believed that in voting 'yes' they were giving Aboriginal people citizenship, or the right to vote, or a conflation of the two. In fact Aboriginal people had (at least technically) been citizens since 1948* and had had the right to vote (at federal elections) since 1962 with the passage of the *Commonwealth Electoral Act*. In fact the reforms in the 1967 referendum were quite modest, giving the Commonwealth

---

*In 1948 the *Nationality and Citizenship Act* created the category of Australian citizen, which included Aboriginal people by virtue of the fact that they had been born in Australia. In reality, however, citizenship for Aboriginal and Torres Strait Islander people existed 'in name only' according to John Chestermann in *Civil Rights* (p. ix) and, as noted by Chris Cuneen in *Unfinished Constitutional Business?* (p. 48), Indigenous people continued to experience 'systematic exclusion' from 'the rights, entitlements and privileges of citizenship' due to ongoing discrimination both in law and in administrative practices. More substantive changes to the citizenship status of Aboriginal people did not emerge until the 1960s when, as Nicholas Peterson and Will Sanders explain in *Citizenship and Indigenous Australians* (p. 14), the restrictions that had been enshrined in various 'protection' acts began to be wound back.

Government the power to make laws in relation to (although not necessarily for the benefit of) Aboriginal people and to allow Aboriginal people to be counted in the census. The significance of the referendum lies not so much in the reality of the changes it brought about, but in the 'myth-making' upon which the success of the referendum rested.[11] Frances Peters-Little argues that a 'compassionate' understanding of these myths in fact tells us much about the reality of Aboriginal life at the time of the referendum, thereby explaining at least some of the significance attached to the event.[12]

Despite the modest reality behind these changes to the Constitution, however, both the campaign and the organisation behind it suggest that Australia did engage in some adaptive change during this period. FCAATSI, formed in 1958 through a coming together of representatives from State and Territory organisations working to advance Indigenous rights, was the principal national body campaigning for greater rights for Aboriginal and Torres Strait Islander peoples towards the end of the assimilation era. Unlike other organisations—either the white philanthropic, humanitarian bodies concerned with protecting 'tribal' Aboriginal people in the north from the impact of colonialism, or the parallel bodies of Indigenous activists more concerned with helping their members in the south-east of Australia to access better services—FCAATSI was both multiracial and national in focus. For much of the next fifteen years the organisation would see black and white working together to end assimilation and strive for greater equality for Aboriginal and Torres Strait Islander peoples.[13] Eventually, however, the organisation would split along racial lines, when the Aboriginal membership asserted their desire to control the executive in line with wider demands for Indigenous self-determination that characterised the early 1970s, and it eventually folded in 1978.[14]

Activists in FCAATSI capitalised on the mood of the 1960s, and the wider climate of social change that was a hallmark of the decade. More specifically, however, advocates for the yes vote in the referendum 'spoke often of their sense of a growing public interest in Aboriginal affairs and an increasingly sympathetic attitude towards the circumstances of Aborigines'.[15] The decade also saw the 1963 bark petitions presented to Federal Parliament by the Yolngu at Yirrkala and the 1966 Wave Hill strike by the Gurindji people, events which created a surge of national mobilisation among Aboriginal activists.[16] FCAATSI activists had pressed for the referendum through petitions that eventually persuaded the Menzies Government to somewhat reluctantly introduce the bill in 1965. Advocates for the yes vote then set about building on their years of letter writing and signature collecting to continue their consciousness-raising efforts in the wider community. They engaged in a media campaign using print, radio and television, along with a constant round of community meetings and public speaking engagements, and developed campaign materials with the appealing image of an Aboriginal child's face and the simple message to 'vote yes'.[17] FCAATSI maintained an approach to campaign communication that involved the 'intentional simplification of complex issues'[18] in a deliberate effort to engage people in support of the yes vote, rather than risk losing them to a complex explanation of constitutional law less likely to produce a positive response.

The exceptionally high yes vote in the 1967 referendum would suggest that this strategy was a wise one. In a country notoriously conservative when it comes to changing its Constitution (only eight out of 44 referenda have ever been passed), 1967 was a remarkable triumph. But historical acclaim for the success of this referendum is more muted. Today, the symbolism of the referendum seems to far outweigh its actual impact on Indigenous lives, and even the interpretation of the high level of support achieved in 1967 can be questioned. Murray Goot and Tim Rowse suggest that support for 'abstract equality', as evident in the yes vote, was not matched by a higher level of 'warmth' towards Aboriginal and Torres Strait Islander people, nor by a desire to see them become more socially included in all areas of Australian society.[19] The fragility of this public sentiment is well understood by Indigenous people, and the academic John Maynard has questioned whether a similar referendum held today would achieve 'even thirty percent' support, suggesting that since the high point of 1967 there has been a concerted campaign to undermine the 'collaboration between Aboriginal people and non-Aboriginal people who supported us'.[20] Given current plans to hold a referendum on constitutional recognition for Indigenous people in 2013 it is likely that Maynard's fears will be tested.

Another consideration here is the role played by collective guilt. An event such as a referendum provides a moment in which it *appears* that the collective guilt of the nation is being put on trial. In voting yes, the Australian public was able to demonstrate an apparent break with the past and thus to briefly feel better about themselves. What was missing in this process, however, was the underlying adaptive work required to make this change more meaningful and sustainable. In this sense it could be argued that the strategy of intentionally simplifying the issues being addressed by the referendum may, in the long run, have backfired. Australians believed they were voting for equal citizenship—for political equality. Many Australians—both Indigenous and non-

Indigenous—still believe that to this day. Believing themselves to have voted for equality, non-Indigenous Australians could wipe their hands of the problem. They had 'given' Aboriginal people equality; now it was up to them to make use of it. Any future failings were a problem belonging to Aboriginal and Torres Strait Islander peoples. As the arguments in this book make clear, however, that sentiment is far from the truth, and it is evident today that Indigenous people are a long way from enjoying equality with non-Indigenous people and even further from a situation of mutual recognition. Indeed, not even twenty years after the referendum it was more widely recognised that there was much more work to be done.

Reconciliation

Reconciliation has for some time been a problematic word in Australian political culture. Intended to deal with 'unfinished business' through a process of 'confronting the legacy of the past and re-aligning the relationship between Aboriginal and Torres Strait Islander people and government and the peoples of Australia', in reality the Australian version of reconciliation was undermined by our collective guilt quite early on.[21] Originally emerging in the context of 'transitional' countries where recognising past wrongs was seen as an important means of supporting the transition to democracy, over time the politics of reconciliation has 'migrated' to established Western democracies as an influential framework for thinking about the continuing impact of historical injustice on oppressed and marginalised groups within those societies.[22] This attention to historical injustice was certainly intended in the Australian process as well; however, a reluctance to face the facts of historical injustice in

Australia's colonial past quickly led to a more insipid framework built around the idea of 'practical reconciliation'.[23]

The Australian reconciliation process originally developed out of a recommendation in the Royal Commission Into Aboriginal Deaths in Custody Report.[24] In 1991 the then Labor Government, under Prime Minister Bob Hawke, created (with bipartisan support) the Council for Aboriginal Reconciliation (CAR) and set out the timeline for the formal process, which would conclude in 2001. Hawke's Minister for Aboriginal Affairs, Robert Tickner, who had been instrumental in developing the Australian process, has since outlined what he saw as the three objectives for reconciliation in Australia. First, Tickner argued that the process needed to educate non-Indigenous Australians about Aboriginal and Torres Strait Islander cultures and the extent of disadvantage still experienced by Indigenous people, with the intent of building a community-based movement focused on addressing Indigenous rights. Second, the process needed to get on to the public agenda what Tickner—in an attempt to get away from the apparently polarising word 'treaty'—described as a 'document of reconciliation'. Through the formal reconciliation process Tickner hoped there could be some agreement on the terms of such a document and a further agreement on how it might be achieved. Finally, Tickner envisaged that the reconciliation process would build a social movement that would drive the nation to 'address indigenous aspirations, human rights and social justice'.[25] Each of these objectives suggest that Tickner was proposing an adaptive process, one that would both acknowledge the injustices of our past and, through this acknowledgement, reframe the relationship between Indigenous and non-Indigenous Australia on a more just and equitable basis. Sadly, the more challenging aspects of these objectives were diluted at the outset, with Hawke's advisers removing the emphasis on justice in Tickner's original proposal, leaving little chance that the process could respond to the adaptive challenge.[26]

The process was diluted further upon the election of the Howard Government in 1996. Although he maintained that he supported the reconciliation process, John Howard differentiated his version of reconciliation from previous ways of thinking by emphasising the need to adopt 'practical measures' to address Indigenous disadvantage.[27] Reconciliation under the banner of practicality was primarily aimed at reducing material disadvantage in Indigenous communities; hardly a new approach given that it had been central to Indigenous policy in all governments since the 1970s.[28] Despite compelling arguments pointing to the 'false dichotomy' between practical and symbolic reconciliation, Howard remained committed to his view that there was a 'direct tradeoff' between these two approaches.[29] This view was underscored with the handing over of the Final Report of the Council on Aboriginal Reconciliation (including its Declaration Towards Reconciliation) to Federal Parliament in December 2000. Both the report and the declaration met with opposition from the government, leading them to publish an alternative version.[30] When the then Chair of ATSIC used Corroboree 2000 to again call for a treaty, Howard responded by arguing that 'an undivided nation does not make a treaty with itself'.[31]

Many Aboriginal and Torres Strait Islander people became disillusioned with the direction of the reconciliation process quite early. Kevin Gilbert, for example, expressed his anger at the expectation that Indigenous people reconcile themselves 'to massacre, to the removal of us from our land, from the taking of our land'. For Gilbert and others who shared his view the reconciliation process would achieve nothing if it did not 'promise justice'.[32] This disillusionment escalated rapidly following Howard's denunciation of much in the *Bringing them Home* report and most particularly following his lectern-thumping tirade during the 1997 reconciliation conference, during which many in the audience stood and turned their backs on him. In delivering this speech a visibly angry Howard insisted that reconciliation would 'not work' if it was 'premised solely on a sense of national guilt and shame'. Instead, Howard argued, the Australian reconciliation process should 'focus on addressing the root causes of current and future disadvantage among our Indigenous people'.[33] Shortly after this event the original chair of the CAR, Patrick Dodson, resigned in anger, later arguing that what he termed the 'mourning period' of Australian history could only come to an end when 'the proper protocols and practical arrangements have been carried out'.[34] Howard's suggestion that current Indigenous disadvantage was somehow disconnected from the nation's past would not enable the proper protocols to take place, nor would it inform a new relationship between Indigenous and non-Indigenous Australians. In essence, the focus on 'practical reconciliation' meant that our adaptive work was avoided once again.

Howard's derailing of the reconciliation process drew heavily on legitimatory arguments that underpinned his criticism of the so-called 'black armband' view of history discussed in Chapter 2. Fundamentally, however, his stance was one of a classic high identifier, wishing to defend a vulnerable national identity from supposed attack. This view misses the point of reconciliation work. Philosopher Trudy Govier argues that people pursuing reconciliation are 'seeking to build relationships of moral equality, relationships that are not overwhelmed by the facts of past oppression and wrongdoing, and relationships that maintain a capacity for cooperation'.[35] Howard's focus on the 'practical' over what he described as the 'symbolic' overlooked this need to reframe and rebuild relationships on fundamentally different terms. At the very least, reconciliation demands a recognition that 'others are human beings like ourselves', and an acknowledgement that this equality between groups 'must sometimes be sufficient to establish the foundation for living together in peace'.[36] The goal of reconciliation in this political sense is for each group to grant the other legitimacy based on a relationship that has been negotiated to allow them both to share the territory on just terms.[37]

Howard's approach also neglected the psychological needs underpinning reconciliation work. Reconciliation is necessarily about changing relations between groups from one of 'hostility and conflict' to one of 'mutual acceptance, respect, and future cooperation'. This type of change in intergroup relations is dependent on psychological change in group values, beliefs and norms, which affects both beliefs about one's own group and views about 'former adversaries', guiding aspirations for the future intergroup relationship.[38] Mick Dodson describes this reshaping of relationships between Indigenous and non-Indigenous people as the 'soft tissue' of reconciliation, 'less tangible, more amorphous' than the political aspects of reconciliation work but no less critical to its successful outcome.[39] Reconciliation processes are inevitably unsettling, drawing attention to discomforting aspects of the past and present in ways that are likely to produce some kind of backlash. In Australia the reconciliation process drew attention to the 'great divide' between the descendants of those who 'waged the war' against Indigenous people and Indigenous people themselves. Reconciliation demanded that we acknowledge both the divide and the violence on which it is predicated, simultaneously demanding that we 'explore the entanglements of memory, connection, and commitment'.[40] Considerations of trust were essential to the work being attempted, recognising that trust must play a key role in future cooperation between groups.[41] For many, John Howard's intervention in the reconciliation process had the effect of rendering both the process and the intentions behind it as untrustworthy.

The response of the wider Australian public to the reconciliation process has been mixed. On the one hand there is both anecdotal and survey evidence to show that the majority of Australians supported the process and the aims of the CAR.[42] Mick Dodson has suggested that the idea of reconciliation is 'broadly accepted' and that the 'fruits of reconciliation, based on respect and trust, are strongly desired'.[43] At the same time, however, there have been persistent feelings of 'concern, embarrassment and shame' about the nation's failure to solve the challenge of Indigenous disadvantage that tempered existing racism. Many Australians also felt 'perplexed and confused' about how to make progress in this area, becoming 'caught between calling for inspired leadership and compassion and the comforts of racism and cynicism'.[44] It certainly seems that there was much goodwill and some change in relationships between non-Indigenous and Indigenous Australians during the period of the formal reconciliation process. A national sample of 1,007 people surveyed for Reconciliation Australia's Reconciliation Barometer[45] indicated that 91 per cent of the general population believed that the relationship between Indigenous and other Australians is important for the country. However, much like the work of FCAATSI and the success of the 1967 referendum, goodwill and support have not been enough to achieve a more substantial change in either political or interpersonal relationships and nor is there much indication that these deeper changes are desired. The Reconciliation Barometer also indicated that only 59 per cent of the wider population believe that Indigenous people hold a 'special place as the first Australians'.[46] As former Australian Parliamentary Fellow Angela Pratt has argued, while the formal reconciliation process in Australia did introduce a new and broad 'moral language' with which to speak about issues of Indigenous social justice, it did not 'help to resolve any of the questions these issues raised'.[47]

If reconciliation is to have any meaning in Australia it requires that, as a nation, we face up to our history in ways that will allow all of us to move forward, psychologically and politically.[48] In postcolonial contexts it is particularly important that reconciliation deal with historical injustice in ways that allow for a healing of relationships between colonising culture and Indigenous people.[49] It will never be enough for individual Australians to make the kind of 'personal moral adjustments' that Peter Sutton advocates.[50] While it is true that we each have an individual responsibility to pursue reconciliation and to do our own, personal adaptive work, the challenge facing the nation is inherently collective and will only be responded to effectively through public, collective and national means. Nor will it be effective if we attempt to avoid the discomfort that is an inevitable part of any reconciliation process by developing a 'more celebratory'—and therefore more palatable—model of reconciliation designed to appease white anxieties, such as that advocated by Australian lawyer Macgregor Duncan and his colleagues.[51] Officially recognising past wrongs through a process of reconciliation, including through achieving constitutional recognition of Indigenous peoples and/or by formalising a treaty or similar document of reconciliation, will not in and of itself reframe a more just Australian society, but it is a necessary first step.[52] Australia has yet to take this step. We still prefer to 'paper over the darker aspects' of this history by 'shifting blame to those most affected'.[53] We continue to avoid our adaptive challenge.

Apology and forgiveness

Around the world, there is a growing recognition that admitting responsibility and guilt for past injustice is now a 'liberal marker of national stability and strength rather than shame'.[54] Australia, however, was a long time coming to this conclusion. As discussed in Chapter 2 of this book, an apology to the Stolen Generations was first recommended in the *Bringing them Home* report from the National Inquiry into the Separation of Aboriginal and Torres Strait Islander Children from Their Families in May 1997. In 1998, on the anniversary of the release of the report, the first Sorry Day was held involving hundreds of community activities and the first signing of Sorry Books. Hundreds of books were circulated around Australia, collecting many hundreds of thousands of signatures. Each official Sorry Book contained an apology that read:

> By signing my name in this book, I record my deep regret for the injustices suffered by Indigenous Australians as a result of European settlement and, in particular, I offer my personal apology for the hurt and harm caused by the forced removal of children from their families and for the effect of government policy on the human dignity and spirit of Indigenous Australians.
>
> I would also like to record my desire for Reconciliation and for a better future for all our peoples. I make a commitment to a united Australia which respects this land of ours, values Aboriginal and Torres Strait Islander heritage and provides justice and equity for all.[55]

In the face of this 'apology movement' Prime Minister Howard's persistent rejection of the call to apologise became a polarising issue in the Australian community and an 'unhelpful simplification' of some of the wider issues raised in discussions of reconciliation.[56]

It was not until the change of government in November 2007 that there was a firm decision to proceed with a national apology. The 2008 apology was not a blanket apology to all Aboriginal and Torres Strait Islander peoples for the human injustice perpetrated as a part of Australia's colonial project. Rather, Prime Minister Rudd apologised specifically for past policies of child removal and for the damage done to families who had had their children taken away. On 13 February 2008, during the first sitting of the new parliament, the new prime minister, Kevin Rudd, made a moving speech in the House of Representatives that produced an outpouring of emotion around the country. In a moment that had been long anticipated, Rudd acknowledged that:

> The time has now come for the nation to turn a new page in Australia's history by righting the wrongs of the past and so moving forward with confidence to the future. We apologise for the laws and policies of successive Parliaments and governments that have inflicted profound grief, suffering and loss on these our fellow Australians. We apologise especially for the removal of Aboriginal and Torres Strait Islander children from their families, their communities and their country. For the pain, suffering and hurt of these Stolen Generations, their descendants and for their families left behind, we say sorry. To the mothers and the fathers, the brothers and the sisters, for the breaking up of families and communities, we say sorry. And for the indignity and degradation thus inflicted on a proud people and a proud culture, we say sorry.[57]

In the aftermath of the apology, many Australians have pointed to the event as an 'enobling, patriotic moment', as 'an instance of one's country being put right' following the recognition of past wrongs. Many people felt a sense of a burden being lifted, and enjoyed a moment of hope that this was finally an end to the culture wars that 'had so deeply scarred the national soul'.[58] It is likely, however, that those feeling a sense of relief following the apology were those who might be described as having a low level of national identification, as discussed in Chapter I. For low identifiers the act of apology tends to be welcomed as a means of demonstrating their willingness to confront the past. For high identifiers, however, apology is more likely to be construed as inviting claims for financial reparations and, more significantly, an apology may be experienced as threatening to the national image.[59]

There are many ways in which the act of apology would seem to go to the heart of Australia's adaptive challenge. An apology requires the acknowledgement of past wrongs, the acceptance of responsibility for these wrongs and a declaration of sorrow or regret.[60] Apologies are intended to 'promote reconciliation and healing' where there has been a history of political and interpersonal conflict and violence. In attempting to atone for this violence, apologies may be the 'most inexpensive and least difficult actions' available to the governments or others involved.[61] Apology can transform the experience of victimisation into a process of mourning, allowing past victims to begin a process of rebuilding.[62] But the act of apology may also change the dynamics in the relationship: those making the apology are entirely in the hands of the injured party as 'they alone can provide release or redemption by virtue of their forgiveness'.[63] Apology, like the idea of reconciliation itself, does not look only to the past. In contributing to the repair of a relationship apology must necessarily look backward in recognition of past wrongs and injustice. Just as importantly, however, apology also looks forward in a commitment to making amends and improving the relationship in the present and the future.[64]

Relationships are really at the heart of an apology, as transitional justice expert Martha Minow has suggested:

> An apology is not a soliloquy. Instead, an apology requires communication between a wrongdoer and a victim; no apology occurs without the involvement of each party. Moreover, the methods for offering and accepting an apology both reflect and help to constitute a moral community. The apology reminds the wrongdoer of community norms because the apology admits to violating them. By retelling the wrong and seeking acceptance, the apologizer assumes a position of vulnerability before not only the victims but also the larger community of literal or figurative witnesses.[65]

However, Minow has also argued that apologies are 'inevitably inadequate'. In the Australian case this inadequacy was amplified by the refusal to even discuss the question of compensation. Where apologies are not accompanied by 'direct and immediate actions', which may include paying compensation to those who have been harmed, an official apology may seem 'superficial, insincere, or meaningless'.[66]

There are also limits to the type of forgiveness that is possible following the making of an apology. Recognising the limits of forgiveness can be painful, particularly if either party is seeking 'a full accounting, total justice, or a kind of annihilation of the past'. There are many wrongs—including the genocide committed as part of the Australian colonial project—that can never be put right. Nevertheless, past wrongs must be acknowledged and a part of this process will involve also acknowledging that complete reparation may not be possible. This acknowledgement is not some type of 'collective amnesia'; rather it is 'an acknowledgment of the full scope of a given horror and the inability of a subsequent generation or generations, not directly responsible for that horror, to put things right. The events stand.'[67] An apology will not fully alleviate the distress about past injustice because on its own such an action can only partially restore equity.[68] Nevertheless, it remains the case that there is a 'certain correspondence' between the intergenerational trauma experienced by the children and grandchildren of the victims of historical injustice and the children and grandchildren of the perpetrators. Both groups are 'connected by the same crime', and while it may not be possible for these later generations to personally offer apology or provide forgiveness, they are able to experience themselves as 'intertwined'; as two groups who have 'something to talk about and work out'.[69]

The making of an apology does not mean that a dispute is resolved or that issues of historical, human injustice are settled. An apology can be a first step, part of a process of negotiating a settlement, but it is unlikely that an apology will ever be an end result that is satisfactory for all concerned.[70] For some the Australian apology was a step towards getting reconciliation 'back on track',[71] but there are many other steps that can be taken to build on the moment of apology. Political philosopher Bashir Bashir suggests that these might involve:

> . . . activities such as the creation of national symbols, public holidays, museums, memorials, and introducing new curricula in the education system to commemorate the past injustices. The talk of these activities is not to romanticize and perpetuate guilt or victimhood. Rather, they are significant because of their social and pedagogical influence. They help citizens to understand differently their history and its connection to current political, social, and economic inequalities.[72]

Australia has taken some of these steps, albeit in a tentative manner. There is a new—and hotly contested—national history curriculum, there has been much wringing of hands about whether the National Museum of Australia achieves the right balance between tales of genocide and tales of settler heroism[73] and there has been an unproductive debate about whether the national war memorial should commemorate the war waged by Aboriginal people in defence of their country (it currently does not).[74] But there continues to be great resistance to advancing these proposals; resistance that is grounded in our collective guilt and the fear that fully acknowledging past wrongs will somehow diminish us as a nation. Nothing could be further from the truth. It is only when we find a way to more fully engage in the adaptive work we have to do that we will be able to reshape our national identity—perhaps not always with pride, but at least with acceptance.

Finding a way forward

From his eight years as chair of the Council for Aboriginal Reconciliation, Patrick Dodson formed the firm view that there is a 'huge reservoir of goodwill towards Indigenous people on the part of millions of Australians'. The three examples suggested here—the successful campaign for the 1967 referendum, the decade of the formal reconciliation process, and the response to the 2008 apology to the Stolen Generations—certainly suggest that he is right in his assessment. However, Dodson also argues that in order to engage that goodwill in a more meaningful process of 'national transformation' what is required is 'bold and imaginative government leadership'.[75] Patrick Dodson's brother Mick also acknowledges the many connections shared by

Indigenous and non-Indigenous Australians, but suggests that for reconciliation to advance we need as a nation to 'go down deeper. To see what makes it work—and what is still missing.' For Mick Dodson the challenge is personal as well as political, and he suggests that Australians need to contemplate how we regard one another and examine 'how this has shaped our potential to achieve reconciliation at the deepest, personal level'.[76]

The apology, the reconciliation process, the 1967 referendum—these and many other examples are a clear indication that Australia would like to see a profound change in the relationship between Indigenous and non-Indigenous people. And yet despite this desire, and despite the efforts of hundreds of thousands of people—in dedicated organisations, in governments and just in their own communities—Australia remains profoundly stuck. With the exception of the 1967 referendum, none of these forms of engagement changed the institutional relationship between peoples. Wherever it seemed that progress was to be made, political will seemed to fail and the opportunity to make more profound change slipped away. Goodwill and optimism generated in the community are eroded by cynicism and confusion. In the eternal hope of avoiding a genuine engagement with our collective guilt people wonder why each small step has not been enough. Why are Aboriginal and Torres Strait Islander peoples still struggling? Didn't we change the Constitution? Didn't we try to reconcile? Didn't we even say sorry?

This dynamic has been evident throughout the post-invasion history of this territory. Political support has come and gone, but there have always been those prepared to unsettle their fellow citizens rather than allow them to feel relaxed and comfortable in the face of widely acknowledged historical injustice. Henry Reynolds has written at length about those who heard 'the whisperings at the bottom of their hearts' and who argued passionately—and often with great unpopularity—for 'the cause of justice and equality, reparation and regret and who often paid a high price for their principled dissent'. Reynolds suggests that these dissenters offered the colonists a choice from Australia's earliest days, but when given this choice it was the colonial project that triumphed, with the colonists preferring 'violent dispossession to purchase, treaty and negotiations; seeking for several generations to create a racially homogenous nation which had no place for Aborigines who it was comfortably expected would "die out" on cue'.[77] In some ways we have made great progress since these times, and in other ways we have made no progress at all. It is certainly high time that we made different choices.

Chapter 6

Unsettling ourselves

The phenomenon of collective guilt is not unique to Australia. Around the world other settler colonies are also grappling with their legacies of historical and human injustice. Attempts to recognise the past and develop more adaptive responses are not infrequent, but are often met with resistance and backlash as the nation seeks to restore equilibrium and to urgently feel good about itself again. This response will never be adequate and it will never free us from our burden of guilt. As US anti-racist activist and writer Tim Wise has suggested, it is quite understandable that we all 'wish to be free from the pain'. But it is not—and never will be—acceptable 'that in seeking that freedom we should ignore the pain by which we have come this far already'.[1] This is a question of justice, but it is also a recognition of what is possible. We will only ever be free from guilt, from our sense of illegitimacy, when we fully engage in our adaptive work, and when we recognise that we need first to unsettle ourselves.

There is a leap to be made from our current resistance to this work to a place where the work can actually begin. Columbia University Professor of International and Public Affairs Elazar Barkan has argued that for the necessary work of restitution to take place at some point:

> ... government and public opinion have to recognise that accepting responsibility for the injustice, assuming the burden of guilt, and paying restitution are in their best interests. At a minimum such demands often dramatically contradict the public's self-perception and necessitate the rewriting of a heroic national history as one that inflicted pain and suffering and even perpetrated crimes. A creative and feasible plan for restitution thus has to stimulate a serious public discussion.[2]

The need for public discussion, in the form of dialogue, is an issue to which I will return later in this chapter. It is worth acknowledging here, however, as Ron Heifetz also does, that such efforts towards what he calls a 'politics of inclusion' are 'not faint hearted efforts at making everybody happy enough'. Inclusion means more than merely taking a range of perspectives into account and attempting to find the most banal and least offensive middle ground. That is just another form of work avoidance. To really be inclusive requires 'challenging people, hard and steadily, to face new perspectives on familiar problems, to let go of old ideas and ways of life long held sacred'. This work will inevitably mean that some parties will feel a sense of loss and, if they are unwilling to change, will express their outrage in ways that cannot be avoided.[3] This is the nature of adaptive work. But while this work is inherently difficult, it is also true that many of us are urgently seeking ways to create what Deborah Bird Rose describes as a 'moral presence for ourselves' that 'engages with our moral relationship with the past, acknowledges our violence, and works dialogically towards alternatives'.[4]

Having explored the dimensions of the adaptive challenge facing Australia, this chapter considers what the dominant culture in Australia might need to relinquish in order to forge a new relationship with Indigenous people. It argues that the most crucial aspect of Australia's adaptive challenge will involve facing up to the reality of our colonial past and the extent of the harms done to Aboriginal and Torres Strait Islander peoples. The challenge will be to find a new response to our history that does not see us 'stuck' in our guilt but allows us to forge a new relationship between Indigenous and non-Indigenous Australia, creating a nation that is better equipped for contemporary challenges. The chapter considers the processes (such as a new dialogue towards reconciliation) and institutional changes (such as constitutional reform) that will be required if Australia is to allow itself to be unsettled and transformed.

Facing the challenge

Reflecting on the suffering endured by Aboriginal and Torres Strait Islander peoples over the 220-plus years since their lands were first invaded is painful. We have developed an 'habitual blindness' towards uncomfortable past events,[5] although we cannot help but know at some level that 'we are here through dispossession and death'.[6] Accepting the multitude of ways in which the generations alive today—*our* generations—share responsibility for past and present suffering is difficult. There is, as Trudy Govier suggests, a 'powerful incentive' to protect ourselves, to attend only selectively to our history and to ignore or repress unwelcome stories of the past. The problem, as Govier articulates, is that through our very denial we continue to reveal our complicity:

> We may ignore the protestations of those who suffer in the aftermath of wrongs, fail to listen, and fail to hear and understand. We may become so oblivious to cries and protestations, to reports of abuse and suffering, that we ignore the evidence and act as though the harmed

> people barely exist at all. We can choose to ignore many facts, problems, and cries of pain. Then, as a result of ignoring, we know little about these others with whom we are in a relationship flawed by denial. If wrongs are claimed, if we are called upon to acknowledge and reconcile, we then plead that we did not know. At this point, the choice presupposed in ignoring is highly salient. We *did* notice something; we *did* know something. We knew enough to know that we wanted to avoid paying attention to a situation, choosing instead to ignore it. We chose to ignore evidence and failed to discover truths that we could have suspected and did suspect—truths that would be unsettling because they would be incompatible with favoured views of our communities and selves. We knew enough to know that we did not want to know more.[7]

It may be counterintuitive, but in fact our continued denial, our refusal to engage in this work and to find a moral presence for ourselves, comes at great cost. Colonisation not only damages Indigenous people, it also disfigures the coloniser.[8] Turning away from what we see in the mirror does not make our reflection any more attractive. Nevertheless, we have a tendency to anaesthetise ourselves from our true feelings about Australia's history. Even when we are confronted with the reality of the past and its contemporary implications we prefer to remain emotionally removed, dissociating ourselves from a situation that is unbearable to confront. But as Frances Kendall asks, 'What do we pay for this daily anaesthetising, this process of dissociating? What does it cost us?'[9]

Heifetz suggests that work avoidance can take many forms including 'Holding on to past assumptions, blaming authority, scapegoating, externalising the enemy, denying the problem, jumping to conclusions, or finding a distracting issue', all in order to deny our discomfort, restore a sense of stability and avoid taking responsibility for a complex challenge.[10] At a political level it seems that an anaesthetised, work-avoiding population is more inclined to replace involvement with denial, and to allow scepticism to breed along with collective guilt.[11] The cynical voice that suggests we have genuinely tried to make amends (through the formal reconciliation process, through weak government policies of self-determination, through apology) reinforces the view that the problem lies with Aboriginal and Torres Strait Islander peoples whom we subtly suggest are wilfully clinging to a divisive manner of living and are therefore not *our* problem.[12] When the challenge also involves racial differences—as in Australia—there is a further tendency to choose a 'colourblind, transcendence-seeking optimism', which does little more than stifle the more difficult dialogue to be had about the racial dynamics that continue to be a feature of Indigenous–non-Indigenous relations.[13] In Australia this false optimism is magnified by the 'uniquely Australian temptation' of believing our national mantra of 'she'll be right, mate'.[14] And layered over all of this is the blanket of collective guilt that smothers our desire to find that moral presence for ourselves. Our fear of criticism and our anxieties about being required to face this guilt prevent us from doing the real, adaptive work that is required.

Nationalism revisited: Can we ever be relaxed and comfortable?

It should be evident from earlier chapters in this book that a large part of what is in the way of our adaptive challenge is our defensive national identity. Our 'narcissistic insecurities' about our place in the world rest in large part on our concern that there is an 'emptiness' at the centre of Australian national identity.[15] It would seem inevitable that such an emptiness will persist for as long as we feel the need to deny aspects of our history. Rather than an identity shaped by what is real—as confronting and difficult as that reality might be—we have instead chosen to shape an identity that is over-reliant on myth and folklore. Such an identity will always have a certain hollowness to it.

One of our most concerted efforts to create a more powerful national identity has been the resurgence of the 'Anzac myth' as a narrative of Australian heroism. Mark McKenna has argued that the increasing prominence of Anzac 'at the vanguard of a new wave of patriotism' that emerged in the early 1980s was in part a response to Australian denial of historical injustice and colonial atrocity. Knowledge of Indigenous dispossession was a constant thorn in the side of other national days of celebration that were based on the commemoration of the British invasion and settlement. As the 1988 bicentenary began to loom on the horizon there was a heightened sense of political anxiety about how the nation would 'celebrate' the anniversary of the arrival of the First Fleet in Sydney Harbour, and an increasingly polarised public debate on the event that McKenna suggests marks the beginning of the 'history wars' discussed in Chapter 2. As Australia Day increasingly became a 'lightning rod' for political disputes, Anzac Day emerged as a 'less complicated and less divisive alternative'. The events at Gallipoli Cove took on the mantle of 'the only true crucible of national identity', accompanied by an unspoken sense of relief that national pride in Anzac need not be haunted by the spilling of Aboriginal blood in the frontier wars, the taking of Aboriginal land and children, or the contemporary effects of these traumas on Indigenous people around Australia.[16] Where the story of the founding of the nation became 'immersed in forgetting', the story of Anzac became 'enmeshed in remembrance'; where the first story was 'literally unspeakable', Anzac was allowed to become 'liturgical'.[17] Anzac allowed us to wash ourselves clean of the stains of our history.

Today the Anzac myth stands in as 'White Australia's creation myth', but not without cost. Historian Marilyn Lake has argued that the focus on Anzac has contributed to the militarisation of Australian history in the school curriculum, which in turn has 'sidelined' other nation-building narratives emphasising social justice and democratic equality. This central place of Anzac in our national narrative also contributes to an over-emphasis on the values of the military—specifically mateship, courage and sacrifice (although not, Lake notes, obedience, conformity, aggression or the capacity to kill)—as foundational for our wider national values.[18] This myth-making about Anzac also seems beyond criticism, despite the questions it raises. Henry Reynolds asks, for example, what the rhetoric about Anzac says about the first hundred years of settlement—what of the other people from all walks of life who contributed to the federation of Australia? Moreover, like Lake, Reynolds questions whether values that privilege the importance of war are really the values that should be passed on to our children with such determination.[19] The danger in over-emphasising a narrative like the Anzac myth is that it becomes a 'touchstone' that cements a version of national identity that speaks for, and to, only some Australians, leaving us ill equipped to deal with contemporary diversity.[20] Anzac is not capable of taking on the role of Australia's central narrative,[21] but for as long as we fail to acknowledge our collective guilt, an inadequate and problematic myth such as this will be required to paper over the holes in our heart.

This was never more evident than during the years of the four Howard governments, between 1996 and 2007. One reason for John Howard's electoral success was his uncanny ability to identify the Australian *zeitgeist*. In the mid 1990s Howard began to articulate his ideological opposition to Prime Minister Paul Keating's willingness to repudiate aspects of Australian history and take responsibility—as in his famous Redfern Park speech—for historical injustices against Aboriginal and Torres Strait Islander peoples.[22] As the kind of high identifier discussed in Chapter 1, Howard had his own psychological need to promote a more positive view of Australian history and national identity. But he also read the mood of the Australian public and, recognising their discomfort at being asked to acknowledge past wrongs, moved swiftly to reassure them that it was desirable and legitimate to want to feel 'relaxed and comfortable'.

Anzac proved the perfect vehicle, helping Howard to recuperate national identity by 'replacing collective guilt and self-hatred with a new cultural confidence'.[23] Through the lens of Anzac, white Australians could see themselves as 'heroic and sacrificial' rather than venal or cruel, and the real blood that was shed on our own shores could be erased by 'the reticulated retelling of the Anzac blood-letting'.[24] Anzac became the '"positive" counter-narrative' to reconciliation and the 'black armband' view of history, allowing Howard to harnass a 'more defensive national mood'. The mythology surrounding Anzac became a 'vehicle for national self-congratulation', eventually infecting Australia Day as well through Howard's active promotion of a simplistic and unreflective nationalism.[25] Time has shown the ugliness of this type of nationalism, most evident in the racially motivated riots at Cronulla beach in December 2005, where drunk and angry young Anglo men engaged in overt displays of Australian national symbols as they verbally and physically attacked young men of 'Middle Eastern appearance'.

So one part of our adaptive challenge must be to question our reliance on narratives such as the Anzac myth in order to maintain a sense of pride in our country. Why is it that while shameful aspects of our history—the dispossession of Aboriginal people, the unjustified removal of their children—can only be 'wheeled out for ceremonial apology' before we are required to 'move on', Anzac is 'held in a state of perpetual remembrance'?[26] Once we have rejected such myths as central to our national identity we open up the space to ask questions about what other forms of collective sentiment might be possible.

For example, might it be possible for us to together craft what Tim Soutphommasane describes as a 'progressive' style of patriotism, in which it is possible to love this country but still work towards a new political relationship between Indigenous and non-Indigenous peoples? Harder still, is it possible for us to even speak of a single national identity, of an inclusive national identity, without acknowledging that many Aboriginal and Torres Strait Islander people do not share a sense of unity with non-Indigenous Australians? Can we speak of historic injustice and the contemporary aspirations of Indigenous people despite the persistent anxiety expressed by the wider population about the need for social cohesion and national identity?[27] Soutphommasane argues that a more progressive patriotism is not only desirable, it is essential to the success of any progressive political agenda. I remain unconvinced by this argument. To me it seems that we are not prepared to advance a new politics based on a 'basic sentiment of solidarity'[28] until we have engaged in the more difficult task of facing our adaptive challenge and acknowledging our collective guilt. This may mean that—at least temporarily—we need to pick apart any assumed solidarity in order to fully explore the dimensions of injury, exclusion, guilt and responsibility that continue to plague our sense of who we are. We cannot rebuild until we have undone. We cannot feel good about ourselves until we understand why we feel so bad.

One possible support for this difficult work, as discussed in Chapter 4, may be the values that many Australians purport to hold dear. Research in applied psychology has suggested that there is a strong correlation between the values of reconciliation and egalitarian views.[29] Even high Australian identifiers may be persuaded that it is entirely consistent with our 'historical self-stereotype' as an egalitarian nation concerned with humanitarian values that we now take bolder, more difficult and confronting steps to acknowledge our collective guilt as a means of forging a new relationship between Indigenous and non-Indigenous Australia.[30] Groups that self-stereotype in this way are known to be more likely to want to make amends for past wrongs, at least where the behaviour of the dominant group is recognised as being at odds with values of fairness and egalitarianism. This depends, however, on 'how values and ideologies are socially constructed, reinterpreted, and applied in specific historical contexts'.[31] There are certainly obstacles to the deployment of positive Australian values in the process of difficult adaptive work, not least the fact that this work will, at another level, profoundly threaten our sense of who we are and the values that we cherish.[32] But we should recognise some values of 'Australianness' as a potential resource in the work we need to do.

Remembering and forgetting

One unavoidable step in the adaptive work involved in acknowledging our collective guilt is for the nation to have another difficult conversation about memory and history. This will never be a straightforward process and there will always be contestation about the content of our history. Our task is not to agree on one 'correct' version of the past. And nor is our task to create an open sore at which the nation can endlessly pick. A collective past that is full of trauma—as Australia's history is—can be the most difficult terrain to navigate. The past continues to have a 'moral claim' on each of us. We carry a moral burden from the past in the present; our memory continues to resist the violence of our history and in remembering we refuse to submit to amnesia about the facts of this nation's founding on this territory.[33] At the same time, however, while the nation does experience an 'intense desire for relief from the burden of guilt', we have developed little in the way of a real appreciation of the legacy of the past in the margins of Australian society.[34] While we may not be allowed to forget, neither have we yet been entirely willing to remember all there is to know about our past and its continuing effects in the present.

But while it is understandable to want to unburden ourselves of this traumatic past, we must recognise that repressing the facts of our history will never set us free. We cannot forget the things that make us most uneasy, as much as we might want to. To forget would mean no longer thinking about the places where disturbing or uncomfortable things have happened or still happen. This would lead us to forgetting the many traumas and losses for which we remain accountable, 'insulating ourselves against the absences that surround us'.[35] In many ways we are very good at this in Australia. How else do we explain the fact that the vast majority of Australians seem unperturbed by the shocking poverty endured by many Aboriginal and Torres Strait Islander peoples? It seems they have indeed insulated themselves from the trauma that has led to the unconscionable circumstances existing within our midst. But to continue to insulate ourselves from this confronting reality must also mean that we ignore the accountability that gives our lives 'moral gravity'; that we would have to 'forget who and where we really are'.[36]

At the same time, however, we need to guard against an endless fixation on past trauma, which Bernhard Schlink argues can become little more than 'the flipside of repression'.[37] There is a 'dark side' to memory that, if ignored, can sustain grievances between people and even fuel ongoing conflict.[38] An endless fixation on trauma can also prolong the pain of those who have suffered. For members of the Stolen Generations, for example, public events such as the tenth anniversary of the *Bringing them Home* report have:

> . . . raised the ghosts of those experiences—the trauma, the grief and the memories—which, left unresolved, can re-traumatise people and create a 'limbo' world in which they have not been able to go home.[39]

If we are as a nation to 'detraumatise', what is needed—for victims and perpetrators and for their descendants—is to become able to both remember and to forget. We need to find ways to leave the past in the past, while also embracing the need for remembrance.[40] Finding a way to make progress in our adaptive challenge will also involve seeking a pathway between 'too much memory and too much forgetting'.[41] We can neither will ourselves into amnesia nor engage in obsessive brooding about the past. Neither path will help us to create a shared future. To do this we must find ways to both understand and confront the elements of our past that prevent us from making adaptive change, while also breaking with the past by righting past injustice and agreeing that future relations will be conducted on a just basis.[42] This work is both challenging and complex, as Martha Minow has suggested:

> What's needed, then, is not memory but remembering, not retrieval of some intact picture but instead a dynamic process of both tying together and distinguishing fragments of past and present. What's needed, paradoxically, is a process for reinterpreting what cannot be made sensible, for assembling what cannot be put together, and for separating what cannot be severed from both present and future.[43]

It is only when we have found the ability to acknowledge past wrongs and break the bonds of solidarity with the perpetrators of historic injustice that our past can actually become our history. When this is possible, the past will no longer dominate our collective stories or our national identity, rather our history will become integrated into our understanding of who we are.[44] To achieve this, however, we must find a way of moving on from a defensiveness about our past, and we must also recognise that we will not deal with our history through endless rounds of rational argument. Instead, to deal with our adaptive challenge and our guilt about the past, as Lorenzo Veracini has suggested 'Something else is needed'.[45]

Beginning a dialogue

That debates about Australian history have been cast as a 'war' says much about the way in which we have conducted that particular conversation. Wars can only ever involve opponents locked in battle, with the expectation that eventually one side will be the victor, having vanquished their foe. This is no way for us to resolve the complex challenges we face. We need to think seriously about an alternative form of engagement that will enable us to do some adaptive work. There are many ways in which perpetrators (and their descendants) and victims (and their descendants) can engage in new political negotiation that 'enables the rewriting of memory and historical identity in ways both can share'.[46] Martha Minow suggests processes for 'deliberating, constructing, disputing, accepting, rejecting, and reconsidering potential responses' to a history of violence and trauma.[47] All of these processes can take place under an umbrella we can call dialogue.

Dialogue is increasingly understood as a crucial element in adaptive work aimed at achieving more just and ethical relations among cultural groups.[48] James Tully has stated unequivocally that reconciliation 'should be dialogical',[49] arguing that the way for Indigenous and non-Indigenous people to work out their relations together is through 'dialogues of negotiation in which they meet as equals'.[50] Paul Keal suggests that dialogue based in ideas of collective responsibility 'is a necessary prelude to settling historical injustices that might involve redistribution issues'.[51] Dialogue, as a form of political intervention, is designed to engage people in divided societies in a process of listening to one another deeply in order to challenge and change their own views about the other group. Through working together to solve difficult social and political issues, groups engaged in dialogue can dispel their misconceptions about each other and build mutual trust, respect and understanding. Through such processes, previously opposed groups can find ways of working together towards the creation of a more just and inclusive society.[52] Dialogue enables a form of relationship through which mutual understanding and even agreement can be reached, meaning that 'consent can replace coercion and confrontation'.[53]

Intercultural dialogue in particular has been suggested as a useful means of working with some of the seemingly immovable relationships that are typical of settler colonies, as it recognises participants both as individuals and as member of groups within institutional and historical contexts.[54] When Indigenous and non-Indigenous people engage in dialogue it is unavoidable that they will bring their cultural understandings and world views with them. This makes the process intercultural and therefore all the more challenging.[55] An effective intercultural dialogue cannot assume a 'Western' superiority if what is desired is a meaningful 'conversation between cultures'.[56] But intercultural dialogue also assumes that people from different cultural backgrounds, and with very different perspectives on a shared and difficult history, may be able to come to know each other better. Participants in dialogue cannot assume that their world views are 'hermetically-sealed chambers of meaning', unknowable to other participants. Rather, participants should be encouraged to think of their world views as more like 'distant but open horizons, understandable through vigorous interpretive effort'. This requires some level of trust and a commitment to dialogue rather than coercion or manipulation. These attitudes and preconditions are themselves very difficult to achieve, most especially in circumstances where one group has experienced violence and injustice at the hands of the other. Nevertheless, these conditions are worth striving for in order to achieve a successful process.[57] Intercultural dialogue can assist non-Indigenous people to understand better the claims of Indigenous groups and can highlight the constitutional injustices that persist when minority cultural recognition is denied by the dominant culture.[58]

As a process, facilitated dialogue differs quite markedly from other forms of communication such as debate and conversation. As William Isaacs has put it, dialogue is 'a conversation with a center, not sides'.[59] Well-designed dialogue is intended to create a space for more meaningful and potentially transformative engagement in an environment in which people can listen to one another openly and creatively, enabling them to work towards a shared understanding of what the problem is, of their part in it, and of what they must do to address it.[60] It is a process of 'shared inquiry, a way of thinking and reflecting together' that takes place '*within* and *between*' the participants.[61] Dialogue creates opportunities for people, who may seem intractably opposed, to change the way they view and relate to each other, often discovering 'shared values and concerns which may lead to collaborative actions that were previously unthinkable'.[62]

Openness is a key concept to the type of transformative, adaptive dialogue that I am proposing here. As Deborah Bird Rose notes, however, while this may seem obvious, it is in fact very challenging. Openness is 'risky'; it suggests that there cannot be a known or even a presumed outcome but requires that we make ourselves available to others, which can make us feel vulnerable. This may be especially true for Indigenous participants. But openness also allows for the possibility that we might be destabilised in a creative way, that we may be surprised and challenged, and even changed.[63] 'Thinking together' in a process of dialogue requires that you 'relax your grip on certainty and listen to the possibilities that result simply from being in a relationship with others—possibilities that might not otherwise have occurred'.[64] To these ends, understanding more about the 'situatedness' of both Indigenous and non-Indigenous participants in a process of dialogue can only be enriching, even if it is challenging. Rose suggests that both Indigenous and non-Indigenous people in Australia are situated in 'damaged places', but contends that an 'ethical dialogue' requires that participants are able to 'acknowledge and understand our particular and harshly situated presence'.[65]

Dialogue practitioners Maggie Herzig and Laura Chasin argue that 'the need for dialogue in our public life is less well understood than the need for debate and activism'. Indeed, in the absence of sufficient dialogue the constructive impact of debate and activism has diminished, leaving public rhetoric constrained by polarising assertions and demonising stereotypes. In such a political climate, meaningful dialogue rarely happens without considerable thought and planning.[66] Internationally there has been far more attention to the theory and practice of dialogue than we have seen in Australia.[67] Various styles of dialogue have been used extensively at organisation, individual and system levels, showing the greatest promise at social and national levels.[68] In Australia, however, processes of structured, facilitated dialogue have been almost completely absent from efforts to address long-standing issues such as reconciliation with Indigenous Australians.[69]

Dialogue can be a process through which Indigenous and non-Indigenous Australians can agree to a new relationship, one that may be written down as a treaty and subsequently reviewed and renewed over time.[70] It is not necessary—and nor should it be intended—that a process of dialogue will reinforce national unity or produce a shared vision or set of values among participants. Dialogue may be full of conflict, but through engaging with the perspectives of people who challenge our own views we can allow conflicting frames of reference to become productive resources for 'social learning', revealing hidden or ignored aspects of our social system.[71] Indeed, if dialogue is directed towards agreement-making, or the formalising of a new relationship between Indigenous and non-Indigenous people in Australia, it is essential that all affected by the negotiations are a part of the exchange of reasons. Where this does not take place it is likely that any agreed-upon norm of mutual recognition that was achieved through the process of dialogue would seem to be a 'sell-out', or an unacceptable compromise.[72]

Certainly dialogue will not provide a solution to all of the challenges involved in acknowledging our collective guilt and engaging in the adaptive work required to establish a new relationship between Indigenous and non-Indigenous people in this country.[73] Nevertheless, as we search for some way of reframing these conversations and rethinking our national selves, formalised processes of dialogue would seem to offer a highly promising path towards negotiating new forms of mutual recognition.

Can we decolonise ourselves?

To be relieved of our burden of collective guilt, Australia must find a way to break the bonds of solidarity with the perpetrators of historical and human injustice. To truly break the bonds with the past we must begin, through processes such as dialogue, to rethink who we are as a nation. Our new thinking must inform new agreements and the formalising of a new relationship between Indigenous and non-Indigenous Australia. What the late political philosopher Iris Marion Young called the 'postcolonial project' entails a commitment to confronting the legacies of colonialism in all their guises as an essential task in creating a more just society.[74] In Australia this necessitates a process of internal decolonisation. It requires that we work towards a new relationship of mutual recognition between Indigenous and non-Indigenous Australia that will allow us to live together in this territory. It must start with a frank acknowledgement of the illegitimacy of our founding, and the desire to acknowledge the sovereign peoples who were usurped in that process.

Australia, like New Zealand and Canada, is simultaneously colonial and postcolonial. Currently, however, we are post-colonial only in terms of the technical reality that we are no longer governed by the 'ex-colonial master society', having freed ourselves from the limiting and hegemonic cultural and political focus on Britain.[75] In many ways, however, Australia is still best described as colonial rather than postcolonial. Ann Curthoys has argued that the difficulty many non-Indigenous Australians have in acknowledging the violence, dispossession and child removal of Australia's history demonstrates psychological elements of a colonial mentality.[76]

In this context, internal decolonisation means moving away from the kinds of policies discussed in Chapter 3, policies that emphasise coercion and control over self-determination even in the face of Indigenous resistance.[77] Decolonising will allow non-Indigenous Australians the moral presence we crave, based on a fundamentally different relationship. As Rose suggests, this new relationship radically rewrites the terms of the old one:

> Against domination it asserts relationality, against control it asserts mutuality, against hyperseparation it asserts connectivity, and against claims that rely on an imagined future it asserts engaged responsiveness in the present.[78]

Crucial to Australia's efforts to decolonise the relationship between Indigenous and non-Indigenous people will be the commitment to a relationship of mutual recognition as 'equal, co-existing and self-governing peoples and cultures'. Mutual recognition must first be accepted by both peoples as appropriate and, subsequently, must also receive public affirmation in the nation's public institutions and symbols. Mutual recognition on these terms will allow Indigenous and non-Indigenous Australia to develop a relationship of coexistence, in which we are able to live alongside one another, governing our own affairs, in a relationship that is respectful of political diversity in representation and in governance arrangements.[79]

I do not outline this future relationship out of a naive view that it may somehow be easy to achieve. Far from it. I agree with James Tully when he suggests that real reconciliation between Indigenous people and the settler colonial orders present in their territories may be the most difficult of cases in which to attempt to achieve mutual recognition.[80] It is difficult for many reasons, not least the need to free ourselves from 'deep-seated prejudices and habits of thought and behaviour inherited from the colonial past'.[81] By their continuing presence alone, Indigenous people in any settler state present a significant challenge to the state's self-perception of itself as just, unified and sovereign.[82] These challenges can be threatening to the decolonisation process as, in assuming a defensive stance, the settler colonial order may continue to resist the deeper challenge inherent in any process of negotiating a new relationship. As the Mohawk scholar Taiaiake Alfred points out, a real commitment to a structural change in the relationship between Indigenous and non-Indigenous people must respond to a 'deeper challenge', going to 'the very foundations of the colonial state and culture'. Without acknowledging this deeper challenge, any change in the relationship that is negotiated in a still-colonial context runs the risk of merely entrenching social and political injustice.[83] Further, as Gillian Cowlishaw points out, until there is acceptance of the historical basis of the moral claims to injury made by Aboriginal and Torres Strait Islander peoples, the fundamental changes to our social and political institutions that are required will barely be contemplated.[84] The challenges to this work are immense.

At the same time, however, I know of no other way forward. Indigenous and non-Indigenous people must engage in new negotiations, through processes of intercultural dialogue, with the aim of achieving a new relationship that is acceptable to both parties. This will not take the form of a final settlement but should reflect 'an ongoing partnership negotiated by free peoples based on principles they can both endorse'.[85] As it is a relatively new phenomenon, we have few models of internal decolonisation to guide us, and as it involves a process of dialogue we cannot presume the outcome in advance while also maintaining a commitment to openness. We can only commit to 'working it out, step by step, dialogically with and among each other', allowing a new relationship to be shaped by all who hold a stake in living together in this territory: Indigenous and non-Indigenous, recent immigrant, settler immigrants and members of the oldest living culture on the planet.[86]

We must also acknowledge that reconciliation, mutual recognition and decolonisation—the requirements of a newly framed relationship between Indigenous and non-Indigenous—are not just a utopian goal. These intentions are not, in fact, a 'goal' or and end point at all. Rather, the work that lies ahead involves a process of building relationships based on trust where now exists only resentment, animosity and suspicion:

> It is not possible to simply *will* trusting and cooperative relationships into existence . . . Reconciliation should not be understood as some kind of end state that can be quickly reached and painlessly maintained. Changed attitudes and actions will emerge after work has been done, and improved relationships will be sustainable only if there are practices for the handling of fresh conflicts that arise. The challenges of reconciliation are real, and meeting them is no easy matter.[87]

What matters is that we understand how much of this effort is ours, attached to the non-Indigenous population of this territory. The political focus on Indigenous people in Australia has almost always been on their perceived deficits—of culture, of civility, of modernity—seen through a lens incapable of recognising difference. We have maintained this view because it has helped us to feel better about the violence and oppression that constituted the founding of the Australian nation and about which we continue to feel collective guilt. It is time for us to recognise that this guilt we feel is in fact an urge to make things right, to create a just relationship, to decolonise ourselves.

There can be no mastering of our past, no denying or avoiding the collective guilt we experience and that continues to deny us a moral presence in this country. It will not be possible to wash ourselves clean of our moral stain, no matter how honourable our intentions in the present.[88] There is, however, the possibility that we might one day learn to live more consciously with the ever-present questions and emotions that the past releases into the present.[89] This is a profound challenge, but it is one well worth the effort; as anti-racism educator Frances Kendall suggests, 'We have only ourselves and our courage to roll up our intellectual, emotional and physical sleeves and do what we know, in our unanaesthetised selves, is right.'[90] There is, as Rose points out, 'no single clear path towards decolonisation'.[91]

What lies ahead will be challenging, slow, and ultimately unsettling. But if we do not take up this challenge we will condemn ourselves to repeat the cycle of guilt, blame and denial *ad infinitum*. We have resisted this challenging path for long enough. Surely it is time we tried a new approach.

Epilogue: Beyond white guilt

During the 2010 federal election campaign both major parties committed to holding a referendum on the question of Indigenous recognition in the Australian Constitution. During the strange days between the election, which resulted in a hung parliament, and the formation of a minority government by the Australian Labor Party, the question of a referendum also found its way into negotiations between Prime Minister Julia Gillard and the Greens and Independent MPs whose support she needed in order to be able to govern. In the text of the written agreements between Gillard and the Greens member for Melbourne, Adam Bandt, and the two Independent members Tony Windsor (New England) and Rob Oakeshott (Lyne), is the simple commitment to hold a referendum 'during the 43rd Parliament or at the next election on Indigenous constitutional recognition'.[1] At the time of writing it remains unclear whether the proposals to hold a referendum on Indigenous recognition will involve merely a statement in a new preamble or more meaningful change to the body of the Constitution. Either proposal is likely to prove problematic, but for different reasons, and so will need to be considered carefully in any campaign leading up to a referendum vote.

If the minority ALP federal government does indeed hold for a full three-year term the proposed referendum will present the nation with an opportunity to make real progress on some of the challenges set out in this book. As noted in Chapter 5, referenda in Australia are notoriously difficult to pass. A 'double majority'—that is, a majority of voters in a majority of States plus an overall majority across the nation—is required for a successful 'yes' vote. This is a very high bar. Nevertheless, as constitutional scholars George Williams and David Hume have argued, referendum success is possible where a proposal is supported by: bipartisanship; popular ownership; popular education; sound and sensible proposals; and a modern referendum process.[2] Of these five pillars it is primarily popular ownership and education that concern Australia's adaptive challenge and our collective guilt; however, these two factors may have a direct impact on the level of bipartisan support given to a proposed referendum.

If a referendum on meaningful constitutional recognition is to succeed, there is an enormous amount of work to be done. Although a referendum is, in many ways, a technical solution, much of the work required for success in this case will need to be adaptive. There will be a great need for community education, to help the wider population to understand why constitutional change is needed and how it will benefit Aboriginal and Torres Strait Islander peoples, and to dispel any fears about what such a change might mean. And there will also be a need for some careful work to engage the underlying adaptive issues and dilute the predictable reactions from the high identifiers in politics and in the wider community. Those of the 'If it's not broke, don't fix it' brigade will need to be persuaded that it is, in fact, broken.

The demands for adaptive work will be less if the proposal is just for recognition in a new preamble as this type of change will primarily be symbolic. If, however, the proposal is for change to the body of the Constitution it will be necessary for us to face some harder facts about the founding of this nation. In its 2010 concluding comments to Australia's country report, the United Nations Committee on the Elimination of Racial Discrimination (CERD) was highly critical of the extent to which racism remains embedded in Australian institutions, including the Constitution. In particular CERD noted its regret that Australia has made only 'limited progress towards Constitutional acknowledgement of Australia's Indigenous peoples' combined with 'slow implementation of the principle of Indigenous peoples' exercising meaningful control over their affairs'. CERD recommended that Australia increase its efforts to 'ensure a meaningful reconciliation with Indigenous peoples', reminding the government that any measures to amend the Constitution should 'include the recognition of Aboriginal and Torres Strait Islanders as First Nations Peoples' and recommending that Australia consider treaty negotiations in order to 'build a constructive and sustained relationship with Indigenous peoples'.[3] Acknowledging the merit in these criticisms and recommendations will prove difficult for the Australian government. They do, however, go to the heart of the adaptive challenge we face and the work that lies ahead in acknowledging our collective guilt. They remind us that the 'cure' for the disease of colonialism 'involves difficult and painful treatment and extraction and reshaping of present conditions of existence'.[4] We must surgically extract the coloniser still resident in us all.[5]

Learning from our past, finding a way forward

There is often a tendency, when thinking about making progress on an issue, to want to draw a line under past events in order that we are able to move forward. In this instance such a strategy would be a terrible mistake. While there are no doubt many who feel that we should stop debating our history, we must still find a way to learn from our past. Bernhard Schlink reminds us that the lessons of the past concern more than just individual morality but also, and more importantly, pertain to 'societal and state institutions in which individual morality must be preserved if it is to have the power to resist'.[6] This is not an impossible challenge, but it does foreshadow some of the ways in which our relationship with our national history needs to be recuperated. Historian Grace Karskens suggests some of the ways in which history might help to inform our present challenges, writing of the ways in which a recuperated history of sites in Sydney, for example, could provide 'incomparable teaching tools' through which:

> ... important lessons could be taught; cross-cultural stories about those early years of co-existence, about intimacy and enmity, adaptation and continuity, dispossession and reparation, contempt and respect. But we would first have to abandon narratives about the settlers' transformation of 'empty' wasteland into something useful, beautiful and civilised ... We would have to rethink those old ways of telling landscape history which seem to validate dispossession as 'inevitable', as history's 'proper course' ...[7]

In this sense, Karskens reminds us that the past is both a key part of our challenge and a potential resource in the work we have to do. Having been informed by the debates in the 'history wars' we are all now aware that history is contested and constructed through the lens with which we understand it. While the past remains, as Schlink reminds us, 'unassailable and irrevocable',[8] it can in many ways be revisited. We cannot undo the atrocities that were committed in the founding of this nation, nor can we undo the many wrongs that have been done since. But we can relearn our past and understand that the choices made by our predecessors were not 'inevitable' but were just that—choices. Understanding massacre, dispossession and child removal as acts that were poor and unjustifiable choices allows us to take a step towards breaking the bonds of solidarity we share with the perpetrators of historical injustice.

From these resources in our history we can begin to think about the present-day strategies or tools we might deploy in order to more fully break with the past and begin to chart a new future. Bashir Bashir and Will Kymlicka outline some of the 'tools or techniques of reconciliation' that might be brought to bear in these efforts, including 'reparations and compensation, apologies, commemorations and memorials, truth telling initiatives, rehabilitation, and amnesties'.[9] Australia has the opportunity to build on the 2008 Apology to the Stolen Generations in taking our efforts towards reconciliation a few steps further. These efforts must take place at a collective level. We are not able to identify, shame, or punish individual wrongdoers as might be the case in countries where injustice has been more recent. But nor would this be desirable. As a nation of diverse peoples we all continue to enjoy the many benefits of living on land that belongs legitimately only to a few. To somehow distance ourselves from past perpetrators would be little more than an effort to sidestep our collective guilt by suggesting that these perpetrators of injustice are not really part of us.[10] For as long as we refuse to acknowledge our collective guilt we must accept that these perpetrators *are* us. To attempt to distance ourselves would do little more than reinscribe our bonds of solidarity with these same perpetrators.

We might also give thought to why we might consider pursuing these strategies. This book has argued that it will only be by taking action to address historic injustice that we will be able to make genuine adaptive change in this country. I am convinced that a majority of Australians would like to see progress in the relationship between Indigenous and non-Indigenous Australia. But this should not be solely because we want to feel better about ourselves. Along with the tools they outline, Bashir and Kymlicka also suggest a number of goals for reconciliation, which include 'nation-building, individual and collective healing after trauma, the pursuit of justice in its various forms (retributive, restorative, distributive), the consolidation of the rule of law, and democratization'.[11] Some of these goals—if pursued with integrity—may in fact make us feel *less* comfortable about ourselves. But if we can commit to working towards the mutual recognition of Indigenous and non-Indigenous peoples as 'equal, coexisting and self governing peoples' we may conceivably set ourselves on a path towards decolonisation and freedom, for Indigenous peoples and for all Australians 'who long to free themselves and their children from any further complicity in a democratic society that contains a regime of inequality within'. This in turn will help to preserve and enhance liberal democratic values in ways that are appropriate to our culturally diverse and postcolonial age, rather than stuck in our colonial past.[12]

In a renewed process of reconciliation and decolonisation it is likely that we will have to come to accept the fact that we are unlikely to ever achieve definitive and final solutions to the wrongs that are at the root of our nationhood. But if our desire is to create in Australia what James Tully describes as 'dialogical civic freedom', or the freedom for all citizens to have an effective say in dialogue over how they are governed, then we will need to appreciate that there will always be reasonable disagreements over how we resolve conflicts and the solutions we might pursue.[13] It will only be through dialogue over our disagreements that we will achieve a deeper understanding of one another, which is a requirement of any meaningful reconciliation process. Understanding 'works against all that separates us and toward all that would bring us together' and without understanding participants in a process of reconciliation will be unable to acknowledge each other as equals.[14] It would be a mistake, however, to presume such understanding. Like every other aspect of this adaptive challenge, understanding will take patience and effort from all involved.

Nevertheless, if we commit to tackling our adaptive challenge we may find that over time we are able to understand each other better, making more genuine connections with one another and developing a view of our nation and our history that is more shared than contested.[15] To do this, those of us who are white will need to 'rein in our instincts to feel self-righteous' by virtue of our desire to make change, recognising that there is the 'potential for connection and transcendence' in every interaction we have while engaged in this work.[16] Making genuine change in this country, engaging *deeply* in our adaptive work, will require all sections of the community. As Schlink reminds us, 'Moral pathos not undergirded by moral engagement, and moral engagement not carried by contemporary concern, are not genuine'. He cautions that the next generation 'keenly senses that hollowness'.[17] Change cannot be made without our genuine moral engagement in the work that lies ahead.

Can we craft a new national story?

Central to our adaptive challenge will be our capacity to craft a new national story. If, as argued in Chapter 1, the Australian nation is a creation of our own hearts and imaginations, then it is time for us to reshape our creation in ways that allow us to break from heroic fictions and equip us for a reconciled future. It is our task, as citizens, to replace the 'official nationalism' of government policy[18] with a new narrative that can engage the minds of other citizens.[19] This narrative must be more than myth. Our national stories have proven inadequate and unsatisfying precisely because they rest on shaky foundations. Our nation must come to rest on a greater 'historical consciousness'. We must understand the chains that keep us connected to 'them' in the past and 'us' in the present, fostering a new kind of 'moral engagement' with the way the past continues to shape our present and our future.[20] Or as Martha Minow suggests, we need to find our way between vengeance and forgiveness through recollection, affirmation, and a process of 'facing who we are, and who we could become'.[21] Our continued reliance on national stories of past heroics only limits our capacity to find new ways of living together.

The crafting of a new national story should not, however, degenerate into what Bashir and Kymlicka describe as a 'nation-building reconciliation' in which past divisions are overcome and replaced with a new shared sense of nationhood:

> Aspiring to achieve a harmonious and integrated society, the process of reconciliation converts people, through confession and acknowledgement, into non-racial citizens of a 'rainbow nation'. This model implies that were it not for artificial divisions created by earlier oppressive policies, the various groups in a divided society would and should feel that they belong together in a unified political community, and that the goal of reconciliation is to move people away from older divisive identities to a new shared national identity.[22]

Nation-building in this sense is not appropriate to a postcolonial context, where what is required is the kind of mutual recognition

Tully advocates. Indeed, some have criticised nation-building as being the cause of historical injustice towards Indigenous peoples, and argue that it can never be the solution to this injustice.[23] Aboriginal and Torres Strait Islander peoples do not, for the most part, want to be absorbed into the Australian nation as this model of reconciliation would suggest. Rather, our new national narrative must recognise that on this territory Indigenous and non-Indigenous peoples can peacefully coexist, recognising each other as distinct and self-governing peoples. This is what justice will look like.

There should be nothing about crafting a new national story that insists we cannot feel good about some aspects of our past. We can both celebrate our achievements and acknowledge past wrongs. We can open up our national identity to scrutiny, we can have fruitful dialogue about how we might interpret or reinterpret our history, and we can question the official nationalism that maintains the bonds of solidarity with past perpetrators of injustice. This process may be full of contradiction: as Tim Soutphommasane has suggested, it can be difficult to make sense of a patriotism that 'involves pride as well as shame, celebration as well as criticism'.[24] But contradiction may just be an integral part of who we are, contradictions that Australian scholars John Docker and Gerhard Fischer[25] suggest are 'overlapping and unresolved': 'colonial versus invaders, majority versus innumerable minorities, white against black or coloured . . .' and so on. These contradictions are as much a part of our national story as any simplistic heroic narrative about the birth of our nationhood on the shores at Gallipoli.

To take these steps towards a different kind of relationship between Indigenous and non-Indigenous Australia we must believe that such a transformation is possible. We must 'engage with thinking beyond the impossible'.[26] As discussed in Chapter 3, too much of our recent focus has been on policy made to address an alleged lack or deficit in Indigenous culture. Time and again we have seen that such an approach does not create change and in fact merely perpetuates the internal colonisation of this territory. It is time to imagine a different approach, one in which non-Indigenous Australians start from a belief that we have the capacity to *change ourselves* and our institutions.[27] Beginning to decolonise the relationship between Indigenous and non-Indigenous people will require—at minimum—a constitution that recognises Indigenous sovereignty and/or a treaty that formalises a new relationship between Indigenous and non-Indigenous Australia. Beyond this, we may also want to consider what Barkan describes as 'restitution agreements' through which we can 'fuze polarized antagonistic histories into a core of shared history to which both sides can subscribe and from which each will benefit'. By sorting out 'seemingly irreconcilable differences' restitution can foster relationships involving 'overlapping plural identities' and provide 'incentive for protagonists to engage in dialogue'.[28]

Legal scholar Roy Brooks has argued that demands for redress for past injustice must be the responsibility of legislators rather than judges simply because legislators are able to achieve more than judges can. Internationally, redress movements carried by the legislative realm have been successful in reaching 'the hearts and minds of lawmakers and citizens alike'. This success, however, has largely depended on the degree of public and private pressure brought to bear on legislators. In other words, the success of these movements is based in politics and passion rather than logic, argument, justice or culture.[29] Our guilt is collective rather than individual, and we must collectively bring pressure to bear on our political leaders. Governments do not tend to do the right thing simply because it is the right thing to do. Governments only do the right thing when the voting public demand it of them. We must let our political leaders know of our need to break the bonds of solidarity with the past, to break free of our collective guilt, and to work at developing a new relationship between Indigenous and non-Indigenous peoples in this country.

Next steps

Reforming our Constitution to reflect a new form of mutual recognition between Indigenous and non-Indigenous peoples is an aspiration that will take much effort. A changed constitution may create the political conditions in which new relationships may be realised, and new institutional arrangements developed. Such reform will not be a solution in and of itself, but it will be a tangible manifestation of our desire to decolonise. But a process of decolonisation will still ask some tough questions of non-Indigenous Australians—the colonisers. Once we understand the import of colonisation and become conscious of our own position, will we accept the situation? Will we agree to continue living in privilege, ignoring the distress of those who are colonised? Will we continue to be usurpers, affirming the oppression and injustice experienced by the original inhabitants of the colony? Will we accept being colonisers, allowing privilege and illegitimacy to become habit, under the constant gaze of the usurped? Will we adjust to this position and censure ourselves from speaking of what we know to be wrong?[30] We do not yet know the answers to these questions in Australia, but there seems to be a growing sense that we must find the answers if we are to reform and rebuild our relationships. This sense comes from the fact that, as Robert Jensen has argued:

> Somewhere down in our guts we understand that in an oppressive system . . . the unearned privileges with which we live are based on the suffering of others. We know that we have things because others don't. We may not want to give voice to that feeling, but it is impossible to ignore completely. And it doesn't feel good, in part, because to be fully human is to seek communion with others, not separation from them, and one cannot find that connection under conditions in which unjust power brings unearned privilege. To be fully human is to reject a system that conditions your pleasure on someone else's pain.[31]

What Jensen emphasises is that relationships will be central to whatever path lies ahead, whether that be a campaign to change the Constitution or some other path towards decolonisation and true reconciliation. Indigenous and non-Indigenous lives are 'entangled' and yet we are barely engaged in the conversations we most need to be having.[32] As Trudy Govier suggests, however:

> It is exactly because people must live and work together that reconciliation matters. If past divides persist to structure present and future relationships, there will be little security in the new structures. In all this, relationships are fundamental; it matters how people see each other and how they feel about each other.[33]

For these reasons it seems essential that we must find ways of fostering, nurturing, supporting and resourcing new forms of dialogue. As a nation, or as many nations trying to find a way to live together, we must find better ways to communicate, to listen to one another openly and deeply. Adam Kahane reminds us of the African proverb that says, 'If you want to walk fast, walk alone. If you want to walk far, walk together.' However, Kahane also suggests that our toughest social challenges require that we walk both fast and far and together:

> When we are on smooth and familiar ground, we may be able to do this easily, even without paying attention. But in order to move forward fluidly on the uneven and unsteady and unfamiliar ground on which we increasingly find ourselves, we need a way to build our capacity for employing both our power and our love collectively.[34]

Kahane emphasises the need for power and love based on his extensive experience of working on tough problems requiring the rebuilding of relationships. We need power so that we might lose our fear of offending or hurting others and so act with purpose. We need love so that we might lose our fear of being embarrassed or hurt and so hold back our openness. Kahane insists that 'Our way forward is not without these fears but through them.'[35] Any new dialogue in Australia will need to involve power and love, hope and fear, and a genuine commitment to change.

In our work to reform and rebuild our relationships we will no longer be able to suppress or deny our collective guilt. Rather, as Kahane suggests, we may come to recognise that in our work to heal ourselves and others 'our wound becomes our gift'. Our willingness to admit that we 'are a part of, rather than apart from, the woundedness of our world' opens up the capacity for us to take risks in a new dialogue, to stumble and fall, and hence to learn and to grow.[36] If we can acknowledge our collective guilt it may goad us towards change, towards accepting that acting on our guilt might actually free us. As David Williams points out, 'if we live in dread of guilt, we must construct a temple of illusions'. Once we accept that moral purity is not, and never has been, a possibility, we can explore new possibilities for the future. Once we have 'tasted' guilt and found that it did not poison us, we may find instead that it 'merely opened our eyes'.[37]

There is woundedness on both sides of the Indigenous–non-Indigenous relationship. This book has focused on the non-Indigenous side of the relationship and efforts that we must make to break the bonds of solidarity with our past. It is not for me to say what Aboriginal and Torres Strait Islanders need to do to heal; all I am able to offer is a willingness to listen and to support Indigenous aspirations. Non-Indigenous desires to 'atone' for the wrongs of our history cannot rest on Indigenous cooperation: it is the right of the hurt to not agree to be healed just because we say the time is right.[38] Bernhard Schlink reminds us that reconciliation is the most demanding and difficult way in which to achieve closure in the wake of an injury, and the extent to which reconciliation is able to occur will depend on the level of our efforts to achieve it.[39] Too often in Australia, our efforts in the direction of reconciliation have foundered on our collective guilt. To avoid acknowledging this guilt we have gone to extraordinary lengths to assert the legitimacy of our founding as a nation and the sincerity of our efforts to 'improve' Indigenous lives ever since. It is time to break this pattern and to get beyond white guilt.

Notes

Foreword

1 Northern Territory (Board of Enquiry into the Protection of Aboriginal Children from Sexual Abuse) (Mr Rex Wild QC and Ms Patricia Anderson, Chairs), June 2007.
2 Wurridjal v The Commonwealth (2009) 237 CLR 309 at 394–5 [214].

Introduction

1 Ian Tyrrell, 'The Cooks River and environmental history', adapted from the 2004 Botany Bay Forum, University of New South Wales, Sydney, 30 November 2004, <http://iantyrrell.wordpress.com/cooks-river/>.
2 Murray Goot and Tim Rowse, *Divided Nation?: Indigenous affairs and the imagined public,* Melbourne University Press, Melbourne, 2007, p. 154.
3 Deborah Bird Rose, *Reports from a Wild Country: Ethics for decolonisation,* UNSW Press, Sydney, 2004, p. 6.
4 Elazar Barkan, *The Guilt of Nations: Restitution and negotiating historical injustices,* The Johns Hopkins University Press, Baltimore, 2000, p. xi.
5 Gillian Cowlishaw, *Blackfellas, Whitefellas and the Hidden Injuries of Race,* Blackwell, Malden, MA, 2004, p. 176.
6 Craig McGarty and Ana-Maria Bliuc, 'Refining the meaning of the "collective" in collective guilt: Harm, guilt and the apology in Australia', in Nyla Branscombe and Bertjan Doosje (eds),

Collective Guilt: International perspectives, Cambridge University Press, Cambridge, UK, 2004, p. 112.

7 ibid., p. 121.

8 Ghassan Hage, *White Nation: Fantasies of White supremacy in a multicultural society*, Routledge, New York, 2000, p. 19.

9 Henry Reynolds, *Why Weren't We Told? A personal search for the truth about our history*, Viking, Melbourne, 1999, p. xv.

10 Donald Horne, *The Lucky Country: Australia in the sixties*, Penguin Books, Melbourne, 1964.

11 Anna Clark, 'Flying the flag for mainstream Australia', *Griffith Review 11: Getting Smart*, 2006; Marian Sawer, 'Governing for the mainstream: Implications for community representation', *Australian Journal of Public Administration*, Vol. 61, No. 1, 2002; Simon Jackman, 'Pauline Hanson, the mainstream and political elites: The place of race in Australian political ideology', *Australian Journal of Political Science*, Vol. 33, No. 2, 1998.

12 Peter Sutton, *The Politics of Suffering: Indigenous Australia and the end of liberal consensus*, Melbourne University Publishing, Melbourne, 2009, p. 202.

13 Ann Curthoys, 'An uneasy conversation: The multicultural and the indigenous', in John Docker and Gerhard Fischer (eds), *Race, Colour and Identity in Australia and New Zealand*, UNSW Press, Sydney.

14 Sara Ahmed, 'The politics of bad feeling', *Australian Critical Race and Whiteness Studies Association Journal*, Vol. 1, 2005, p. 78.

15 Cowlishaw, *Blackfellas*, p. 240.

16 Ronald A. Heifetz, *Leadership Without Easy Answers*, The Bellknap Press of Harvard University Press, Cambridge, MA, 1994, pp. 2, 22.

17 ibid., pp. 72–3.

18 Sarah Maddison, *Black Politics: Inside the complexity of Aboriginal political culture*, Allen & Unwin, Sydney, 2009.

19 Heifetz, *Leadership Without Easy Answers*, p. 73.
20 ibid., p. 254.
21 ibid., p. 38.
22 ibid., pp. 86–7.
23 ibid., p. 30.
24 ibid., p. 238.
25 Frances E. Kendall, *Understanding White Privilege: Creating pathways to authentic relationships across race*, Routledge, New York, 2006, p. 86.
26 Shelly Tochluk, *Witnessing Whiteness: First steps towards an antiracist practice and culture*, Rowman & Littlefield Education, Lanham, Maryland, 2008, p. 56.
27 Shelby Steele, *White Guilt: How blacks and whites together destroyed the promise of the civil rights era*, Harper Perennial, New York, 2006, p. 24.
28 McGarty and Bliuc, 'Refining the meaning of the "collective"', in Branscombe and Doosje, *Collective Guilt*, p. 114.
29 Sonia Roccas, Yechiel Klan and Ido Liviatan, 'Exonerating cognitions, group identification and personal predictors of collective guilt among Jewish-Israelis', in Branscombe and Doosje, *Collective Guilt* p. 131.
30 Brian Lickell, Toni Schmader and Marchelle Barquissau, 'The evocation of moral emotions in intergroup contexts: The distinction between collective guilt and collective shame', in Branscombe and Doosje, *Collective Guilt*, p. 39.
31 Robert Jensen, *The Heart of Whiteness: Confronting race, racism and white privilege*, City Lights, San Francisco, 2005, p. xix.
32 Lickell et al., 'Evocation of moral emotions', in Branscombe and Doosje, *Collective Guilt*, p. 47.
33 Jensen, *Heart of Whiteness*, p. xviii.
34 Barkan, *Guilt of Nations*, pp. 316–17.
35 Emina Subăsić and Katherine Reynolds, 'Beyond "practical" reconciliation: Intergroup inequality and the meaning of

non-Indigenous identity', *Political Psychology*, Vol. 30, No. 2, 2009, pp. 248–9.

36 Aarti Iyer, Colin Wayne Leach and Anne Pederson, 'Racial wrongs and restitutions: The role of guilt and other group-based emotions', in Branscombe and Doosje, *Collective Guilt*, p. 271.

37 Branscombe and Doosje, *Collective Guilt*, p. ix.

38 Kendall, *Understanding White Privilege*, p. 103.

39 Branscombe and Doosje, *Collective Guilt*, pp. 4, 5.

40 Lickell et al., 'Evocation of moral emotions', in Branscombe and Doosje, *Collective Guilt*, p. 40.

41 McGarty and Bliuc, 'Refining the meaning of the "collective"', in Branscombe and Doosje, *Collective Guilt*, p. 120.

42 David C. Williams, 'In praise of guilt: How the yearning for moral purity blocks reparations for Native Americans', in Federico Lenzerini (ed.) *Reparations for Indigenous Peoples: International and comparative perspectives*, Oxford University Press, Oxford, 2008, p. 229.

43 Subăsić and Reynolds, 'Beyond "practical" reconciliation', p. 249.

44 Branscombe and Doosje, *Collective Guilt*, p. 29.

45 Diana Eades, 'Aboriginal English', in Stephen A. Wurm, Peter Mülhäusler and Darrell T. Tryon (eds), *Atlas of Languages of Intercultural Communication in the Pacific, Asia and the Americas*, Vol. II.I, Mouton de Gruyter, Berlin, 1996, p. 136.

46 Lickell et al., 'Evocation of moral emotions', in Branscombe and Doosje, *Collective Guilt*, pp. 43, 48, 52.

47 Kendall, *Understanding White Privilege*, p. 85.

48 Jensen, *Heart of Whiteness*, p. 47.

49 Maddison, *Black Politics*.

50 Cowlishaw, *Blackfellas*, p. 80.

51 Lickell et al., 'Evocation of moral emotions', in Branscombe and Doosje, *Collective Guilt*, p. 38.

52 Roccas et al., 'Exonerating cognitions', in Branscombe and Doosje, *Collective Guilt*, p. 135.
53 Branscombe and Doosje, *Collective Guilt*, pp. 20, 24–5.
54 Kendall, *Understanding White Privilege*, p. 81.
55 Robyn Mallett and Janet Swim, 'Collective guilt in the United States: Predicting support for social politics that alleviate social injustice', in Branscombe and Doosje, *Collective Guilt*, p. 67.
56 Martha Augoustinos and Amanda Le Conteur, 'On whether to apologise to Indigenous Australians: The denial of white guilt', in Branscombe and Doosje, *Collective Guilt*, pp. 251–2.
57 Lorenzo Veracini, 'Settler collective, founding violence and disavowal: The settler colonial situation', *Journal of Intercultural Studies*, Vol. 29, No. 4, 2008, p. 364.
58 Barkan, *Guilt of Nations*, p. 345.
59 Branscombe and Doosje, *Collective Guilt*, p. 7.
60 ibid., p. x.
61 Irene Watson, 'Aboriginal Sovereignties: Past, present and future (im)possibilities', in Suvendrini Perera (ed.), *Our Patch: Enacting Australian sovereignty post-2001*, Network books, The API Network, Perth, 2007, p. 42.
62 Jensen, *Heart of Whiteness*, p. xx.
63 Williams, 'In praise of guilt', in Lenzerini, *Reparations for Indigenous Peoples*, p. 231.
64 Lickell et al., 'Evocation of moral emotions', in Branscombe and Doosje, *Collective Guilt*, p. 52.
65 Martha Minow, *Between Vengeance and Forgiveness: Facing history after genocide and mass violence*, Beacon Press, Boston, 1998, p. 21.
66 ibid.
67 Iyer et al., 'Racial wrongs and restitutions', in Branscombe and Doosje, *Collective Guilt*, p. 273.

Chapter 1 The long colonial shadow

1. Benedict Anderson, *Imagined Communities: Reflections on the origins and spread of nationalism*, Verso, London, 2006, pp. 6–7.
2. Michael Freeman, 'Past wrongs and liberal justice', *Ethical Theory and Moral Practice*, Vol. 5, No. 2, Pardoning Past Wrongs, 2002, p. 201.
3. Williams, 'In praise of guilt', in Lenzerini, *Reparations for Indigenous Peoples*, p. 246.
4. W.E.H. Stanner, *The Dreaming and Other Essays*, Black Inc, Melbourne, 2009 [1968], p. 118.
5. Lickell et al., 'Evocation of moral emotions', in Branscombe and Doosje, *Collective Guilt*, p. 35.
6. Bernhard Schlink, *Guilt about the Past*, University of Queensland Press, St Lucia, 2009, p. 8.
7. Lickell et al., 'Evocation of moral emotions', in Branscombe and Doosje, *Collective Guilt*, p. 49.
8. Branscombe and Doosje, *Collective Guilt*, pp. x, 3, 17, 22.
9. Schlink, *Guilt about the Past*, pp. 12, 14, 19–20.
10. ibid., pp. 12–14.
11. Branscombe and Doosje, *Collective Guilt*, pp. 3, 4.
12. McGarty and Bliuc, 'Refining the meaning of the "collective"', in Branscombe and Doosje, *Collective Guilt*, p. 114.
13. Iyer et al., 'Racial wrongs and restitutions', in Branscombe and Doosje, *Collective Guilt*, p. 263.
14. Michael J. Halloran, 'Indigenous reconciliation in Australia: Do values, identity and collective guilt matter?', *Journal of Community and Applied Social Psychology*, Vol. 17, 2007, p. 13.
15. Schlink, *Guilt about the Past*, p. 1.
16. ibid., pp. 15–16.
17. ibid., p. 18.
18. Gabriele Schwab, *Haunting Legacies: Violent histories and transgenerational trauma*, Columbia University Press, New York, 2010, p. 3.

19 Schlink, *Guilt about the Past,* p. 21.
20 Bashir Bashir, 'Accommodating historically oppressed social groups: Deliberative democracy and the politics of reconciliation', in Will Kymlicka and Bashir Bashir (eds), *The Politics of Reconciliation in Multicultural Societies,* Oxford University Press, Oxford, 2008, p. 58.
21 Lickell et al., 'Evocation of moral emotions', in Branscombe and Doosje, *Collective Guilt,* p. 42.
22 Barkan, *Guilt of Nations,* p. 344.
23 Cowlishaw, *Blackfellas,* p. 240.
24 Williams, 'In praise of guilt', in Lenzerini, *Reparations for Indigenous Peoples,* p. 249.
25 Schmitt et al., 'Gender inequality and the intensity of men's collective guilt', in Branscombe and Doosje, *Collective Guilt,* p. 84.
26 Mark McKenna, 'Anzac Day: How did it become Australia's national day?', in Marilyn Lake and Henry Reynolds (eds), *What's Wrong with Anzac? The militarisation of Australian history,* UNSW Press, Sydney, 2010, p. 121.
27 Craig Calhoun, *Nations Matter: Culture, history and the cosmopolitan dream,* Routledge, Abingdon, UK, 2007, p. 1.
28 ibid., p. 27.
29 Anderson, *Imagined Communities,* p. 159.
30 Barkan, *Guilt of Nations,* p. xxxix.
31 Anthony Moran, 'White Australia, settler nationalism and Aboriginal assimilation', *Australian Journal of Politics and History,* Vol. 51, No. 2, 2005, p. 171.
32 Ashis Nandy, 'Australia's polyglot ghosts and monoglot ghostbusters: A demonic foreword', in J.V. D'Cruz, Bernie Neville, Devika Goonewardene and Philip Darby (eds), *As Others See Us,* Australian Scholarly Publishing, Melbourne, 2008, pp. xiii, xxii.
33 Williams, 'In praise of guilt', in Lenzerini, *Reparations for Indigenous Peoples,* p. 246.

34 James Tully, *Public Philosophy in a New Key: Volume 1, Democracy and civic freedom*, Cambridge University Press, Cambridge, 2008.
35 Lickell et al., 'Evocation of moral emotions', in Branscombe and Doosje, *Collective Guilt*, pp. 39–40.
36 Roccas et al., 'Exonerating cognitions', in Branscombe and Doosje, *Collective Guilt*, p. 140.
37 Branscombe and Doosje, *Collective Guilt*, pp. 97–8.
38 John Howard, 'Opening Address to the Australian Reconciliation Convention, The Hon. John Howard, MP, The Prime Minister', Melbourne, 27 May 1997, <http://www.auslii.edu.au/au/other/IndigLRes/car/1997/4/pmspoken.html>.
39 Meredith J. Green and Christopher C. Sonn, 'Examining discourses of whiteness and the potential for reconciliation', *Journal of Community and Applied Social Psychology*, Vol. 15, 2005, p. 483.
40 Rose, *Reports from a Wild Country*, p. 58.
41 Kendall, *Understanding White Privilege*, p. 93.
42 Elizabeth Povinelli, *The Cunning of Recognition: Indigenous alterities and the making of Australian multiculturalism*, Duke University Press, Durham, 2002, p. 154.
43 ibid.
44 Subăsić and Reynolds, 'Beyond "practical" reconciliation', p. 249.
45 ibid.
46 Branscombe and Doosje, *Collective Guilt*, p. ix.
47 Stephen Hills, '"The Grand Experiment of the Civilisation of the Aborigines": Perspectives on a missionary endeavour in Western Australia', in *Evangelists of Empire? Missionaries in colonial history*, Amanda Barry, Joanna Cruikshank, Andrew Brown-May and Patricia Grimshaw (eds), University of Melbourne eScholarship Research Centre, Melbourne, 2008, <http://msp.esrc.unimelb.edu.au/shs/missions>.
48 Maddison, *Black Politics*, p. 208.

49 Dominik J. Schaller and Jürgen Zimmerer, 'From the Guest Editors: Raphael Lemkin: the "founder of the United Nations' Genocide Convention" as a historian of mass violence', *Journal of Genocide Research,* Vol. 7, No. 4, 2005, p. 447.

50 See Human Rights Web, United Nations Convention on the Prevention and Punishment of the Crime of Genocide, 1997, for the full text. <http://www.hrweb.org/legal/genocide.html>.

51 Christopher Powell, 'The morality of genocide', in Adam Jones (ed.), *New Directions in Genocide Research,* Routledge, New York, 2011.

52 Ann Curthoys, 'Constructing national histories', in Bain Attwood and Stephen Foster (eds), *Frontier Conflict: The Australian experience,* National Museum of Australia, Canberra, 2003, p. 198.

53 Keith Windschuttle, 'Doctored evidence and invented incidents in Aboriginal historiography', in Attwood and Foster, *Frontier Conflict,* p. 110.

54 Carmel Bird (ed.), *The Stolen Children: Their stories,* Random House, Sydney, 1998, p. 6.

55 Powell, 'The morality of genocide', 2011.

56 Christopher Powell, 'The Moralization Of Genocide In Canada', paper presented at the Prairie Perspectives conference, Truth and Reconciliation event, Winnipeg, 17 June 2010, p. 5.

57 Bernard Smith, *The Spectre of Truganini,* 1980 Boyer Lectures, Australian Broadcasting Corporation, Sydney, 1980, p. 10.

58 Cowlishaw, *Blackfellas,* p. 203.

59 Raymond Evans, 'The country has another past: Queensland and the History Wars', in Frances Peters-Little, Ann Curthoys and John Docker (eds), *Passionate Histories: Myth, memory and Indigenous Australia,* ANU E-Press, Canberra, 2010, p. 13.

60 Smith, *Spectre of Truganini,* p. 52.

61 Paul Keal, *European Conquest and the Rights of Indigenous Peoples: The moral backwardness of international society,* Cambridge University Press, Cambridge, 2003, p. 174.

62 ibid., p. 173.
63 Tully, *Public Philosophy in a New Key*, p. 235.
64 Powell, 'The Moralization Of Genocide', p. 5.
65 Macgregor Duncan, Andrew Leigh, David Madden and Peter Tynan, *Imagining Australia: Ideas for our future*, Allen & Unwin, Sydney, 2004, p. 11.
66 Marilyn Lake, 'Introduction: What have you done for your country?', in Marilyn Lake and Henry Reynolds (eds), *What's Wrong with Anzac? The militarisation of Australian history*, UNSW Press, Sydney, 2001, pp. 20–1.
67 Tim Soutphommasane, *Reclaiming Patriotism: Nation-building for Australian progressives*, Cambridge University Press, Melbourne, 2009, p. 2.
68 ibid., p. 54.
69 King quoted in Adam Kahane, *Power and Love: A theory and practice of social change*, Berrett-Koehler Publishers, San Francisco, 2010, p. 8.
70 ibid., p. 8.
71 Cowlishaw, *Blackfellas*, p. 100.
72 ibid., p. 175.

Chapter 2 History and identity

1 Stanner, *The Dreaming and Other Essays*, pp. 188–9.
2 Tom Griffiths, 'The language of conflict', in Attwood and Foster, *Frontier Conflict*, p. 138.
3 Barkan, *Guilt of Nations*, p. x.
4 Bashir, 'Accommodating historically oppressed social groups', in Kymlicka and Bashir, *Politics of Reconciliation*, p. 54.
5 Jensen, *Heart of Whiteness*, p. 28.
6 Donald W. Shriver, 'Where and when in political life is justice served by forgiveness?', in Nigel Biggar (ed.), *Burying the Past:*

Making peace and doing justice after civil conflict, Georgetown University Press, Washington, DC, 2003, pp. 26, 31.

7 Jensen, *Heart of Whiteness*, p. 26.

8 Trudy Govier, *Taking Wrongs Seriously: Acknowledgment, reconciliation and the politics of sustainable peace*, Humanity Books, New York, 2006, p. 177.

9 Tuomas Forsberg, 'The philosophy and practice of dealing with the past: Some conceptual and normative issues', in Biggar, *Burying the Past*, p. 67.

10 Henry Reynolds, *This Whispering in our Hearts*, Allen & Unwin, Sydney, 1998, p. xvi.

11 Patrick Wolfe, *Settler Colonialism and the Transformation of Anthropology: The politics and poetics of an ethnographic event*, Cassell, London, 1999, p. 169.

12 Wolfe, *Settler Colonialism*, p. 27.

13 Nadim N. Rouhana, 'Reconciling history and equal citizenship in Israel: Democracy and the politics of historical denial', in Kymlicka and Bashir, *Politics of Reconciliation*, p. 73.

14 Wolfe, *Settler Colonialism*, p. 2.

15 Stanner, *The Dreaming and Other Essays*, p. 119.

16 Rose, *Reports from a Wild Country*, p. 4.

17 Barkan, *Guilt of Nations*, pp. 159–60.

18 Veracini, 'Settler collective, founding violence and disavowal', p. 364.

19 Wolfe, *Settler Colonialism*, p. 31.

20 Rose, *Reports from a Wild Country*, p. 35.

21 Sean Brennan, Larissa Behrendt, Lisa Strelein and George Williams, *Treaty*, The Federation Press, Sydney, 2005, pp. 58–9.

22 Lorna Lippmann, *Generations of Resistance: The Aboriginal struggle for justice*, Longman Cheshire, Melbourne, 1981, p. 93.

23 Briggs quoted in Maddison, *Black Politics*, p. 110.

24 George Morgan, *Unsettled Places: Aboriginal people and urbanisation in New South Wales*, Wakefield Press, Kent Town, 2006, p. 15.

25 Frances Peters-Little, *The Community Game: Aboriginal self-definition at the local level,* Research Discussion Paper No. 10, Australian Institute for Aboriginal and Torres Strait Islander Studies, Canberra, 2000, p. 4.
26 Roy L. Brooks, 'The age of apology', in Roy Brooks (ed.), *When Sorry Isn't Enough: The controversy over apologies and reparations for human injustice,* New York University Press, New York, 1999, p. 7.
27 Rose, *Reports from a Wild Country,* p. 5.
28 Stanner, *The Dreaming and Other Essays,* p. 119.
29 Soutphommasane, *Reclaiming Patriotism,* p. 53.
30 Attwood and Foster, *Frontier Conflict,* p. 13.
31 Soutphommasane, *Reclaiming Patriotism,* p. 17.
32 Curthoys, 'Constructing national histories', in Attwood and Foster, *Frontier Conflict,* p. 185.
33 Reynolds, *Why Weren't We Told?,* p. 245.
34 Attwood and Foster, *Frontier Conflict,* p. 12.
35 McKenna, 'Anzac Day', in Lake and Reynolds, *What's Wrong with Anzac?,* p. 123.
36 Curthoys, 'Constructing national histories', in Attwood and Foster, *Frontier Conflict,* p. 187.
37 Geoffrey Blainey, 'Drawing up a balance sheet of our history', *Quadrant,* July–August 1993. Black armbands, as a symbol of mourning, have been a feature of twentieth-century Aboriginal politics in Australia; see Mark McKenna, *Different Perspectives in Black Armband History,* Research paper 5 1997–98, Parliamentary Library, Parliament of Australia, <http://www.aph.gpv.au/library/pubs/rp/1997–98/98rp05.htm>.
38 John Howard, 'The Liberal tradition: The beliefs and values which guide the Federal Government', Sir Robert Menzies Lecture, 18 November 1996, <http://www.menzieslecture.org/1996.html>.
39 Soutphommasane, *Reclaiming Patriotism,* p. 54.
40 See Ron Brunton, 'Betraying the victims: The "Stolen Genera-

tions" Report', *IPA Backgrounder*, Vol. 10, No. 1, 1998; Reynolds, *Why Weren't We Told?*; Keith Windschuttle, *The Fabrication of Aboriginal History, Volume One: Van Diemen's Land 1803–1847*, Macleay Press, Sydney, 2002; Robert Manne (ed.), *Whitewash: On Keith Windschuttle's Fabrication of Aboriginal History*, Black Inc, Melbourne, 2003; Stuart Macintyre and Anna Clark, *The History Wars*, Melbourne University Publishing, Melbourne, 2003 among others.

41 Evans, 'The country has another past', in Peters-Little et al., *Passionate Histories*, p. 10.
42 Rose, *Reports from a Wild Country*, p. 30.
43 Julie Marcus, *A Dark Smudge upon the Sand: Essays on race, guilt and the national consciousness*, LhR Press, Sydney, 1999, pp. 12–13.
44 Human Rights and Equal Opportunities Commission, *Bringing them Home*, pp. 36–7.
45 Coined by historian Peter Read in the 1980s, the term 'stolen generation' has, according to Robert Manne, taken on a similar significance for Indigenous Australians as the term 'the Holocaust' has for Jews; Robert Manne, 'In denial: the stolen generation and the Right', *Quarterly Essay*, Issue 1, 2001, p. 82.
46 Robert Manne, *The Barren Years: John Howard and Australian political culture*, Text Publishing, Melbourne, 2001, p. 38.
47 McKenna, 'Anzac Day', in Lake and Reynolds, *What's Wrong with Anzac?*, p. 123.
48 Augoustinos and Le Conteur, 'On whether to apologise', in Branscombe and Doosje, *Collective Guilt*, pp. 255–6.
49 Evans, 'The country has another past', in Peters-Little et al., *Passionate Histories*, p. 12.
50 ibid., p. 13.
51 Goot and Rowse, *Divided Nation?*, p. 160.
52 Soutphommasane, *Reclaiming Patriotism*, p. 53.
53 Wolfe, *Settler Colonialism*, p. 33.
54 Rose, *Reports from a Wild Country*, p. 23.

55 Schlink, *Guilt about the Past,* p. 50.
56 Anderson, *Imagined Communities,* p. 204.
57 Curthoys, 'Constructing national histories', in Attwood and Foster, *Frontier Conflict,* p. 185.
58 Rose, *Reports from a Wild Country,* pp. 13–14.
59 Curthoys, 'Constructing national histories', in Attwood and Foster, *Frontier Conflict,* p. 198.
60 John Docker and Gerhard Fischer (eds), *Race, Colour and Identity in Australia and New Zealand,* UNSW Press, Sydney, 2000, p. 11.
61 Susanne Schech and Jane Haggis, 'Migrancy, whiteness and the settler self in contemporary Australia', in Docker and Fischer, *Race, Colour and Identity,* p. 232.
62 Cowlishaw, *Blackfellas,* pp. 5–6.
63 Attwood and Foster, *Frontier Conflict,* p. 13.
64 Roccas et al., 'Exonerating cognitions', in Branscombe and Doosje, *Collective Guilt,* pp. 135–6.
65 Curthoys, 'Constructing national histories', in Attwood and Foster, *Frontier Conflict,* p. 187.
66 Govier, *Taking Wrongs Seriously,* p. 49.
67 Kevin Gilbert, *Because a White Man'll Never Do It,* Angus & Robertson Classics, HarperCollins Publishers, Sydney, 2002 [1973], p. 11.
68 Judy Atkinson, *Trauma Trails, Recreating Song Lines: The transgenerational effects of trauma in Indigenous Australia,* Spinifex Press, Melbourne, 2002, p. 70.
69 Alan Atkinson, 'Historians and moral disgust', in Attwood and Foster, *Frontier Conflict,* p. 119.
70 Reynolds, *Why Weren't We Told?,* p. 258.
71 Heifetz, *Leadership Without Easy Answers,* p. 235.
72 See Maddison, *Black Politics,* p. xxxvii.
73 Rachel Seider, 'War, peace and the politics of memory in Guatemala', in Biggar, *Burying the Past,* p. 210.

74 Ahmed, 'The politics of bad feeling', p. 83.
75 Forsberg, 'The philosophy and practice of dealing with the past', in Biggar, *Burying the Past,* p. 67.
76 Rose, *Reports from a Wild Country,* p. 11.
77 Forsberg, 'The philosophy and practice of dealing with the past', in Biggar, *Burying the Past,* p. 74.
78 Cowlishaw, *Blackfellas,* p. 243.
79 Barkan, *Guilt of Nations,* pp. xxi, xxii.
80 Bashir, 'Accommodating historically oppressed social groups', in Kymlicka and Bashir, *Politics of Reconciliation,* pp. 49, 53.
81 Schlink, *Guilt about the Past,* pp. 26–8.
82 Rose, *Reports from a Wild Country,* pp. 15, 16, 18.
83 Bashir Bashir and Will Kymlicka, 'Introduction: Struggles for inclusion and reconciliation in modern democracies', in Kymlicka and Bashir, *Politics of Reconciliation,* pp. 11–12.

Chapter 3 Intervention and redemption

1 Wolfe, *Settler Colonialism,* p. 169.
2 Stanner, *The Dreaming and Other Essays,* p. 120.
3 ibid.
4 Tully, *Public Philosophy in a New Key,* p. 255.
5 Povinelli, *The Cunning of Recognition,* p. 154.
6 Freeman, 'Past wrongs and liberal justice', p. 218.
7 Ahmed, 'The politics of bad feeling', p. 77.
8 ibid., p. 82.
9 John Howard and Amanda Vanstone, 'Transcript of the Prime Minister The Hon. John Howard MP Joint Press Conference with Senator Amanda Vanstone', Parliament House, Canberra, 15 April 2004.
10 Melinda Hinkson, 'Media images and the politics of hope', in *Culture Crisis: Anthropology and politics in Aboriginal Australia,*

Jon Altman and Melinda Hinkson (eds), UNSW Press, Sydney, 2010, p. 23.

11 For discussion of this, see Maddison, *Black Politics*, pp. 26–8.

12 Amanda Vanstone, 'Message from the Minister', in *Australian Government Feature: Indigenous Affairs—Sharing Responsibility*, 2005, <http://www.indigenous.gov.au/rpa/koori_mail.ins.pdf>.

13 Michael Morrissey, 'The Australian state and Indigenous people 1900–2006', *Journal of Sociology*, Vol. 42, No. 4, 2006, p. 352.

14 Human Rights and Equal Opportunities Commission, *Bringing them Home*, pp. 36–7.

15 Parliamentary Debate, House of Representatives, Questions without Notice: Aboriginals: Stolen Generations, 3 April 2000, 15008.

16 Hinkson, 'Media images and the politics of hope', in Altman and Hinkson, *Culture Crisis*, p. 230.

17 Rex Wild and Patricia Anderson, *Ampe akelyernemane meke mekarle: Little children are sacred*, Report of the Northern Territory Board of Inquiry into the protection of children from sexual abuse, 2007, <www.nt.gov.au/dcm/inquirysaac/pdf/bipacss_final_report.pdf>.

18 Melinda Hinkson, 'In the name of the child', in *Coercive Reconciliation: Stabilise, Normalise, Exit Aboriginal Australia*, John Altman and Melinda Hinkson (eds), Arena Publications, Melbourne, 2007, p. 1.

19 Malcolm Brough, 'National emergency response to protect children in the Northern Territory', Media release, 21 June 2007.

20 Andrew Lattas and Barry Morris, 'The politics of suffering and the politics of anthropology', in Altman and Hinkson, *Culture Crisis*, p. 62.

21 Peter Yu, Bill Gray and Marcia Ella Duncan, Report of the NTER Review Board, Department of Families, Housing, Community Services and Indigenous Affairs, Canberra, 2008,

<http://www.nterreview.gov.au/docs/report_nter_review/docs/Report_NTER_Review_October08.pdf>.

22 Misha Schubert, 'UN delegate blasts "demeaning" NT intervention', *The Age*, 28 August 2009, <http://www.theage.com.au/national/un-delegate-blasts-demeaning-nt-intervention–20090827-fl6q.html>.

23 *Sydney Morning Herald*, 'Indigenous poverty "outrageous": Amnesty', 18 November 2009.

24 Jenny Macklin, 'Strengthening the Northern Territory Emergency Response', joint media release with Warren Snowdon MP, member for Lingiari, 25 November 2009, <http://www.jennymacklin.fahcsia.gov.au/mediareleases/2009/Pages/strengthenening_nter_25nov2009.aspx.

25 Lattas and Morris, 'The politics of suffering', in Altman and Hinkson, *Culture Crisis*, p. 84.

26 Australian Human Rights Commission, *Submission to the Senate Community Affairs Committee on the Welfare Reform and Reinstatement of the RDA Bill 2009 and other Bills*, 10 February 2010.

27 Alastair Nicolson, *Social Security and Other Legislation Amendment (Welfare Reform and Reinstatement of Racial Discrimination Bill 2009): Notes and Comment*, 2005, <http://stoptheintervention.org/rda-new-legislation/notes-and-comment-by-prof-nicholson>.

28 Sutton, *The Politics of Suffering*.

29 Melinda Hinkson, 'Introduction: Anthropology and the culture wars', in Altman and Hinkson, *Culture Crisis*, p. 1.

30 See for example Ron Brunton, *Black Suffering, White Guilt? Aboriginal disadvantage and the Royal Commission into Deaths in Custody*, IPA Current Issues, Institute of Public Affairs, Perth, 1993; Gary Johns (ed.), *Waking up to Dreamtime: The illusion of Aboriginal self-determination*, Media Masters, Singapore, 2001.

31 Elizabeth Povinelli, 'Indigenous politics in late liberalism', in Altman and Hinkson, *Culture Crisis*, pp. 23–5.

32 Peter Billings, 'Social welfare experiments in Australia: More trials for Aboriginal families?', *Journal of Social Security Law*, Vol. 17, No. 3, 2010, p. 180.
33 Noel Pearson, 'An end to the tears', *The Australian*, 23 June 2007.
34 Noel Pearson, 'White guilt, victimhood and the quest for a radical centre', *Griffith Review*, 16, 2007, pp. 17, 26.
35 Cape York Institute, *From Hand Out to Hand Up: Cape York welfare reform project, design recommendations*, Cape York Institute for Policy and Leadership, Cairns, 2007, p. 44, my emphasis.
36 Atkinson, *Trauma Trails*, p. 68.
37 Pearson, 'White guilt', p. 53.
38 Sutton, *The Politics of Suffering*, pp. 11–12.
39 ibid., p. 41.
40 Cowlishaw, *Blackfellas*, p. 195.
41 Jon Altman, 'What "liberal consensus"?', *New Matilda*, 16 July 2009, <http://newmatilda.com/2009/07/16/what-liberal-consensus>.
42 See for example Harvard Project on American Indian Economic Development, *The State of Native Nations: Conditions under US policies of self-determination*, Oxford University Press, New York, 2008; Miriam Jorgensen (ed.), *Rebuilding Native Nations: Strategies for governance and development*, University of Arizona Press, Tucson, 2007.
43 Watson, 'Aboriginal Sovereignties', in Perera, *Our Patch*, pp. 24, 28.
44 Veracini, 'Settler collective', p. 367.
45 Tim Rowse, 'Mabo and moral anxiety', *Meanjin*, 2, 1993, pp. 229–52.
46 Cowlishaw, *Blackfellas*, p. 173.
47 James Tully, 'Recognition and dialogue: The emergence of a new field', *Critical Review of International Social and Political Philosophy*, Vol. 7, No. 3, 2004, pp. 89–90.
48 Rouhana, 'Reconciling history', in Kymlicka and Bashir, *Politics of Reconciliation*, p. 75.

49 Rose, *Reports from a Wild Country*, p. 23.
50 ibid.
51 Wolfe, *Settler Colonialism*, p. 34.
52 Watson, 'Aboriginal Sovereignties', in Perera, *Our Patch*, p. 28.
53 ibid., pp. 28–9.
54 Wolfe, *Settler Colonialism*, p. 2.
55 Tully, *Public Philosophy in a New Key*, p. 260.
56 ibid., p. 262.
57 Heifetz, *Leadership without Easy Answers*, pp. 46–7.
58 Tess Lea, *Bureaucrats and Bleeding Hearts: Indigenous health in northern Australia*, UNSW Press, Sydney, 2008, pp. x–xi.
59 Povinelli, 'Indigenous politics in late liberalism', in Altman and Hinkson, *Culture Crisis*, p. 26.
60 Curthoys, 'Constructing national histories', in Attwood and Foster, *Frontier Conflict*, p. 199.
61 Tully, 'Recognition and dialogue', p. 91.
62 Lea, *Bureaucrats and Bleeding Hearts*, pp. 11–12.
63 Gillian Cowlishaw, 'Helping anthropologists, still', in Altman and Hinkson, *Culture Crisis*, p. 52.
64 Lea, *Bureaucrats and Bleeding Hearts*, p. 15, emphasis in the original.
65 Cowlishaw, 'Helping anthropologists, still', in Altman and Hinkson, *Culture Crisis*, p. 50.
66 Lea, *Bureaucrats and Bleeding Hearts*, p. x.
67 Pearson, 'White guilt', p. 49.
68 Emma Kowal, 'Is culture the problem or the solution? Outstation health and the politics of remoteness', in Altman and Hinkson, *Culture Crisis*, pp. 189–92.
69 Hinkson, 'Introduction', in Altman and Hinkson, *Culture Crisis*, p. 13.
70 Tully, 'Recognition and dialogue', p. 91.

Chapter 4 Not just empty vessels

1 Pearson quoted in Marcia Langton, 'The shock of the new: A postcolonial dilemma for Australianist anthropology', in Altman and Hinkson, *Culture Crisis*, p. 94.
2 Maddison, *Black Politics*, pp. xxxvii–xxxviii.
3 Goot and Rowse, *Divided Nation?*, pp. 18, 28.
4 Kowal, 'Is culture the problem or the solution?', in Altman and Hinkson, *Culture Crisis*, p. 192.
5 Povinelli, 'Indigenous politics in late liberalism', in Altman and Hinkson, *Culture Crisis*, p. 18.
6 Sutton, *The Politics of Suffering*, pp. 10–11.
7 Smith, *The Spectre of Truganini*, p. 10.
8 Meaghan Morris, 'Beyond assimilation: Aboriginality, media history and public memory', *Rouge*, 2004, <http://www.rouge.com.au/3/beyond.html>.
9 Smith, *The Spectre of Truganini*, p. 34.
10 Helene S. Lorenz and Mary Watkins, 'Depth psychology and colonialism: Individuation, seeing through, and liberation', Unpublished paper, 2000, <http://www.pacifica.edu/gems/creatingcommunityw/DepthPsychologyColonialism.pdf>.
11 Stanner, *The Dreaming and Other Essays*, pp. 186–91.
12 Tim Rowse, 'Indigenous politics', in *The Australian Study of Politics*, R.A.W. Rhodes (ed.), Palgrave Macmillan, Basingstoke, 2009, pp. 314–15.
13 Geoffrey Gray, *A Cautious Silence: The politics of Australian anthropology*, Aboriginal Studies Press, Canberra, 2007, p. 3.
14 ibid., p. 17.
15 ibid., p. 20.
16 Aileen Moreton-Robinson, *Talkin' up to the White Woman: Indigenous women and feminism*, University of Queensland Press, Brisbane, 2000, p. 93.
17 Reynolds, *Why Weren't We Told?*, p. 2.

18 Reconciliation Australia, Australian Reconciliation Barometer, Reconciliation Australia, Canberra, 2008.
19 Dodson, Mick 'Respect. Relationships. We have come so far', *Sydney Morning Herald*, 17 January 2010.
20 ibid.
21 ibid., p. 257.
22 Cowlishaw, 'Helping anthropologists, still', in Altman and Hinkson, *Culture Crisis*, p. 48.
23 Albert Memmi, *The Colonizer and the Colonized*, Beacon Press, Boston, 1965, p. 71.
24 Cowlishaw, *Blackfellas*, p. 24.
25 Tochluk, *Witnessing Whiteness*, p. 20.
26 Jensen, *Heart of Whiteness*, pp. 54–5.
27 Cowlishaw, *Blackfellas*, p. 13.
28 Pearson, 'White guilt', p. 28.
29 ibid., p. 29.
30 ibid., pp. 30–1.
31 Hage, *White Nation*, p. 29.
32 Reynolds, *Why Weren't We Told?*, p. 42.
33 Hage, *White Nation*, pp. 31–2.
34 ibid., p. 32.
35 Meredith J. Green and Christopher C. Sonn, 'Problematising the discourses of the dominant: Whiteness and reconciliation', *Journal of Community and Applied Social Psychology*, Vol. 16, 2006, p. 381.
36 Green and Sonn, 'Examining discourses of whiteness', pp. 478, 480.
37 Jensen, *Heart of Whiteness*, pp. xvii–xviii.
38 Kendall, *Understanding White Privilege*, p. 1.
39 Subăsić and Reynolds, 'Beyond "practical" reconciliation', p. 262.
40 Wendy Brady and Michelle Carey, 'Talkin' up whiteness: A black and white dialogue', in Docker and Fischer, *Race Colour and Identity*, pp. 275, 279.

41 Schech and Haggis, 'Migrancy, whiteness and the settler self', in Docker and Fischer, *Race, Colour and Identity*, p. 237.
42 Cowlishaw, *Blackfellas*, p. 11.
43 Kendall, *Understanding White Privilege*, p. 38.
44 Kowal, 'Is culture the problem or the solution?', in Altman and Hinkson, *Culture Crisis*, p. 186.
45 Green and Sonn, 'Examining discourses of whiteness', p. 479.
46 Green and Sonn, 'Problematising the discourses of the dominant', p. 382.
47 Elaine Thompson, *Fair Enough: Egalitarianism in Australia*, UNSW Press, Sydney, 1994, p. 128.
48 Heifetz, *Leadership without Easy Answers*, p. 23.
49 ibid., pp. 31–2.
50 Subăsić and Reynolds, 'Beyond "practical" reconciliation', pp. 250–1.
51 Tully, *Public Philosophy in a New Key*, p. 232.
52 Heifetz, *Leadership without Easy Answers*, p. 25.
53 Keal, *European Conquest and the Rights of Indigenous Peoples*, pp. 157, 161.
54 Govier, *Taking Wrongs Seriously*, pp. 52–3.
55 Wolfe, *Settler Colonialism*, p. 177.
56 Australian Broadcasting Corporation, 'Ill woman says her race stopped people from helping', *PM*, ABC Radio National, 7 March 2006, <http://www.abc.net.au/pm/content/2006/s1586142.htm>.
57 Green and Sonn, 'Examining discourses of whiteness', p. 480.
58 Rose, *Reports from a Wild Country*, pp. 1–2.
59 Jackie Huggins, *Sister Girl: The writings of an Aboriginal activist and historian*, University of Queensland Press, St Lucia, 1998, p. x.
60 Maddison, *Black Politics*, p. xxxviii.
61 Heifetz, *Leadership without Easy Answers*, p. 62.
62 Jensen, *Heart of Whiteness*, p. 80.

63 Goot and Rowse, *Divided Nation?*, p. 164.
64 Moreton-Robinson, *Talkin' up to the White Woman.*
65 Reynolds, *Why Weren't We Told?*, p. 257.

Chapter 5 Referendum, reconciliation and apology

1 Inga Clendinnen, *Dancing with Strangers,* Text Publishing, Melbourne, 2008.
2 Ann Curthoys, *Freedom Ride: A Freedom Rider Remembers,* Allen & Unwin, Sydney, 2002.
3 Russel Ward, *The Australian Legend,* second edition, Oxford University Press, Melbourne, 1966.
4 Curthoys, 'Constructing national histories', in Attwood and Foster, *Frontier Conflict,* pp. 193–3.
5 Reynolds, *This Whispering in our Hearts,* p. xiv.
6 Holding quoted in Goot and Rowse, *Divided Nation?*, pp. 62, 75.
7 Mick Dodson, 'How well do we know each other?', The annual ANU Reconciliation Lecture, Australian National University, Canberra, 5 June 2009, p. 4.
8 Rose, *Reports from a Wild Country,* p. 22.
9 Tully, *Public Philosophy in a New Key,* p. 241.
10 Jennifer Clark, *Aborigines and Activism: Race, Aborigines and the coming of the sixties to Australia,* University of Western Australia Press, Perth, 2008, p. 123.
11 Bain Attwood and Andrew Markus, 'Representation matters: The 1967 referendum and citizenship', in Nicolas Peterson and Will Sanders (eds), *Citizenship and Indigenous Australians: Changing conceptions and possibilities,* Cambridge University Press, Cambridge, 1998, p. 131.
12 Frances Peters-Little, 'Remembering the referendum with compassion', in Peters-Little et al., *Passionate Histories.*
13 Sue Taffe, *Black and White Together: FCAATSI, The Federal Council of*

Aborigines and Torres Strait Islanders 1958–1973, University of Queensland Press, Brisbane, 2005, pp. 4, 12–13.

14 Jack Horner, *Seeking Racial Justice: An insider's memoir of the movement for Aboriginal advancement, 1938–1978*, Aboriginal Studies Press, Canberra, 2004; Taffe, *Black and White Together*.

15 Clark, *Aborigines and Activism*, p. 185.

16 Francesca Merlan, 'Indigenous movements in Australia', *Annual Review of Anthropology*, Vol. 34, 2005, p. 484.

17 Clark, *Aborigines and Activism*, pp. 198–201.

18 Sue Taffe, 'The role of FCAATSI in the 1967 referendum: Mythmaking about citizenship or political strategy', in Tim Rowse (ed.), *Contesting Assimilation*, API Network, Perth, 2005, p. 294.

19 Goot and Rowse, *Divided Nation?*, p. 59.

20 Quoted in Maddison, *Black Politics*, p. 38.

21 Mick Dodson, 'Unfinished business: A shadow across our relationships', in *Treaty—Let's get it Right!*, Hannah McGlade (ed.), Aboriginal Studies Press, Canberra, 2003, p. 31.

22 Bashir and Kymlicka, 'Introduction', in Kymlicka and Bashir, *Politics of Reconciliation*, pp. 3–4.

23 Angela Pratt, Catriona Elder and Cath Ellis, '"Papering over differences": Australian nationhood and the normative discourse of reconciliation', in *Reconciliation, Multiculturalism, Identities: Difficult dialogue, sensible solutions*, Mary Kalantzis and Bill Cope (eds), Common Ground Publishing, Melbourne, 2001; Subăsić and Reynolds, 'Beyond "practical" reconciliation'.

24 Royal Commission into Aboriginal Deaths in Custody, *National Report*, Vol. 1, Australian Government Publishing Service, Canberra, 1991.

25 Robert Tickner, *Taking a Stand: Land Rights to Reconciliation*, Allen & Unwin, Sydney, 2001, p. 33.

26 Andrew Gunstone, *Unfinished Business: The Australian formal reconciliation process*, Australian Scholarly Publishing, Melbourne, 2007, p. 37.

27 John Howard, Address to Corroboree 2000, Council for Aboriginal Reconciliation, Sydney, 27 May 2000, <http://www.austlii.edu.au/au/orgs/car/media/Prime%20Minister's%20address%20to%20Corroboree%202000.htm>.
28 Maddison, *Black Politics*, p. 11.
29 Jon Altman, 'Practical reconciliation and the new mainstreaming: Will it make a difference to Indigenous Australians?', *Dialogue*, Vol. 23, No. 2, 2004, p. 39.
30 Will Sanders, 'Never even adequate: Reconciliation and Indigenous affairs', in *Howard's Second and Third Governments: Australian Commonwealth Administration 1998–2004*, C. Aulich and R. Wettenhall (eds), UNSW Press, Sydney, 2005, p. 156.
31 Quoted in Sanders, 'Never even adequate', p. 156.
32 Gilbert, quoted in Mudrooroo, *Us Mob: History, culture, struggle. An introduction to Indigenous Australia*, HarperCollins Publishers, Sydney, 1995, p. 228.
33 Howard, 'Opening Address to the Australian Reconciliation Convention'.
34 Patrick Dodson, *Beyond the Mourning Gate: Dealing with unfinished business*, The Wentworth Lecture, 12 May 2000, AATSIS, Canberra, p. 15.
35 Govier, *Taking Wrongs Seriously*, pp. 12–13.
36 Schlink, *Guilt about the Past*, p. 78.
37 Rouhana, 'Reconciling history', in Kymlicka and Bashir, *Politics of Reconciliation*, pp. 75–6.
38 Subăsić and Reynolds, 'Beyond "practical" reconciliation', pp. 245–6.
39 Dodson, 'How well do we know each other?', p. 3.
40 Rose, *Reports from a Wild Country*, p. 185.
41 Govier, *Taking Wrongs Seriously*, p. 21.
42 Halloran, 'Indigenous reconciliation in Australia', p. 2.
43 Dodson, 'How well do we know each other?', p. 4.
44 Green and Sonn, 'Problematising the discourses of the

dominant', p. 380; Green and Sonn, 'Examining discourses of whiteness', p. 483.
45 Reconciliation Australia, *Australian Reconciliation Barometer: Comparative report,* Reconciliation Australia, Canberra, 2008, p. 5.
46 ibid
47 Pratt et al., 'Papering over differences', in Kalantzis and Cope, *Reconciliation, Multiculturalism, Identities,* p. 157.
48 Brennan et al., *Treaty,* p. 122.
49 Subăsić and Reynolds, 'Beyond "practical" reconciliation', p. 246.
50 Sutton, *Politics of Suffering,* p. 203.
51 Duncan et al., *Imagining Australia,* pp. 33–5.
52 Seider, 'War, peace and the politics of memory in Guatemala', in Biggar, *Burying the Past,* p. 229.
53 David Cooper, 'Escaping from the shadowland: Campaigning for Indigenous justice in Australia', *Indigenous Law Bulletin,* Vol. 16, Issue 10, 2005, p. 15.
54 Barkan, *Guilt of Nations,* p. xxix.
55 Sorry Books, MS3569, Australian Institute of Aboriginal and Torres Strait Islander Studies, Canberra, 1998–2002, <http://www.aiatsis.gov.au/collections/docs/findingaids/MS3569_sorry.pdf>.
56 Goot and Rowse, *Divided Nation?,* p. 141.
57 Kevin Rudd, 'Apology to Australia's Indigenous peoples', House of Representatives, Parliament House, Canberra, 13 February 2008, <http://www.pm.gov.au/media/Speech/2008/speech_0073.cfm>.
58 Soutphommasane, *Reclaiming Patriotism,* pp. 4, 15.
59 Branscombe and Doosje, *Collective Guilt,* 2004.
60 Aaron Lazare, *On Apology,* Oxford University Press, New York, 2004.
61 Minow, *Between Vengeance and Forgiveness,* p. 114.

62 Barkan, *Guilt of Nations*, p. 323.
63 Augoustinos and Le Conteur, 'On whether to apologise' in Branscombe and Doosje, *Collective Guilt*, p. 240.
64 Govier, *Taking Wrongs Seriously*, pp. 67–9.
65 Minow, *Between Vengeance and Forgiveness*, p. 114.
66 ibid., p. 116.
67 Jean Bethke Elshtain, 'Politics and forgiveness', in Biggar, *Burying the Past*, pp. 49–50.
68 Robyn Mallett, and Janet Swim, 'Collective guilt in the United States: Predicting support for social policies that alleviate social injustice', in Branscombe and Doosje, *Collective Guilt*, p. 67.
69 Schlink, *Guilt about the Past*, pp. 70–1.
70 Barkan, *Guilt of Nations*, p. xxix.
71 Isabelle Auguste, 'On the significance of saying "sorry": Apology and reconciliation in Australia', in Peters-Little et al., *Passionate Histories*, p. 321.
72 Bashir, 'Accommodating historically oppressed social groups', in Kymlicka and Bashir, *Politics of Reconciliation*, pp. 57–8.
73 See Keith Windschuttle, 'How not to run a museum: People's history at the postmodern museum', *Quadrant*, September 2001, <http://www.sydneyline.com/National%20Museum.htm>; Dawn Casey, 'Battleground of ideas and histories', in Dimity Reed (ed.) *Tangled Destinies: National Museum of Australia*, Images Publishing Group, Mulgrave, Victoria, 2002, among others.
74 Australian Broadcasting Corporation, 'War memorial battle over frontier conflict recognition', *The 7.30 Report*, 26 February 2009, <http://www.abc.net.au/7.30/content/2009/s2502535.htm>.
75 Patrick Dodson, 'Reconciliation', in *Dear Mr Rudd: Ideas for a better Australia*, Robert Manne (ed.), Black Inc, Melbourne, 2008, p. 33.
76 Dodson, 'How well do we know each other?', p. 4.
77 Reynolds, *This Whispering in our Hearts*, p. 249.

Chapter 6 Unsettling ourselves

1 Tim Wise, 'Your House is on Ground Zero (and Quite Without Permission)', *Red Room,* 2010, <http://www.redroom.com/blog/tim-wise/your-house-ground-zero-and-quite-without-permission>.
2 Barkan, *Guilt of Nations,* p. 328.
3 Heifetz, *Leadership Without Easy Answers,* pp. 239–40.
4 Rose, *Reports from a Wild Country,* p. 31.
5 Cowlishaw, *Blackfellas,* p. 100.
6 Rose, *Reports from a Wild Country,* p. 6.
7 Govier, *Taking Wrongs Seriously,* p. 52.
8 Memmi, *The Colonizer and the Colonized,* p. 147.
9 Kendall, *Understanding White Privilege,* pp. 33–5.
10 Heifetz, *Leadership Without Easy Answers,* p. 37.
11 Barkan, *Guilt of Nations,* p. xxxix.
12 Cowlishaw, *Blackfellas,* p. 169.
13 Tochluk, *Witnessing Whiteness,* p. 15.
14 Rose, *Reports from a Wild Country,* p. 34.
15 Duncan et al., *Imagining Australia,* pp. 9–10.
16 McKenna, 'Anzac Day', in Lake and Reynolds, *What's Wrong with Anzac?,* pp. 112–121.
17 Evans, 'The country has another past', in Peters-Little et al., *Passionate Histories,* pp. 12–13.
18 Marilyn Lake, 'Introduction: What have you done for your country?', in Lake and Reynolds, *What's Wrong with Anzac?,* pp. 1, 10–11.
19 Henry Reynolds, 'Are nations really made in war?', in Lake and Reynolds, *What's Wrong with Anzac?,* pp. 26, 42–3.
20 Soutphommasane, *Reclaiming Patriotism,* p. 63.
21 Duncan et al., *Imagining Australia,* p. 24.
22 Soutphommasane, *Reclaiming Patriotism,* p. 22.
23 ibid., p. 16.

24 Evans, 'The country has another past', in Peters-Little et al., *Passionate Histories*, p. 12.
25 McKenna, 'Anzac Day', in Lake and Reynolds, *What's Wrong with Anzac?*, pp. 25–7.
26 ibid., p. 133.
27 Soutphommasane, *Reclaiming Patriotism*, p. 32.
28 ibid., p. 40.
29 Halloran, 'Indigenous reconciliation in Australia', p. 14.
30 McGarty and Bliuc, 'Refining the meaning of the "collective"', in Branscombe and Doosje, *Collective Guilt*, p. 122.
31 Michael Schmitt et al. 'Gender inequality and the intensity of men's collective guilt', in Branscombe and Doosje, *Collective Guilt*, p. 84.
32 Williams, 'In praise of guilt', in Lenzerini, *Reparations for Indigenous Peoples*, p. 247.
33 Rose, *Reports from a Wild Country*, p. 30.
34 Cowlishaw, *Blackfellas*, p. 196.
35 Rose, *Reports from a Wild Country*, p. 47.
36 ibid.
37 Schlink, *Guilt about the Past*, p. 36.
38 Freeman, 'Past wrongs and liberal justice', p. 202.
39 Tom Calma, quoted in *Koori Mail*, 'Report anniversary a bittersweet time', 6 June 2007.
40 Schlink, *Guilt about the Past*, p. 36.
41 Minow, *Between Vengeance and Forgiveness*, p. 118.
42 Parekh, quoted in Freeman, 'Past wrongs and liberal justice', p. 202.
43 Minow, *Between Vengeance and Forgiveness*, p. 120.
44 Schlink, *Guilt about the Past*, p. 41.
45 Veracini, 'Settler collective, founding violence and disavowal', p. 374.
46 Barkan, *Guilt of Nations*, p. xviii.
47 Minow, *Between Vengeance and Forgiveness*, p. 122.

48 See for example Mary Jane Collier and Darrin Hicks, 'Discursive plurality: Negotiating cultural identities in public democratic dialogue', *Quest: An African Journal of Philosophy*, XVI, 1–2, 2002; James Tully, *Strange Multiplicity: Constitutionalism in an age of diversity*, Cambridge University Press, Cambridge, 1995; Tully, 'Recognition and dialogue'; Tully, *Public Philosophy in a New Key*; Iris Marion Young, *Justice and the Politics of Difference*, Princeton University Press, Princeton, 1990; Iris Marion Young, 'Communication and the Other', in Seyla Benhabib (ed.), *Democracy and Difference*, Princeton University Press, Princeton, 1996; Bhikhu Parekh, *Rethinking Multiculturalism: Cultural diversity and political theory*, Harvard University Press, Cambridge, MA, 2000, among others.

49 Tully, 'Recognition and dialogue', p. 91.

50 Tully, *Public Philosophy in a New Key*, p. 239.

51 Keal, *European Conquest and the Rights of Indigenous Peoples*, p. 172.

52 Sarah Maddison et al., *Democratic Dialogue: Finding the right model for Australia*, Discussion paper No. 1, Indigenous Policy and Dialogue Research Unit, University of New South Wales, 2009; Bettye Pruitt and Philip Thomas, *Democratic Dialogue: A handbook for practitioners*, General Secretariat of the Organization of American States, International Institute for Democracy and Electoral Assistance, and United Nations Development Program, New York, 2007.

53 Tully, *Public Philosophy in a New Key*, p. 239.

54 Collier and Hicks, 'Discursive plurality', p. 213.

55 Tully, *Public Philosophy in a New Key*, p. 239.

56 Keal, *European Conquest and the Rights of Indigenous Peoples*, p. 164.

57 Michael Rabinder James, 'Critical intercultural dialogue', *Polity*, Vol. 31, No. 4, 1999, p. 590.

58 Tully, *Strange Multiplicity*, pp. 40–1.

59 W. Isaacs, *Dialogue and the Art of Thinking Together*, Doubleday, New York, 1999, p. 19.

60 Elena Diez Pinto, *Towards the Construction of a Dialogue Typology*, Democratic Dialogue Project, United Nations Development Program, Regional Bureau for Latin America and the Caribbean, 2003, p. 2; Pruitt and Thomas, *Democratic Dialogue*.
61 Isaacs, *Dialogue and the Art of Thinking Together*, p. 19.
62 Maggie Herzig and Laura Chasin, *Fostering Dialogue across Divides: A nuts and bolts guide from the public conversations project*, Public Conversations Project, Watertown, Massachusetts, 2006, p. 1.
63 Rose, *Reports from a Wild Country*, p. 22.
64 Isaacs, *Dialogue and the Art of Thinking Together*, p. 19.
65 Rose, *Reports from a Wild Country*, p. 22.
66 Herzig and Chasin, *Fostering Dialogue across Divides*, pp. 1–2.
67 See for example David Bohm, *On Dialogue*, Routledge, London, 1996; Isaacs, *Dialogue and the Art of Thinking Together*; Bela Banathy and Patrick Jenlink, *Dialogue as a Means of Collective Communication*, Kluwer, New York, 2005; Pruitt and Thomas, *Democratic Dialogue*; Adam Kahane, *Solving Tough Problems: An open way of talking, listening and creating new realities*, Berrett-Koehler Publishers, San Fancisco, 2004, among others.
68 Isaacs, *Dialogue and the Art of Thinking Together*, p. 360.
69 M. Davis, 'Indigenous knowledge: Beyond protection, towards dialogue', *Australian Journal of Indigenous Education*, 37, 2008, pp. 25–6.
70 Tully, *Public Philosophy in a New Key*, p. 239.
71 Heifetz, *Leadership Without Easy Answers*, pp. 33, 35.
72 Tully, 'Recognition and dialogue', pp. 92–3.
73 Tully, *Public Philosophy in a New Key*, p. 101.
74 Iris Marion Young, 'Hybrid democracy: Iroquois federalism and the postcolonial project', in Duncan Ivison, Paul Patton and Will Sanders (eds), *Political Theory and the Rights of Indigenous Peoples*, Cambridge University Press, New York, 2000, pp. 237–8.
75 Docker and Fischer, *Race, Colour and Identity*, pp. 5–6.

76 Ann Curthoys, 'An uneasy conversation: The multicultural and the indigenous', in Docker and Fisher, *Race, Colour and Identity*, pp. 21–36.
77 ibid., p. 32.
78 Rose, *Reports from a Wild Country*, p. 213.
79 Tully, *Public Philosophy in a New Key*, pp. 229–30.
80 ibid., p. 223.
81 ibid., p. 230.
82 Barkan, *Guilt of Nations*, p. xxvi.
83 Taiaiake Alfred, *Wasáse: Indigenous pathways of action and freedom*, Broadview Press, Peterborough, Ontario, 2005, p. 180.
84 Cowlishaw, *Blackfellas*, p. 55.
85 Tully, *Public Philosophy in a New Key*, p. 223.
86 Rose, *Reports from a Wild Country*, p. 24.
87 Govier, *Taking Wrongs Seriously*, p. 208.
88 Williams, 'In praise of guilt', in Lenzerini, *Reparations for Indigenous Peoples*, p. 248.
89 Schlink, *Guilt about the Past*, p. 38.
90 Kendall, *Understanding White Privilege*, p. 160.
91 Rose, *Reports from a Wild Country*, p. 1.

Epilogue

1 See Australian Labor Party, *The Australian Greens and the Australian Labor Party—Agreement*, 2010.
2 George Williams and David Hume, *People Power: The history and the future of the referendum in Australia*, UNSW Press, Sydney, 2010.
3 Committee on the Elimination of Racial Discrimination, *Concluding Observations—Australia*, United Nations, New York, 2010.
4 Memmi, *The Colonizer and the Colonized*, p. 147.

5 Jean Paul Sartre, 'Preface', in *The Wretched of the Earth,* Frantz Fanon, Grove Press, New York, 1961, p. lvii.
6 Schlink, *Guilt about the Past,* p. 33.
7 Grace Karskens, *The Colony: A history of early Sydney,* Allen & Unwin, Sydney, 2010, p. 545.
8 Schlink, *Guilt about the Past,* p. 43.
9 Bashir and Kymlicka, 'Introduction', in Kymlicka and Bashir, *Politics of Reconciliation,* p. 12.
10 Lickell et al., 'Evocation of moral emotions', in Branscombe and Doosje, *Collective Guilt,* p. 51.
11 Bashir and Kymlicka, 'Introduction', in Kymlicka and Bashir, *Politics of Reconciliation,* p. 12.
12 Tully, *Public Philosophy in a New Key,* pp. 232, 255.
13 Tully, 'Recognition and dialogue', p. 99.
14 Schlink, *Guilt about the Past,* pp. 84–5.
15 Kendall, *Understanding White Privilege,* p. 39.
16 Jensen, *Heart of Whiteness,* p. 65.
17 Schlink, *Guilt about the Past,* p. 29.
18 Anderson, *Imagined Communities,* p. 159.
19 Soutphommasane, *Reclaiming Patriotism,* p. 30.
20 Attwood and Foster, *Frontier Conflict,* p. 26.
21 Minow, *Between Vengeance and Forgiveness,* p. 147.
22 Bashir and Kymlicka, 'Introduction', in Kymlicka and Bashir, *Politics of Reconciliation,* pp. 14–15.
23 ibid.
24 Soutphommasane, *Reclaiming Patriotism,* pp. 67–8, 80.
25 Docker and Fischer, *Race, Colour and Identity,* p. 6.
26 Watson, 'Aboriginal Sovereignty', in Perera, *Our Patch,* p. 28.
27 Kendall, *Understanding White Privilege,* p. 18.
28 Barkan, *Guilt of Nations,* p. 329.
29 Brooks, 'The age of apology', in Brooks, *When Sorry Isn't Enough,* p. 6.
30 Memmi, *The Colonizer and the Colonized,* p. 18.

31 Jensen, *Heart of Whiteness*, p. xx.
32 Rose, *Reports from a Wild Country*, p. 177.
33 Govier, *Taking Wrongs Seriously*, p. 17.
34 Kahane, *Power and Love*, pp. 121–2.
35 ibid., p. 132.
36 ibid., p. 130.
37 Williams, 'In praise of guilt', in Lenzerini, *Reparations for Indigenous Peoples*, p. 249.
38 Cowlishaw, *Blackfellas*, p. 172.
39 Schlink, *Guilt about the Past*, pp. 87–8.

Bibliography

Ahmed, Sara, 'The politics of bad feeling', *Australian Critical Race and Whiteness Studies Association Journal*, Vol. 1, 2005, pp. 72–85

Alfred, Taiaiake, *Wasáse: Indigenous pathways of action and freedom*, Broadview Press, Peterborough, Ontario, 2005

Altman, Jon, 'Practical reconciliation and the new mainstreaming: Will it make a difference to Indigenous Australians?', *Dialogue*, Vol. 23, No. 2, 2004, pp. 35–46

—— 'What "liberal consensus"?', *New Matilda*, 16 July 2009, <http://newmatilda.com/2009/07/16/what-liberal-consensus>

Anderson, Benedict, *Imagined Communities: Reflections on the origins and spread of nationalism*, Verso, London, 2006

Atkinson, Alan, 'Historians and moral disgust', in Bain Attwood and Stephen Foster (eds), *Frontier Conflict: The Australian experience*, National Museum of Australia, Canberra, 2003, pp. 113–119

Atkinson, Judy, *Trauma Trails, Recreating Song Lines: The transgenerational effects of trauma in Indigenous Australia*, Spinifex Press, Melbourne, 2002

Attwood, Bain and Foster, Stephen (eds), *Frontier Conflict: The Australian experience*, National Museum of Australia, Canberra, 2003

Attwood, Bain and Markus, Andrew, 'Representation matters: The 1967 referendum and citizenship', in Nicolas Peterson and Will Sanders (eds), *Citizenship and Indigenous Australians: Changing conceptions and possibilities*, Melbourne, 1998, pp. 118–140

Augoustinos, Martha and Le Conteur, Amanda, 'On whether to apologise to Indigenous Australians: The denial of white guilt', in Nyla Branscombe and Bertjan Doosje (eds), *Collective Guilt:*

International perspectives, Cambridge University Press, Cambridge UK, 2004, pp. 236–261

Auguste, Isabelle, 'On the significance of saying "sorry": Apology and reconciliation in Australia', in Frances Peters-Little, Ann Curthoys and John Docker (eds), *Passionate Histories: Myth, memory and Indigenous Australia*, ANU E Press, Canberra, 2010, pp. 309–321

Australian Broadcasting Corporation, 'Ill woman says her race stopped people from helping', *PM*, ABC Radio National, 7 March 2006, <http://www.abc.net.au/pm/content/2006/s1586142.htm>

——, 'War memorial battle over frontier conflict recognition', *The 7.30 Report*, 26 February 2009, <http://www.abc.net.au/7.30/content/2009/s2502535.htm>

Australian Human Rights Commission, *Submission to the Senate Community Affairs Committee on the Welfare Reform and Reinstatement of the RDA Bill 2009 and other Bills*, 10 February 2010, <http://www.aph.gov.au/senate/committee/clac_ctte/soc_sec_welfare_reform_racial_discrim_09/submissions/sub76.pdf>

Australian Labor Party, *The Australian Greens and the Australian Labor Party—Agreement 2010*, <http://www.alp.org.au/getattachment/255f5397-f9da–41c8–97c3–72287595d2eb/government-agreements/>

Australians for Native Title and Reconciliation, *Sea of Hands*, n.d., <http://www.antar.org.au/sea_of_hands>

Banathy, Bela and Jenlink, Patrick, *Dialogue as a Means of Collective Communication*, Kluwer, New York, 2005

Barkan, Elazar, *The Guilt of Nations: Restitution and negotiating historical injustices*, The Johns Hopkins University Press, Baltimore, 2000

Bashir, Bashir, 'Accommodating historically oppressed social groups: Deliberative democracy and the politics of reconciliation', in Will Kymlicka and Bashir Bashir (eds), *The Politics of Reconciliation in Multicultural Societies*, Oxford University Press, Oxford, 2008, pp. 48–69

Bashir, Bashir and Kymlicka, Will, 'Introduction: Struggles for inclusion and reconciliation, in modern democracies', in Will Kymlicka and Bashir Bashir (eds), *The Politics of Reconciliation in Multicultural Societies,* Oxford University Press, Oxford, 2008, pp. 1–24

Billings, Peter, 'Social welfare experiments in Australia: More trials for Aboriginal families?', *Journal of Social Security Law,* Vol. 17, No. 3, 2010, pp. 164–197

Bird, Carmel (ed), *The Stolen Children: Their stories,* Random House, Sydney, 1998

Blainey, Geoffrey, 'Drawing up a balance sheet of our history', *Quadrant,* July–August 1993, pp. 11–15

Bohm, David, *On Dialogue,* Routledge, London, 1996

Brady, Wendy and Carey, Michelle, 'Talkin' up whiteness: A black and white dialogue', in John Docker and Gerhard Fischer (eds), *Race, Colour and Identity in Australia and New Zealand,* UNSW Press, Sydney, 2000, pp. 270–282

Branscombe, Nyla and Doosje, Bertjan (eds), *Collective Guilt: International perspectives,* Cambridge University Press, Cambridge UK, 2004

Branscombe, Nyla and Doosje, Bertjan, 'International perspectives on the experience of collective guilt', in Nyla Branscombe and Bertjan Doosje (eds), *Collective Guilt: International perspectives,* Cambridge University Press, Cambridge, 2004, pp. 3–15

Branscombe, Nyla, Slugoski, Ben and Kappen, Diane, 'The measurement of collective guilt: What it is and what it is not', in Nyla Branscombe and Bertjan Doosje (eds), *Collective Guilt: International perspectives,* Cambridge University Press, Cambridge, 2004, pp. 16–34

Brennan, Sean, Behrendt, Larissa, Strelein, Lisa and Williams, George, *Treaty,* The Federation Press, Sydney, 2005

Brooks, Roy L., 'The age of apology', in Roy Brooks (ed.), *When Sorry Isn't Enough: The controversy over apologies and reparations for human injustice,* New York University Press, New York, 1999, pp. 3–11

Brough, Malcolm, 'National emergency response to protect children in the Northern Territory', Media release, 21 June 2007

Brunton, Ron, *Black Suffering, White Guilt? Aboriginal disadvantage and the Royal Commission into Deaths in Custody*, IPA Current Issues, Institute of Public Affairs, Perth, 1993

——, 'Betraying the victims: The "Stolen Generations" Report', *IPA Backgrounder*, Vol. 10, No.1, 1998

Calhoun, Craig, *Nations Matter: Culture, history, and the cosmopolitan dream*, Routledge, Abingdon, 2007

Cape York Institute, *From Hand Out to Hand Up: Cape York welfare reform project, design recommendations*, Cape York Institute for Policy and Leadership, Cairns, 2007

Casey, Dawn, 'Battleground of ideas and histories', in Dimity Reed (ed.), *Tangled Destinies: National Museum of Australia*, Images Publishing Group, Mulgrave, Victoria, 2002, pp. 18–27

Chesterman, John, *Civil Rights: How Indigenous Australians won formal equality*, University of Queensland Press, Brisbane, 2005

Clark, Anna, 'Flying the flag for mainstream Australia', *Griffith Review 11: Getting Smart*, 2006, pp. 107–112

Clark, Jennifer, *Aborigines and Activism: Race, Aborigines and the coming of the sixties to Australia*, University of Western Australia Press, Perth, 2008

Clendinnen, Inga, *Dancing with Strangers*, Text Publishing, Melbourne, 2008

Collier, Mary Jane and Hicks, Darrin, 'Discursive plurality: Negotiating cultural identities in public democratic dialogue', *Quest: An African Journal of Philosophy*, XVI, 1–2, 2002, pp. 197–219

Committee on the Elimination of Racial Discrimination, *Concluding observations—Australia*, United Nations, New York, 2010, <http://www.ohchr.org/EN/countries/AsiaRegion/Pages/AUIndex.aspx>

Cooper, David, 'Escaping from the shadowland: Campaigning for

Indigenous justice in Australia', *Indigenous Law Bulletin,* Vol. 16, Issue 10, 2005, pp. 15–17

Cowlishaw, Gillian, *Blackfellas, Whitefellas and the Hidden Injuries of Race,* Blackwell, Malden, MA, 2004

——, 'Helping anthropologists, still', in Jon Altman and Melinda Hinkson (eds), *Culture Crisis: Anthropology and politics in Aboriginal Australia,* UNSW Press, Sydney, 2010, pp. 45–60

Cunneen, Chris, 'Consensus and sovereignty: rethinking policing in the light of Indigenous self-determination', in Barbara A. Hocking (ed.), *Unfinished Constitutional Business? Rethinking Indigenous self-determination,* Aboriginal Studies Press, Canberra, 2005, pp. 47–60

Curthoys, Ann, 'An uneasy conversation: The multicultural and the indigenous', in John Docker and Gerhard Fischer (eds), *Race, Colour and Identity in Australia and New Zealand,* UNSW Press, Sydney, 2000, pp. 21–36

——, *Freedom Ride: A freedom rider remembers,* Allen & Unwin, Sydney, 2002

——, 'Constructing national histories', in Bain Attwood and Stephen Foster (eds), *Frontier Conflict: The Australian experience,* National Museum of Australia, Canberra, 2003, pp. 185–200

Davis, M., 'Indigenous knowledge: Beyond protection, towards dialogue', *Australian Journal of Indigenous Education,* 37, 2008, pp. 25–33

Díez Pinto, Elena, *Towards the Construction of a Dialogue Typology,* Democratic Dialogue Project, United Nations Development Program, Regional Bureau for Latin America and the Caribbean, 2003

Docker, John and Fischer, Gerhard, 'Adventures of identity', in *Race, Colour and Identity in Australia and New Zealand,* John Docker and Gerhard Fischer (eds), UNSW Press, Sydney, 2000, pp. 3–20

Dodson, Mick, 'Unfinished business: A shadow across our

relationships', in Hannah McGlade (ed.), *Treaty—Let's get it Right!*, Aboriginal Studies Press, Canberra, 2003, pp. 30–40

——, 'How well do we know each other?', The annual ANU Reconciliation Lecture, Australian National University, Canberra, 5 June 2009

——, 'Respect. Relationships. We have come so far', *Sydney Morning Herald*, 17 January 2010

Dodson, Patrick, *Beyond the Mourning Gate: Dealing with unfinished business*, The Wentworth Lecture, 12 May 2000, AIATSIS, Canberra

——, 'Reconciliation', in Robert Manne (ed.), *Dear Mr Rudd: Ideas for a better Australia*, Black Inc, Melbourne, 2008, pp. 28–41

Doosje, Bertjan, Branscombe, Nyla, Spears, Russell and Manstead, Antony, 'Consequences of national ingroup identification for responses to immoral historical events', in Nyla Branscombe and Bertjan Doosje (eds), *Collective Guilt: International perspectives*, Cambridge University Press, Cambridge, 2004, pp. 95–111

Duncan, Macgregor, Leigh, Andrew, Madden, David and Tynan, Peter, *Imagining Australia: Ideas for our future*, Allen & Unwin, Sydney, 2004

Eades, Diana, 'Aboriginal English', in Stephen A. Wurm, Peter Mülhäusler and Darrell T. Tryon (eds), *Atlas of Languages of Intercultural Communication in the Pacific, Asia and the Americas*, Vol II.1, Mouton de Gruyter, Berlin, 1996, pp. 133–142

Elshtain, Jean Bethke, 'Politics and forgiveness', in Nigel Biggar (ed.), *Burying the Past: Making peace and doing justice after civil conflict*, Georgetown University Press, Washington, DC, 2003, pp. 45–64

Evans, Raymond, 'The country has another past: Queensland and the History Wars', in Frances Peters-Little, Ann Curthoys and John Docker (eds), *Passionate Histories: Myth, memory and Indigenous Australia*, ANU E-Press, Canberra, 2010, 9–38

Forsberg, Tuomas, 'The philosophy and practice of dealing with the past: Some conceptual and normative issues', in Nigel

Biggar (ed.), *Burying the Past: Making peace and doing justice after civil conflict*, Georgetown University Press, Washington, DC, 2003, pp. 65–84

Freeman, Michael, 'Past wrongs and liberal justice', *Ethical Theory and Moral Practice*, Vol. 5, No. 2, *Pardoning Past Wrongs*, 2002, pp. 201–220

Gilbert, Kevin, *Because a White Man'll Never Do It*, Angus & Robertson Classics, HarperCollins Publishers, Sydney 2002 [1973]

Goot, Murray and Rowse, Tim, *Divided Nation? Indigenous affairs and the imagined public*, Melbourne University Press, Melbourne, 2007

Govier, Trudy, *Taking Wrongs Seriously: Acknowledgment, reconciliation, and the politics of sustainable peace*, Humanity Books, New York, 2006

Gray, Geoffrey, *A Cautious Silence: The politics of Australian anthropology*, Aboriginal Studies Press, Canberra, 2007

Green, Meredith J. and Sonn, Christopher C, 'Examining discourse of whiteness and the potential for reconciliation', *Journal of Community and Applied Social Psychology*, Vol. 15, 2005, pp. 478–492

——, 'Problematising the discourses of the dominant: Whiteness and reconciliation', *Journal of Community and Applied Social Psychology*, Vol. 16, 2006, pp. 379–395

Griffiths, Tom, 'The language of conflict', in Bain Attwood and Stephen Foster (eds), *Frontier Conflict: The Australian experience*, National Museum of Australia, Canberra, 2003, pp. 135–149

Gunstone, Andrew, *Unfinished Business: The Australian formal reconciliation process*, Australian Scholarly Publishing, Melbourne, 2007

Hage, Ghassan, *White Nation: Fantasies of White supremacy in a multicultural society*, Routledge, New York, 2000

Halloran, Michael J., 'Indigenous reconciliation in Australia: Do values, identity and collective guilt matter?', *Journal of Community and Applied Social Psychology*, Vol. 17, 2007, pp. 1–18

Harvard Project on American Indian Economic Development, *The State of Native Nations: Conditions under U.S. policies of self-determination*, Oxford University Press, New York, 2008

Heifetz, Ronald A., *Leadership Without Easy Answers*, The Bellknap Press of Harvard University Press, Cambridge, MA, 1994

Herzig, Maggie and Chasin, Laura, *Fostering Dialogue across Divides: A nuts and bolts guide from the public conversations project*, Public Conversations Project, Watertown, Massachusetts, 2006

Hills, Stephen, '"The Grand Experiment of the Civilisation of the Aborigines": Perspectives on a missionary endeavour in Western Australia', in Amanda Barry, Joanna Cruickshank, Andrew Brown-May and Patricia Grimshaw (eds), *Evangelists of Empire? Missionaries in colonial history*, University of Melbourne eScholarship Research Centre, Melbourne, 2008, <http://msp.esrc.unimelb.edu.au/shs/missions>

Hinkson, Melinda, 'In the name of the child', in Jon Altman and Melinda Hinkson (eds), *Coercive Reconciliation: Stabilise, Normalise, Exit Aboriginal Australia*, Arena Publications, Melbourne 2007, pp. 1–12

——, 'Introduction: Anthropology and the culture wars', in Jon Altman and Melinda Hinkson (eds), *Culture Crisis: Anthropology and politics in Aboriginal Australia*, UNSW Press, Sydney, 2010, pp. 1–13

——, 'Media images and the politics of hope', in Jon Altman and Melinda Hinkson (eds), *Culture Crisis: Anthropology and politics in Aboriginal Australia*, UNSW Press, Sydney, 2010, pp. 229–247

Horne, Donald, *The Lucky Country: Australia in the sixties*, Penguin Books, Melbourne, 1964

Horner, Jack, *Seeking Racial Justice: An insider's memoir of the movement for Aboriginal advancement, 1938–1978*, Aboriginal Studies Press, Canberra, 2004

Howard, John, 'The Liberal tradition: The beliefs and values which guide the Federal Government', Sir Robert Menzies Lecture, 18 November 1996, <http://www.menzieslecture.org/1996.html>

——, 'Opening Address to the Australian Reconciliation Convention, The Hon. John Howard, MP, The Prime Minister',

Melbourne, 27 May 1997, <http://www.austlii.edu.au/au/other/IndigLRes/car/1997/4/pmspoken.html>

——, Address to Corroboree 2000, Council for Aboriginal Reconciliation, Sydney, 27 May 2000, <http://www.austlii.edu.au/au/orgs/car/media/Prime%20Minister's%20address%20to%20Corroboree%202000.htm>

Howard, John and Vanstone, Amanda, 'Transcript of the Prime Minister The Hon. John Howard MP Joint Press Conference with Senator Amanda Vanstone', Parliament House, Canberra, 15 April 2004

Huggins, Jackie, *Sister Girl: The writings of an Aboriginal activist and historian*, University of Queensland Press, St Lucia, 1998

Human Rights and Equal Opportunities Commission, *Bringing them Home: Report of the national inquiry into the separation of Aboriginal and Torres Strait Islander children from their families*, Human Rights and Equal Opportunities Commission, Sydney, 1997

Human Rights Web, United Nations Convention on the Prevention and Punishment of the Crime of Genocide, <http://www.hrweb.org/legal/genocide.html>

Isaacs, W. *Dialogue and the Art of Thinking Together*, Doubleday, New York, 1999

Iyer, Aarti, Leach, Colin Wayne and Pederson, Anne, 'Racial wrongs and restitutions: The role of guilt and other group-based emotions', in Nyla Branscombe and Bertjan Doosje (eds), *Collective Guilt: International perspectives*, Cambridge University Press, Cambridge, 2004, pp. 262–283

Jackman, Simon, 'Pauline Hanson, the mainstream, and political elites: The place of race in Australian political ideology', *Australian Journal of Political Science*, Vol. 33, No. 2, 1998, pp. 167–186

James, Michael Rabinder, 'Critical intercultural dialogue', *Polity*, Vol. 31, No. 4, 1999, pp. 587–607

Jensen, Robert, *The Heart of Whiteness: Confronting race, racism and white privilege*, City Lights, San Francisco, 2005

Johns, Gary (ed.), *Waking up to Dreamtime: The illusion of Aboriginal self-determination*, Media Masters, Singapore, 2001

Jorgensen, Miriam (ed.), *Rebuilding Native Nations: Strategies for governance and development*, University of Arizona Press, Tucson, 2007

Kahane, Adam, *Solving Tough Problems: An open way of talking, listening and creating new realities*, Berrett-Koehler Publishers, San Francisco, 2004

——, *Power and Love: A theory and practice of social change*, Berrett-Koehler Publishers, San Francisco, 2010

Karskens, Grace, *The Colony: A history of early Sydney*, Allen & Unwin, Sydney, 2010

Keal, Paul, *European Conquest and the Rights of Indigenous Peoples: The moral backwardness of international society*, Cambridge University Press, Cambridge, 2003

Kendall, Frances E., *Understanding White Privilege: Creating pathways to authentic relationships across race*, Routledge, New York, 2006

Koori Mail, 'Report anniversary a bittersweet time', 6 June 2007, p. 41

Kowal, Emma, 'Is culture the problem or the solution? Outstation health and the politics of remoteness', in Jon Altman and Melinda Hinkson (eds), *Culture Crisis: Anthropology and politics in Aboriginal Australia*, UNSW Press, Sydney, 2010, pp. 179–194

Lake, Marilyn, 'Introduction: What have you done for your country?', in Marilyn Lake and Henry Reynolds (eds), *What's Wrong with Anzac? The militarisation of Australian history*, UNSW Press, Sydney, 2010, pp. 1–23

Langton, Marcia, 'The shock of the new: A postcolonial dilemma for Australianist anthropology', in Jon Altman and Melinda Hinkson (eds), *Culture Crisis: Anthropology and politics in Aboriginal Australia*, UNSW Press, Sydney, 2010, pp. 91–115

Lattas, Andrew and Morris, Barry, 'The politics of suffering and the politics of anthropology', in Jon Altman and Melinda Hinkson (eds), *Culture Crisis: Anthropology and politics in Aboriginal Australia*, UNSW Press, Sydney, 2010, pp. 61–87

Lazare, Aaron, *On Apology*, Oxford University Press, New York, 2004

Lea, Tess, *Bureaucrats and Bleeding Hearts: Indigenous health in northern Australia*, UNSW Press, Sydney, 2008

Lickell, Brian, Schmader, Toni and Barquissau, Marchelle, 'The evocation of moral emotions in intergroup contexts: The distinction between collective guilt and collective shame', in Nyla Branscombe and Bertjan Doosje (eds), *Collective Guilt: International perspectives*, Cambridge University Press, Cambridge, 2004, pp. 35–55

Lippmann, Lorna, *Generations of Resistance: The Aboriginal struggle for justice*, Longman Cheshire, Melbourne, 1981

Lorenz, Helene S. and Watkins, Mary, 'Depth psychology and colonialism: Individuation, seeing through, and liberation', Unpublished paper, 2000, <http://www.pacifica.edu/gems/creatingcommunityw/DepthPsychologyColonialism.pdf>

McGarty, Craig and Bliuc, Ana-Maria, 'Refining the meaning of the "collective" in collective guilt: Harm, guilt and the apology in Australia', in Nyla Branscombe and Bertjan Doosje (eds), *Collective Guilt: International perspectives*, Cambridge University Press, Cambridge, 2004, pp. 112–129

Macintyre, Stuart and Clark, Anna, *The History Wars*, Melbourne University Publishing, Melbourne, 2003

McKenna, Mark, *Different Perspectives in Black Armband History*, Research paper 5 1997–98, Parliamentary Library, Parliament of Australia, <http://www.aph.gpv.au/library/pubs/rp/1997–98/98rp05.htm>

——, 'Anzac Day: How did it become Australia's national day?', in Marilyn Lake and Henry Reynolds (eds), *What's Wrong with Anzac? The militarisation of Australian history*, UNSW Press, Sydney, 2010, pp. 110–134

Macklin, Jenny, 'Strengthening the Northern Territory Emergency Response', joint media release with Warren Snowdon MP, member for Lingiari, 25 November 2009, <http://www.

jennymacklin.fahcsia.gov.au/mediareleases/2009/Pages/strengthening_nter_25nov2009.aspx>

Maddison, Sarah, *Black Politics: Inside the complexity of Aboriginal political culture,* Allen & Unwin, Sydney, 2009

Maddison, Sarah, Cronin, Darryl, Williams, Shelley and Coggan, Rochelle, *Democratic Dialogue: Finding the right model for Australia,* Discussion paper No. 1, Indigenous Policy and Dialogue Research Unit, University of New South Wales, 2009

Mallett, Robyn and Swim, Janet, 'Collective guilt in the United States: Predicting support for social policies that alleviate social injustice', in Nyla Branscombe and Bertjan Doosje (eds), *Collective Guilt: International perspectives,* Cambridge University Press, Cambridge, 2004, pp. 56–74

Manne, Robert, *The Barren Years: John Howard and Australian political culture,* Text Publishing, Melbourne, 2001

——, 'In denial: The stolen generation and the Right', *Quarterly Essay,* Issue 1, 2001

——, *Whitewash: On Keith Windschuttle's Fabrication of Aboriginal History,* Black Inc, Melbourne, 2003

Marcus, Julie, *A Dark Smudge upon the Sand: Essays on race, guilt and the national consciousness,* LhR Press, Sydney, 1999

Memmi, Albert, *The Colonizer and the Colonized,* Beacon Press, Boston, 1965

Merlan, Francesca, 'Indigenous movements in Australia', *Annual Review of Anthropology,* Vol. 34, 2005, pp. 437–494

Minow, Martha, *Between Vengeance and Forgiveness: Facing history after genocide and mass violence,* Beacon Press, Boston, 1998

Moran, Anthony, 'White Australia, settler nationalism and Aboriginal assimilation', *Australian Journal of Politics and History,* Vol. 51, No. 2, 2005, pp. 168–193

Moreton-Robinson, Aileen, *Talkin' up to the White Woman: Indigenous women and feminism,* University of Queensland Press, Brisbane, 2000

Morgan, George, *Unsettled Places: Aboriginal people and urbanisation in New South Wales*, Wakefield Press, Kent Town, 2006

Morris, Meaghan, 'Beyond assimilation: Aboriginality, media history and public memory', *Rouge*, 2004,<http://www.rouge.com.au/3/beyond.html>

Morrissey, Michael, 'The Australian state and Indigenous people 1900–2006', *Journal of Sociology*, Vol. 42, No. 4, 2006, pp. 347–354

Mudrooroo, *Us Mob: History, culture, struggle. An introduction to Indigenous Australia*, HarperCollins Publishers, Sydney, 1995

Nandy, Ashis, 'Australia's polyglot ghosts and monoglot ghostbusters: A demonic foreword', in J.V. D'Cruz, Bernie Neville, Devika Goonewardene and Philip Darby (eds), *As Others See Us*, Australian Scholarly Publishing, Melbourne, 2008, pp. xiii–xxv

Nicholson, Alastair, *Social Security And Other Legislation Amendment (Welfare Reform And Reinstatement Of Racial Discrimination Bill 2009): Notes And Comment*, 2005, <http://stoptheintervention.org/rda-new-legislation/notes-and-comment-by-prof-nicholson>

Noonuccal, Oodgeroo, 'The Past', in *My People*, Jacaranda, Brisbane, 1970

Parekh, Bhikhu, *Rethinking Multiculturalism: Cultural diversity and political theory*, Harvard University Press, Cambridge, MA, 2000

Parliamentary Debate, House of Representatives, Questions without Notice: Aboriginals: Stolen Generations, 3 April, 14 August 2000

Pearson, Noel, 'An end to the tears', *The Australian*, 23 June 2007, pp. 17, 22

——, 'White guilt, victimhood and the quest for a radical centre', *Griffith Review*, 16, 2007, pp. 3–58

Peters-Little, Frances, *The Community Game: Aboriginal self-definition at the local level*, Research Discussion Paper No. 10, Australian Institute for Aboriginal and Torres Strait Islander Studies, Canberra, 2000

——, 'Remembering the referendum with compassion', in Frances Peters-Little, Ann Curthoys and John Docker (eds), *Passionate Histories: Myth, memory and Indigenous Australia*, ANU E-Press, Canberra, 2010, pp. 75–97

Peterson, Nicolas and Sanders, Will (eds), *Citizenship and Indigenous Australians: Changing conceptions and possibilities*, Cambridge University Press, Melbourne, 1998

Povinelli, Elizabeth, *The Cunning of Recognition: Indigenous alterities and the making of Australian multiculturalism*, Duke University Press, Durham, 2002

——, 'Indigenous politics in late liberalism', in Jon Altman and Melinda Hinkson (eds), *Culture Crisis: Anthropology and politics in Aboriginal Australia*, UNSW Press, Sydney, 2010, pp. 17–31

Powell, Christopher, 'The Moralization Of Genocide In Canada', paper presented at the Prairie Perspectives conference, Truth and Reconciliation event, Winnipeg, 17 June 2010

——, *Barbaric Civilization: A Critical Sociology of Genocide*, McGill-Queen's University Press, Montréal, 2011

——, 'The morality of genocide', in Adam Jones (ed.), *New Directions in Genocide Research*, Routledge, New York, 2011

Pratt, Angela, *Practising Reconciliation? The politics of reconciliation in the Australian parliament, 1991–2000*, Parliamentary Library, Parliament of Australia, Canberra, 2003

Pratt, Angela, Elder, Catriona and Ellis, Cath, ' "Papering over differences": Australian nationhood and the normative discourse of reconciliation', in Mary Kalantzis and Bill Cope (eds), *Reconciliation, Multiculturalism, Identities: Difficult dialogues, sensible solutions*, Common Ground Publishing, Melbourne, 2001, pp. 135–148

Pruitt, Bettye and Thomas, Philip, *Democratic Dialogue: A handbook for practitioners*, General Secretariat of the Organization of American States, International Institute for Democracy and Electoral Assistance, and United Nations Development Program, New York, 2007

Reconciliation Australia, *Australian Reconciliation Barometer: Comparative report*, Reconciliation Australia, Canberra, 2008

Reynolds, Henry, *This Whispering in Our Hearts*, Allen & Unwin, Sydney, 1998

——, *Why Weren't We Told? A personal search for the truth about our history*, Viking, Melbourne, 1999

——, 'Are nations really made in war?', in Marilyn Lake and Henry Reynolds (eds), *What's Wrong with Anzac? The militarisation of Australian history*, UNSW Press, Sydney, 2010, pp. 24–44

Roccas, Sonia, Klan, Yechiel and Liviatan, Ido, 'Exonerating cognitions, group identification and personal predictors of collective guilt among Jewish-Israelis', in Nyla Branscombe and Bertjan Doosje (eds), *Collective Guilt: International perspectives*, Cambridge University Press, Cambridge, 2004, pp. 130–147

Rose, Deborah Bird, *Reports from a Wild Country: Ethics for decolonisation*, UNSW Press, Sydney, 2004

Rouhana, Nadim N., 'Reconciling history and equal citizenship in Israel: Democracy and the politics of historical denial', in Will Kymlicka and Bashir Bashir (eds), *The Politics of Reconciliation in Multicultural Societies*, Oxford University Press, Oxford, 2008, pp. 70–93

Rowse, Tim, 'Mabo and moral anxiety', *Meanjin*, 2, 1993, pp. 229–252

——, 'Indigenous politics', in R.A.W. Rhodes (ed.), *The Australian Study of Politics*, Palgrave Macmillan, Basingstoke, 2009, pp. 314–324

Royal Commission into Aboriginal Deaths in Custody, *National Report*, Vol. 1, Australian Government Publishing Service, Canberra, 1991

Rudd, Kevin, Apology to Australia's Indigenous peoples, House of Representatives, Parliament House, Canberra, 13 February 2008, <http://www.pm.gov.au/media/Speech/2008/speech_0073.cfm>

Sanders, Will, 'Never even adequate: Reconciliation and Indigenous affairs', in C. Aulich and R. Wettenhall (eds), *Howard's Second and Third Governments: Australian Commonwealth Administration 1998–2004*, UNSW Press, Sydney, 2005, pp. 152–172

Sartre, Jean Paul, 'Preface', in *The Wretched of the Earth*, Frantz Fanon, Grove Press, New York, 1961, pp. xliii–lxii

Sawer, Marian, 'Governing for the mainstream: Implications for community representation', *Australian Journal of Public Administration*, Vol. 61, No. 1, 2002, pp. 39–49

Schaller, Dominik J. and Zimmerer, Jürgen, 'From the Guest Editors: Raphael Lemkin: the "founder of the United Nations' Genocide Convention" as a historian of mass violence', *Journal of Genocide Research*, Vol. 7, No. 4, 2005, pp. 447–452

Schech, Susanne and Haggis, Jane, 'Migrancy, whiteness and the settler self in contemporary Australia', in John Docker and Gerhard Fischer (eds), *Race, Colour and Identity in Australia and New Zealand*, UNSW Press, Sydney, 2000, pp. 231–239

Schlink, Bernhard, *Guilt about the Past*, University of Queensland Press, St Lucia, Brisbane, 2009

Schmitt, Michael, Branscombe, Nyla and Brehm, Jack, 'Gender inequality and the intensity of men's collective guilt', in Nyla Branscombe and Bertjan Doosje (eds), *Collective Guilt: International perspectives*, Cambridge University Press, Cambridge, 2004, pp. 75–92

Schubert, Misha, 'UN delegate blasts "demeaning" NT intervention', *The Age*, 28 August 2009, <http://www.theage.com.au/national/un-delegate-blasts-demeaning-nt-intervention–20090827-f16q.html>

Schwab, Gabriele, *Haunting Legacies: Violent histories and transgenerational trauma*, Columbia University Press, New York, 2010

Shriver, Donald W., 'Where and when in political life is justice served by forgiveness?', in Nigel Biggar (ed.), *Burying the Past: Making peace and doing justice after civil conflict*, Georgetown University Press, Washington, DC, 2003, pp. 25–43

Sieder, Rachel, 'War, peace and the politics of memory in Guatemala', in Nigel Biggar (ed.), *Burying the Past: Making peace and doing justice after civil conflict*, Georgetown University Press, Washington, DC, 2003, pp. 209–234

Smith, Bernard, *The Spectre of Truganini*, 1980 Boyer Lectures, Australian Broadcasting Corporation, Sydney, 1980

Soutphommasane, Tim, *Reclaiming Patriotism: Nation-building for Australian progressives*, Cambridge University Press, Melbourne, 2009

Sorry Books, MS3569, Australian Institute of Aboriginal and Torres Strait Islander Studies, Canberra, 1998–2002, <http://www.aiatsis.gov.au/collections/docs/findingaids/MS3569_sorry.pdf>

Stanner, W.E.H., *The Dreaming and Other Essays*, Black Inc, Melbourne, 2009 [1968]

Steele, Shelby, *White Guilt: How blacks and whites together destroyed the promise of the civil rights era*, Harper Perennial, New York, 2006

Subăsić, Emina and Reynolds, Katherine, 'Beyond "practical" reconciliation: Intergroup inequality and the meaning of non-indigenous identity', *Political Psychology*, Vol. 30, No. 2, 2009, pp. 243–267

Sutton, Peter, *The Politics of Suffering: Indigenous Australia and the end of liberal consensus*, Melbourne University Publishing, Melbourne, 2009

Sydney Morning Herald, 'Indigenous poverty "outrageous": Amnesty', 18 November 2009, <http://news.smh.com.au/breaking-news-national/indigenous-poverty-outrageous-amnesty–20091118-imnr.html>

Taffe, Sue, *Black and White Together: FCAATSI, The Federal Council of Aborigines and Torres Strait Islanders 1958–1973*, University of Queensland Press, Brisbane, 2005

——, 'The role of FCAATSI in the 1967 referendum: Mythmaking about citizenship or political strategy', in Tim Rowse (ed.), *Contesting Assimilation*, API Network, Perth, 2005, pp. 285–298

Thompson, Elaine, *Fair Enough: Egalitarianism in Australia*, UNSW Press, Sydney, 1994

Tickner, Robert, *Taking a Stand: Land rights to reconciliation*, Allen & Unwin, Sydney, 2001

Tochluk, Shelly, *Witnessing Whiteness: First steps towards an antiracist practice and culture*, Rowman & Littlefield Education, Lanham, Maryland, 2008

Tully, James, *Strange Multiplicity: Constitutionalism in an age of diversity*, Cambridge University Press, Cambridge, 1995

——, 'Recognition and dialogue: The emergence of a new field', *Critical Review of International Social and Political Philosophy*, Vol. 7, No. 3, 2004, pp. 84–106

——, *Public Philosophy in a New Key, Volume 1, Democracy and civic freedom*, Cambridge University Press, Cambridge, 2008

Tyrrell, Ian, 'The Cooks River and environmental history', adapted from the 2004 Botany Bay Forum, University of New South Wales, Sydney, 30 November 2004, <http://iantyrrell.wordpress.com/cooks-river/>

Vanstone, Amanda, 'Message from the Minister', in *Australian Government Feature: Indigenous Affairs—Sharing Responsibility*, 2005, <http://www.indigenous.gov.au/rpa/koori_mail_ ins.pdf>

Veracini, Lorenzo, 'Settler collective, founding violence and disavowal: The settler colonial situation', *Journal of Intercultural Studies*, Vol. 29, No. 4, 2008, pp. 363–379

Ward, Russel, *The Australian Legend*, second edition, Oxford University Press, Melbourne, 1966

Watson, Irene, 'Aboriginal Sovereignties: Past, present and future (im)possibilities', in Suvendrini Perera (ed.), *Our Patch: Enacting Australian sovereignty post-2001*, Network Books, The API Network, Perth, 2007 pp. 23–43

Wild, Rex, and Anderson, Patricia, *Ampe akelyernemane meke mekarle: Little children are sacred*, Report of the Northern Territory Board of Inquiry into the protection of children from sexual abuse,

2007, <www.nt.gov.au/dcm/inquirysaac/pdf/bipacsa_ final_report.pdf>

Williams, David C., 'In praise of guilt: How the yearning for moral purity blocks reparations for Native Americans', in Federico Lenzerini (ed.), *Reparations for Indigenous Peoples: International and comparative perspectives*, Oxford University Press, Oxford, 2008, pp. 229–249

Williams, George and Hume, David, *People Power: The history and the future of the referendum in Australia*, UNSW Press, Sydney, 2010

Windschuttle, Keith, 'How not to run a museum: People's history at the postmodern museum', *Quadrant*, September 2001, <http://www.sydneyline.com/National%20 Museum.htm>

——, *The Fabrication of Aboriginal History, Volume One: Van Diemen's Land 1803–1847*, Macleay Press, Sydney, 2002

——, 'Doctored evidence and invented incidents in Aboriginal historiography', in Bain Attwood and Stephen Foster (eds), *Frontier Conflict: The Australian experience*, National Museum of Australia, Canberra, 2003, pp. 99–112

Wise, Tim, 'Your House is on Ground Zero (and Quite Without Permission)', *Red Room*, 2010, <http://www.redroom.com/blog/tim-wise/your-house-ground-zero-and-quite-without-permission>

Wolfe, Patrick, *Settler Colonialism and the Transformation of Anthropology: The politics and poetics of an ethnographic event*, Cassell, London, 1999

Young, Iris Marion, *Justice and the Politics of Difference*, Princeton University Press, Princeton, 1990

——, 'Communication and the Other', in Seyla Benhabib (ed.), *Democracy and Difference*, Princeton University Press, Princeton, 1996, pp. 120–135.

——, 'Hybrid democracy: Iroquois federalism and the postcolonial project', in Duncan Ivison, Paul Patton and Will Sanders (eds), *Political theory and the rights of Indigenous peoples*, Cambridge University Press, New York, 2000, pp. 237–238

Yu, Peter, Gray, Bill and Ella Duncan, Marcia, 'Report of the NTER Review Board', Department of Families, Housing, Community Services and Indigenous Affairs, Canberra, 2008, http://www.nterreview.gov.au/docs/report_nter_review/docs/Report_NTER_Review_October08.pdf

Acknowledgements

I began writing this book while travelling in Canada and the United States on a research trip for another project and completed it at home in Australia. I am grateful to all the traditional owners of the lands through which I travelled, and I particularly acknowledge the traditional owners of the land on which I live and work: the Gadigal people of the Eora nation. I pay my sincere respects to the elders and ancestors of the Eora nation, several generations of whom bore the full brunt of the invasion and early settlement of this country. This book is an acknowledgement of their suffering.

I thank my colleagues in the Indigenous Policy and Dialogue Research Unit at the University of New South Wales for tolerating my absent-mindedness and distraction while I was immersed in writing. I am also grateful for the ongoing financial support I have received from the Australian Research Council, particularly through Discovery Project DP0877157 and Linkage Project LP100100216, which have each contributed to aspects of the work towards this book.

It has again been my privilege to work with Elizabeth Weiss and Rebecca Kaiser at Allen & Unwin, who are the best editors anyone could hope for. My gratitude also to friends and colleagues who read and commented on some or all of the draft manuscript including Christopher Powell, Adam Kahane, Catherine Lumby, Jeff McMullen and Liz Skelton.

And, of course, my family: my lovely, almost-grown children Sam and Eliza and my amazing partner, Emma Partridge, patiently enduring my distraction and preoccupation while I was writing this book. I am so grateful for their forbearance. And for Emma in particular, who is always the first to read every word I write and whose love and reassurance give me the confidence to keep going—you still make every day a good day and you will always be my biggest, biggest love.

Index

Note: references suffixed with n refer to footnotes